Agnostics and atheists ha
in spite of the fact that th
propaganda we need a 1
arguments are. Jeffrey Johnson has chosen the word 'absurdity' to characterise these, and he has chosen well. Chapter by chapter he strips unbelief of any vestige of credibility, then shows with crystal clarity why the biblical case for God stands supreme when contrasted with all other philosophical and religious belief systems. I predict that this book will be as great a help to many of its readers as it has been to me, and I commend it warmly.

— John Blanchard, Author of *Does God Believe in Atheists?*

The Bible doesn't merely state the atheist's creed, it provides us with an assessment of that creed: "The fool has said in his heart, 'There is no God'" (Psalm 14:1). In his new book *The Absurdity of Unbelief*, Jeffrey Johnson ably demonstrates that the Scripture writer isn't hurling insults or engaging in *ad hominem*. Rather, as Johnson shows, the Bible is simply telling the truth. To reject the triune God of Scripture and to replace him with a non-biblical worldview is self-defeating. How does Johnson defend this thesis (and biblical claim)? First, he argues that human beliefs are not neutral but are in certain ways biased and preconditioned. Next, Johnson proceeds, by means of *reductio ad absurdum*, to expose the irrationality of the world's major non-biblical philosophies and unbiblical religions. Finally, Johnson carefully sets forth the arguments and lays out the evidence for the veracity of Christianity, and he concludes with an earnest and humble appeal to receive the gospel of Jesus Christ, which alone can restore true meaning to the world and wherein is found true wisdom from God. *The Absurdity of Unbelief* will challenge the unbeliever's skepticism and will confirm the believer's faith. I highly recommend it!

— Robert R. Gonzales Jr., Author of *Where Sin Abounds*

Jeffrey Johnson's new book, *The Absurdity of Unbelief*, demonstrates the absurdity of most of the worldviews which parade themselves as truth – naturalism, relativism, atheism, existentialism, pantheism, materialism, and the rest. He clearly examines the premises of each system of thought and demonstrates their many contradictions. His scholarship and historical understanding of the entire field of philosophy and the other so-called religions is evident throughout the book. He has done a masterful job in showing that the Christian worldview is the only system that will meet all the tests of logic and ethics. He concludes this excellent work with a passionate call to submit ourselves to the God of the Scriptures who has given us His son, Jesus Christ, who will remove all of our sin and guilt. To trust in any of the other philosophical or religious positions while refusing to accept God's gracious offer of salvation is indeed absurd!

– Curtis C. Thomas, Author of *Practical Wisdom for Pastors*

A major strength of Jeffrey Johnson's *Absurdity of Unbelief* is its step-by-step systematic approach. He explains what faith is (and is not), what factors drive us to adopt our beliefs, how to test them, fatal difficulties on all systems of thought not built on the foundation of Christ, grounds for holding to Christian theism, and a passionate call to faith in Jesus. Along the way he examines Christian and non-Christian thinkers and movements both ancient and contemporary, demonstrating that the principles underlying a biblical apologetic equally apply to all forms of unbelief. I plan on coming back to this book again and again.

–Joseph E. Torres, Editor and coauthor with John M. Frame,
Apologetics: A Justification of Christian Belief,
and blogger at KINGDOMVIEW

As Christians struggle to hold onto a semblance of sanity in the midst of the collapse of Western morality and thought, a sound foundation upon which to stand in explaining our unwillingness to bow the knee to Caesar is a must. In *The Absurdity of Unbelief*, Jeffrey Johnson provides a clear and compelling case for the Christian faith, readable and usable for believer and unbeliever alike.

– James R. White, Director of Alpha and Omega Ministries

THE
ABSURDITY OF

UNBELIEF
A WORLDVIEW APOLOGETIC OF THE CHRISTIAN FAITH

JEFFREY D. JOHNSON

FREE GRACE PRESS

THE ABSURDITY OF UNBELIEF:

A Worldview Apologetic of the Christian Faith

Published by Free Grace Press
1455 Champions Rd.
Conway, AR 72034
freegracepress.com

Cover design by Scott Schaller
scottschallerdesigns.com

ISBN: 978-1-59925-353-4

To my brothers
James & Jason Johnson

Contents

PART 5: The Grounds for Belief

PART 6: The Call to Believe

Preface

One cannot deny logical and ethical absolutes without the use of the laws of logic and ethics in the process. If some say they don't care about logic, then they might as well say that they are okay with sounding absurd. Why would anyone want to take them seriously? If some do not care about being ethical, then why would anyone want to trust them when they admit that lying is okay?

Without God, there is no meaning, no truth, no rationality, and no ethical standard. Because without God – and specifically the God of the Bible – there is no foundation for logic or ethics to be utilized in argumentation at all (as we shall see).

In other words, I don't believe in intellectual atheists anymore than I believe in relativists who take relativism seriously. Sure, there are plenty who call themselves atheists, but deep down, they are lying to themselves. Sure, there are plenty who hold to relativistic thinking, but this does not mean that they truly think it is okay for others to cheat, defraud, exploit, or kill them. No matter how postmodern and open-minded many may think they are, they cannot help but get incensed when others take advantage of them. So, no, I don't believe in atheists or relativists.

Knowing this is a bold way to introduce a book on Christian apologetics, I would only challenge you to try to remain honest with yourself as you read this book. If you happen to be a self-proclaimed atheist, agnostic, or skeptic, see if you can be honest with your conscience and continue to deny the existence of God.

I hope that all skeptics of Christianity read this book, not because I feel I have written the best book on the subject, but because I am persuaded by the coherency of the Christian worldview that Christianity is true. It is the *only* worldview that is intellectually and practically defensible, for it is the *only* worldview that can give a coherent answer to why there are logical and ethical absolutes.

I write with certainty, but that does not mean this book is certain to bring any unbeliever away from his or her unbelief. Even though I am convinced that Christianity is both right and defensible, I am not convinced that this is enough to convince unbelieving skeptics.

The problem with unbelief, as I explain in PART 2, is not a lack of evidence or rational warrant; unbelief is due to a lack of appreciation for the truth. Faith in Christ requires more than just intellectual knowledge of Christ; it requires a love for Christ that comes only by the illumination of the Spirit (as we shall see in chapter 26). This is something that goes beyond the reach of apologetics, for only God can reveal Himself to us in such a way for us to be willing to sell all that we have and follow Him.

Though I cannot be certain this book will be of any eternal value for unbelievers, I can write with the knowledge that apologetics is a great value to those who already love the Lord Jesus. In some ways, apologetics is more helpful for believers than for non-believers. This may sound odd, since believers already have faith in Christ, but just as the gospel is continuously beneficial for believers, Christian apologetics is helpful in strengthening and encouraging the faith of those who already believe – especially if we have a biblical apologetic, *"for faith comes by hearing, and hearing by the Word of God"* (Rom. 10:17).

My aim, though, is not to instruct the reader on how to carry out apologetics, or to discuss the differences between the various apologetical approaches, but to carry out an apologetic. I am not simply seeking to defend the Christian worldview from outside criticism, but to provide an offensive attack on all forms of unbelief.

Because the Christian worldview is the only system of thought that is cohesively consistent with itself, all other possible worldviews are inherently incoherent. It is not sufficient for an atheist or any other skeptic to simply attack the walls of the Christian worldview. They must also defend their own ground. They must protect their own presuppositions and belief systems.

My aim is to show that the castle of unbelief rests on quicksand, and the more unbelievers struggle to defend their worldview, the more they sink under the weight of it. Atheism, deism, naturalism, relativism, existentialism, pantheism, polytheism, and any other non-Christian *ism*, along with Judaism and Islam, are incoherent and, thus, rationally indefensible.

So let us prepare to defend our own castles and see which worldview ultimately ends victorious. Before we head into the battlefield though, I need to thank some very important people for their assistance. None of us fight alone, and this book has definitely not been the effort of a single person.

I would like to begin by thanking Nathan Berry for his encouragement to remain in the battle. Without his kind words the manuscript may have not made it out of the first draft. Thank you!

I would also like to thank Brandon Burks and Mike Cantrell for providing additional fortification for this defense. With their background in theology and philosophy respectively, they were able to give helpful feedback, which, no doubt, has improved the overall presentation of this work.

Robert Gonzales Jr. not only gave an endorsement, he took the time to read the manuscript closely with editorial corrections. He went beyond being helpful. Thank you, brother.

Thom Cole has become a good friend through the process of writing this book. Thom, thank you for all your help, but most of all, thank you for your genuine kindness and friendship. May our covenant God bless you richly.

My blog partner and friend, Keith Throop, has been a major encouragement and blessing to me. This book would not be in its present form without his sacrificial labors. Thank you!

Telling Kathy Bland 'thank you' doesn't seem sufficient. She labored over this manuscript as if it was her own. Not just running through it once, but she carefully worked through multiple drafts. Only love could motivate someone to give so much. From my heart I would like to say, thank you Kathy!

I appreciate the keen eyes of my longtime friend, Greg Stevens. Thank you for proofreading this work. I can't fully explain what your faithful testimony means to me. I am also blessed to be friends with Nina Baker. Thank you, Nina, for your kindness and sweet disposition. May God bless you for helping me. And though Jeffrey Homstad is a new friend, he is already a close friend. God has given you an amazing gift – thank you for using it to help improve the readability of this book.

Lastly, I would like to express my gratitude to Matt Millsap. I appreciate your wisdom and your willingness to invest a bit of your time into this project. Thank you for allowing me to wear your ears out on the subject. I am thankful to have been your pastor, and I pray the Lord's continual blessing on you and your wife, Katie.

My prayer is that this book would be used by God to challenge all forms of unbelief in the believer and unbeliever alike. To Him be the glory!

PART 1

The Nature of Belief

Faith comes by hearing,
and hearing through the Word of God.
Romans 10:17

1

Faith is Not Blind

"In the name of Jesus!" This was the declaration that darted out of the mouth of the misguided driver as he closed his eyes and pulled out into heavy traffic. Some call this, "taking a blind leap of faith," which may partly be true – the cab driver, while operating in his faith that no harm will come to him, took an irrational and "blind" leap into traffic. What happens from here though, is that many then go on to think faith, in general, requires a mindless leap into darkness. It is unfortunate that so many believe this, when in fact, the opposite is true.

There are so many unbiblical views of faith that it has become hard to discern what real faith looks like. One of the more common misconceptions is to think that faith is a knowledge that exists between certainty and doubt. That faith is not full-fledged doubt, but it is not certainty either. If we were certain, we wouldn't need faith to believe. In the words of Paul Tillich (1886-1965), one of the more influential liberal theologians, "Faith comprises both itself and the doubt of itself."[1]

Faith, as it goes, may not be completely irrational, but neither is it always supported by reason. In the same way children are prone to believe in superstitions, such as UFO's, Bigfoot, and the Loch Ness monster, faith in God requires that we become like children and suspend our own better judgment. How else could

[1] Paul Tillich, *Biblical Religion and the Search for Ultimate Reality* (Chicago: The University of Chicago Press, 1955), 85.

we be able to believe in the supernatural miracles of Christ if we don't take a leap of faith? Are not the deity and resurrection of Christ a bit far-fetched? It's as if to say, I have no rational or empirical reason to believe that this chair exists, and I am even less certain that this chair will be able to hold up my weight; by faith, nevertheless, I am able to take a leap in the darkness and sit down.

Faith, according to this way of thinking, is blind. According to the atheist Richard Dawkins, faith is "blind trust in the absence of evidence, even in the teeth of evidence."[2] Or, if evidence or rationale were needed, as some would say, then there would be no need to have faith. Faith is a leap into the darkness, for this is what it means to "walk by faith and not by sight."

Separating Reason from Faith

Much of the confusion, so it seems, centers on the relationship between faith and reason. From those who preach that faith *goes against reason* to those who claim that faith is *independent of reason*, there is a push to *separate* reason from faith.

An example of one who separated reason from faith is Pseudo-Dionysius the Areopagite. Dionysius was the most influential Christian mystic of the fifth century and likely throughout the Middle Ages.

Dionysius built his mystical theology on the idea that God is ineffable (i.e., completely unknowable). He claimed that God transcends all thought and is beyond any human comparisons: "For if all the branches of knowledge belong to things that have being, and if their limits have reference to the existing world,

---

2 Richard Dawkins, *The Selfish Gene* (New York: Oxford, 2006), 198. Dawkins claims that the Bible ridicules Doubting Thomas for asking for evidence before he believed in the resurrection of Christ (Ibid.).

then that which is beyond all Being must also be transcendent above all knowledge."[3]

Dionysius went on to claim that there was no knowable concept that could properly describe God. "We must not then dare to speak, or indeed to form any conception, of the hidden super-essential Godhead." Again, he said, "The One which is beyond thought surpasses the apprehension of thought, and the God which is beyond utterance surpasses the reach of words."[4]

Since God cannot be described using any meaningful language, it is best to understand God by the things that He is not (*Via Negativa*, also known as *apophatic* theology). What is God *not?*

First, according to Dionysius, God is not a person. Man is a personal being; man is personal because he can be distinguished from other persons. Personhood, therefore, is something that is finite, something that is separate from the whole, and something that is distinguishable. God, however, is infinite, simple, and absolute. God transcends all forms of separation; God is *Unity*. Thus, God is beyond personhood; He is "Super-Personal," as Dionysus often stated.

Second, according to Dionysus, since God is Unity, He is not even a conscious being. Why? Because consciousness implies a state of thinking, and thinking implies self-awareness. Self-awareness cannot happen without a thinking object making a distinction between His thoughts and that which is being thought upon. Thus, there is a separation, at least in the mind, between the thinking subject and the object of thought. With God, however, there can be no differentiation or divisions.

[3] Dionysius, "The Divine Names," in *Dionysius the Areopagite on the Divine Names and The Mystical Theology*, trans. C. E. Rolt (Berwick, MA: Ibis Press, 2004), 59.
[4] Ibid., 53.

Third, as we move down the chain of nonsense, God does not even exist. In the words of Dionysius: "He neither was, nor will be, nor hath entered the life-process, nor is doing so, nor ever will, or rather He doth not even exist."[5] Why? According to Dionysius the word *existence* implies a distinction between that which exists and that which does not exist. God is beyond all distinctions. God is Unity.

Fourth, Dionysius went so far as to undermine the foundation of his whole argument. The reason why God is not a person, a conscious being, or even a being that exists, is that He is absolute Unity. According to Dionysius, *Unity* is the one word that best depicted God. God is one, because He is simple, He is without divisions or limitations. God transcends all boundaries.

According to Dionysius, even the word *Unity* comes infinitely short in defining God. Although the word *Unity* might be the best human term to understand God, it remains inadequate in bringing us to any true knowledge of the Unknowable. The term *Unity* fails in that it implies a distinction and separation from that which is plural or divided. God is neither *one* nor *many* – He transcends them both. Thus, God (if He even can be called God at this point) is not even *Unity*. He is, as Dionysius claimed, "Super-Unity." So, in the end, God is beyond essence, consciousness, life, existence, and unity because He is absolute and infinite. Yet, because God is ineffable, He is also beyond being absolute and infinite. God transcends all human words, even the word *transcendence*.

If Dionysius is correct, what is left? Nothing. Dionysius, in an absurd way, would have us believe in an unknowable God that does not even exist. Dionysius' mystical negation greatly influenced the medieval mystics, such as Bernard of Clairvaux (1090-1153), Francis of Assisi (1182-1226), and Bonaventure (1221-1274). For instance, Bonaventure, in his book *The Journey of*

[5] Ibid., 135.

the Mind to God, leaned heavily on the writings of Dionysius. He began his book with these words:

> Wherefore, Dionysius in his "Mystical Theology," wishing to instruct us in these transcendent workings of the soul, sets down prayer as the first condition...By so praying we are led to discern the degrees of the soul's ascent to God. For, inasmuch as, in our present condition, this universe of things is a ladder whereby we may ascend to God.[6]

How does one ascend to God? After contemplating what is revealed, one must begin contemplating that which is not revealed:

> Do thou, O friend, push on boldly to the mystic vision, abandon the work of the senses and the operations of the reasoning faculty, leave aside all things visible and invisible, being and nonbeing, and cleave as far as possible, and imperceptibly, to the unity of Him who transcends all essences and all knowledge.[7]

A few years later, Meister Eckhart (1260-1328) explained the practical way of entering into mystical experiences of mindless activity. He declared: "'Should [we] not pray, or read, or hear a sermon...? No!,' answered Eckhart, 'You may be sure that perfect quiet and idleness is the best you can do. Is it my place to be in the darkness?'" Eckhart responded, "Yes, truly. You could do no better than to go where it is dark, that is, uncon-sciousness."[8]

Conclusion

Dionysius and the mystics who followed him would have us place our faith in nothing. Mystical theology removes our need to have

---

[6] Bonaventure, "The Journey of the Mind to God," in *Late Medieval Mysticism,* ed. Ray C. Petry (Philadelphia: The Westminster Press, 1957), 132.

[7] Ibid., 140-141.

[8] Meister Eckhart, "Another Sermon on the Eternal Birth," in *Late Medieval Mysticism,* ed. Ray C. Petry (Philadelphia: The Westminster Press, 1957), 189.

faith in the God of the Bible. Faith in the truth claims of the Bible is not needed. Why? Because God cannot be known by truth claims. The only thing that can connect us with God, if He can be called *God*, is an unconscious, mystical experience. This is mysticism, and this is truly a blind leap into the darkness

2

Faith is Not Subjectivity

Rather than faith being a blind leap into the darkness, for others it is more of a *subjective* experience that causes a person to embrace that which would otherwise be unbelievable. They believe faith must either be the *cause* or *effect* of a supernatural encounter with the Divine., and that God may be real, but you can only know for sure if you experience Him in some otherwise unbelievable way.

Søren Kierkegaard

We can see traces of such a notion of faith in the writings of Søren Kierkegaard (1813-1855).

Kierkegaard, the father of *existentialism*, had become outraged with the formalism of the Danish National Church. The Church of Denmark was plagued with two problems. The first problem was that the church was largely made up of nominal Christians. To receive a birth certificate, to receive a marriage license, and to receive a burial plot in the church graveyard, a person had to be registered and baptized in the church. This union between state and church may have enlarged the membership of the church, but it also filled it with a roster of unbelievers. Though the Bible may have been preached and Luther's catechism may have been memorized, personal and experiential faith in Christ was no longer required to be a Christian. Kierkegaard was alarmed at the lack of experiential faith within the membership of the church.

The second concern for Kierkegaard was the wave of *rationalism* that had swept across Germany and Denmark. Rationalism had flooded the universities, and as the wave descended, it ended up seeping into the church through the back door. The aftermath of the storm robbed the biblical text of all its supernatural elements. From a rejection of Divine inspiration to a rejection of the recorded miracles, the rationalism of German higher criticism had neutered the supernatural from the Bible altogether.

The concern for Kierkegaard was that without a supernatural religion, Christians were no longer required to have a supernatural faith in a supernatural God. Non-believers were added to the state church without faith, and they were never called to believe in a supernatural God thereafter. The church seemed to have lost its faith altogether.

Immanuel Kant

How did this happen? In the generation that preceded Kierkegaard, theological professors and pastors had been greatly influenced by the writings of Immanuel Kant (1724-1804).

Kant believed that all knowledge begins with experience.

That all our knowledge begins with experience there can be no doubt. For how is it possible that the faculty of cognition should be awakened into exercise otherwise than by means of objects which affect our senses, and partly of themselves produce representations, partly rouse our powers of understanding into activity, to compare, to connect, or to separate these, and so to convert the raw material of our sensuous impressions into a knowledge of objects, which is called experience? In respect of time, therefore, no knowledge of ours is antecedent to experience, but begins with it.[1]

Knowledge begins with experience, but experience is restricted by the limitations of the senses. For instance, our eyes can only see what they are capable of seeing; our ears can only hear the sound waves that our ear drums are capable of detecting; our tongue can only taste that which the taste buds are able to sense; our fingers can only feel the textures that our mechanoreceptors and muscle nerves are capable of perceiving; and, our nose can only smell the aromas that can be sensed by our olfactory receptors. What if there are other aromas, sights, and sounds that existed that we are incapable of perceiving? Who is to say that reality does not consist of other dimensions and properties? Who is to say that if we had a sixth sense, we would not ascertain additional knowledge of the universe? Each of the five senses can only perceive according to their abilities, so who is to say that our senses are properly and fully ascertaining what is real?

In addition to the limitations of the senses, before the incoming sensations are processed, sorted, and cataloged by the mind, they are merely unorganized and indiscernible bits of stimuli. Like observing the confusion of a 500-piece puzzle before it's put together, bare sensations coming from the external world make no sense without the mind processing and putting these disorderly pieces together.

Sensations need to be arranged and processed if knowledge is to be obtained. Though knowledge begins by experience, experience alone does not supply us with knowledge. To construct knowledge, the mind must supply the *à priori* concepts of *space* and *time* to the incoming sensations. As modes of perception, space and time are not observed by the senses, for

---

[1] Immanuel Kant, *Critique of Pure Reason*, trans. J. M. D. Meiklejohn (Amherst, NY: Prometheus Books, 1990), 1.

they are not properties of the external world. Space and time are concepts supplied by the mind to sense experiences. Only afterwards, when the concepts of space and time are applied to sensations, do sensations become perceptions.

Yet, perceptions still do not classify as knowledge, for they still need additional processing. Disjointed perceptions must be filtered and properly filed through the 12 categories of the understanding (such as ideas of cause, unity, reciprocal relation, necessity, contingency, etc.) before they form knowledge.

In short, only after sensations have been processed through the mental concepts of space and time do they become perceptions, and only after perceptions are filtered through the categories of the mind do they form knowledge.[2]

This implies that the mind is not a passive wax tablet that is waiting to be molded and shaped by experience, but rather the mind is an active organ that coordinates and constructs the chaotic sensations (that are gathered by sense experiences from the external world) into ideas. According to Kant, without the mind thus supplying these à priori concepts to experience, knowledge is impossible.[3]

But this has its consequences. This means that order and structure are concepts of the mind and not of the world. The world, as far as we know, is without any order or structure. More importantly, this means that the laws of nature (such as causality)

---

[2] See Ibid., 91.

[3] As Kant stated: "But, though all our knowledge begins with experience, it by no means follows that all arises out of experience. For, on the contrary, it is quite possible that our empirical knowledge is a compound of that which we receive through impressions, and that which the faculty of cognition supplies itself" (Ibid.). In this way, Kant was not suggesting that there were no concepts supplied by cognition, but these concepts (or categories, as he called them) were not initiated until they were simulated by the sensations derived by the senses. For this reason, the categories can never extend further than to the objects of experience. In other words, there is no such thing as pure (unaided) à priori reason/knowledge that is independent of empirical sensations.

are merely the laws of thought. The mind supplies order to the world. In other words, the laws of nature are not in nature but are supplied by the mind.

Though knowledge originates from the external world, knowledge of the external world (as it is in-and-of-itself) is unknowable. We cannot know the world as it is, but only as our minds interpret the world. According to Kant, it is impossible to know reality as it really is; all we know for certain is our perception of reality. Seeing that our internal perceptions are shaped and organized by the *à priori* categories, the external world remains locked behind an unassailable wall. We can only know, according to Kant, the things as they appear to us, not as they are "things-in-themselves."[4]

If Kant was right, then this "wall" (known as the *transcendental wall*) separating *subjective* perception from *objective* reality changes everything. If objective objects of the universe, as things-in-themselves, lie behind the transcendental wall, how much more does an invisible and immaterial God remain unknowable?

Kant, oddly enough, remained religious, for he claimed that he found it necessary to deny the knowledge of God in order to make room for faith in God. But faith in God is not based on any *objective* knowledge. As Bryan Magee, in his book, *The Story of Philosophy*, concluded: "he [Kant] demolished so called 'proofs' of the existence of God, and in doing so reduced to rubble much of the philosophizing of centuries...Since Kant it has been accepted almost universally by serious thinkers that the existence of God is not something that can be proved."[5]

---

[4] Kant, in his book the *Critique of Pure Reason*, divided existence into two spheres, the *noumenal* – the world as it actually is, and the *phenomena* – the world as it appears to us. According to Kant, we can never know the world as it truly is, but only the *phenomena* world of appearance.

[13] Bryan Magee, *The Story of Philosophy* (London: Dorling Kindersley, 2001), 137.

Friedrich Schleiermacher

As you can imagine, the philosophy of Kant had a devastating effect on the church. One such person who was influenced by Kant was Friedrich Schleiermacher (1768–1834), the father of Modern Liberal Theology.

After Schleiermacher left his pietistic home and enrolled in the University of Halle, he began to study the philosophy of Kant. In the process, Schleiermacher became increasingly skeptical of the supernatural claims of Christianity. He eventually wrote home to his concerned father with these words:

> Faith is the regalia of the Godhead, you say. Alas! dearest father, if you believe that without this faith no one can attain to salvation in the next world, nor to tranquility in this – and such, I know, is your belief – oh! then pray to God to grant it to me, for to me it is now lost. I cannot believe that he who called himself the Son of Man was the true, eternal God; I cannot believe that his death was a vicarious atonement.[6]

Schleiermacher, in part, bought into the philosophy of Kant. If God and ultimate reality, as *things-in-themselves*, are locked behind a transcendental wall, then there can be no absolute knowledge of the Divine. This means that the Bible could not have had a divine or supernatural origin. Consequently, once the supernatural is removed from the pages of the Scriptures, then miracles, the deity of Christ, and every other supernatural element must be removed as well.

Christianity can still operate without the supernatural because, according to Schleiermacher, the heart of religion is a *subjective* experience.[7] The Bible is still important, not because it is authoritative in what it says, but because it is a reliable

---

[6] B. A. Gerrish, *A Prince of the Church: Schleiermacher and the Beginnings of Modern Theology* (Philadelphia: Fortress Press, 1984), 25.

[7] That religious experience, for Schleiermacher, was a sense of *dependence*.

expression of the religious experience(s) of the ancient church.[8] On this humanistic foundation, Modern Liberal Theology flourished. Strangely, however, Schleiermacher remained a professing Christian and even became an influential pastor. In the process, he became one of the major contributors to Biblical Higher Criticism, which has had damaging effects on the Church.

And this brings us back to the life of Kierkegaard. How was Kierkegaard to save Christianity from a lack of belief in the supernatural? Is not Christianity destroyed when the supernatural is eliminated? What good is a religion without a supernatural God? Kierkegaard knew that Christianity was supposed to be more than a name; it was supposed to be a "passionate" faith. And with the idea that Christianity is foremost an exercise of passionate faith, Kierkegaard devised a solution that could "leap" believers over Kant's transcendental wall.[9] His solution was not to defend the *objective* certainty of the historicity of the Christian faith, but to stress the inwardness of a passionate faith.

---

[8] See John L. Murphy, *Modernism and the Teaching of Schleiermacher*, Part II (Washington: The Catholic University of America Press, 1961), 15-38.

[9] Though Kierkegaard makes reference to Lessing's ditch (a ditch that separates eternal truths of reason from contingent truths of history), Ronald Green suggests that Kierkegaard had Kant's distinction between the *noumenal and phenomena* realms in mind when he speaks of faith in God as a *leap* (See Ronald Green, *Kierkegaard and Kant: The Hidden Debt*). Gotthold Ephriam Lessing (1729-1781), however, thought it was unreasonable to believe in the historicity of miracles because faith would rest not on the proof exhibited by the miracle, but faith would rest on the fallible testimony of historical witnesses of the miracle. As Lessing stated: "Fulfilled prophecies which I myself experience are one thing; fulfilled prophecies of which I have only historical knowledge that others claimed to have experienced them are another" ("On the proof of the spirit and of power (1777)" in *Lessing: Philosophical and Theological Writings*. Edit. H. B. Nisbet. Cambridge: Cambridge University Press, 2005., 83). After separating the reported historical miracles of Christ from our present day experiences that run contrary to the miraculous, Lessing went on to claim: "That, then, is the ugly great ditch which I cannot cross, however often and however earnestly I have tried to make that leap" (Ibid., 87).

According to Kierkegaard, God is the absolute paradox. He cannot be comprehended by human reasoning, and is "completely different" from us, so any attempt to understand Him ends in failure. When trying to explain God, Kierkegaard would augured, we cannot help but make Him in our own image by erroneously ascribing human qualities to His nature.

God being paradoxical to human reasoning, according to Kierkegaard, does not mean that it is irrational to believe in God. God being paradoxical, however, does mean that any human conception of God leads to *apparent* absurdities or contradictions. This is especially true when we try to make sense of the incarnation. From our finite perspective, it seems absurd that an infinite and timeless God can be united to time and space in a human body. Though this may not be a formal contradiction, it goes beyond the reach of reason.

But where reason comes short, Kierkegaard said, faith takes a "leap." Faith transcends reason and sense perception by providing an existential experience of God. Though reason and sense perception are incapable of giving *objective* evidence of the supernatural, faith (as it is supernaturally wrought by the Spirit) does not need logical reason or empirical proof to believe.

Though *objective* certainty is unobtainable, *objective* certainty is not needed for faith. For faith to take a passionate leap, reason must "set itself aside." According to Ronald Green, professor of religion at Dartmouth, faith for Kierkegaard is "a leap beyond knowledge, a leap into the absurd."[10] However, Stephen Evans, a professor of philosophy at Baylor, reminds us that belief in the absurd is not belief in a logical contraction, but belief in an apparent contradiction – a paradox.[11] For instance, by faith Abraham was willing to do something that, humanly speaking,

[10] Ronald Green, *Kierkegaard and Kant: The Hidden Debt* (Albany: State University of New York Press, 1992), 76.
[11] Stephen Evans, *Passionate Reason: Making Sense of Kierkegaard's Philosophical Fragments* (Bloomington: Indiana University Press, 1992), 88.

appeared to be completely opposed to reason all together. He was willing to follow God and sacrifice his son. "But Abraham had faith," Kierkegaard argued, "and did not doubt. He believed the absurd."[12]

According to Kierkegaard, "truth is subjectivity."[13] "Only in subjectivity is there decision."[14] Only in subjectivity can faith operate. Kierkegaard defined truth as an "objective uncertainty, held fast through appropriation with the most passionate inwardness."[15] Objective uncertainty is what fuels faith: "Without risk, no faith. Faith is the contradiction between the infinite passion of the inwardness and the objective uncertainty. If I am able to apprehend God objectively, I do not have faith; but because I cannot do this, I must have faith."[16] In other words, without doubt, faith is non-existent. According to Kierkegaard, objectivity destroys faith.[17] But this is why faith is needed. By passionate faith, believers can "leap" over the wall of rational doubt and firmly take hold of apparent absurdities.

Karl Barth

Karl Barth (1886-1968), arguably the most influential theological thinker of the twentieth century, agreed with Kierkegaard that the heart of faith is a *subjective* grasping hold of Christ. For Barth, Christ is the objective Word of God. But what about the Bible?

---

[12] Søren Kierkegaard, *Fear and Trembling*, trans. Alastair Hannay (London: Penguin Books, 2003), 54.

[13] Søren Kierkegaard, 'Concluding Unscientific Postscript' in *Kierkegaard's Writings*, Vol. 1. ed. and trans. Howard V. Hong & Edna H. Hong (Princeton: Princeton University Press, 1992), 203.

[14] Ibid.

[15] Ibid.

[16] Ibid., 204.

[17] Kierkegaard claimed that if believers foolishly attempt to fortify their faith through an "objective inquiry," their faith would be lost in the process. When the absurd becomes increasingly probable, then faith has nothing to grasp hold of, "for the absurd is precisely the object of faith, and the only [object] that can be believed" (Ibid., 211). As if to say that faith cannot attach itself to that which is not absurd.

According to Barth, the Bible is authoritative not because it is without human error, but because it gives testimony of Christ and the Holy Spirit may choose to illuminate that testimony to our hearts. Barth claimed: "Scripture is holy and the Word of God, because by the Holy Spirit it became and will become to the Church a witness to divine revelation."[18] In this sense, "The Bible is God's Word so far as God lets it be His Word, so far as God speaks through it."[19]

Therefore, Barth did not view the historicity of the life, death, and resurrection of Christ as a relevant question. Not that he denied the historicity of Christ, but that the answer was not germane to faith. According to Barth, what is germane and important is for the Spirit to reveal Christ, who is the Word of God, to our hearts.

It is not faith in a document but faith in a living person that saves. It is the moment that we believe through the power of the Holy Spirit that the life, death, and resurrection of Christ effectually means something to us. Thus, according to Barth, knowledge of God comes by experiencing a personal relationship with Christ Jesus through faith.

Rudolf Bultmann

Rudolf Bultmann (1884-1976) was even more radical in his attempt to separate faith from reality. He agreed with Kierkegaard and Barth that the main concern in Christianity is faith in Christ, yet belief in the historical Jesus was optional. In his *demythology*, Bultmann attempted to remove the apparent myths from within the pages of Scripture.[20] It is the spiritual truth behind the story that matters, not the historicity of the

---

[18] Karl Barth, *Church Dogmatics*, ed. G. W. Bromiley and T.F. Torrance (Edinburgh: T. & T. Clark, 1936-1969), 1.2, 457.

[19] *Church Dogmatics.*, 1.1.123.

[20] See Rudolf Bultmann, *New Testament and Mythology* (New York: Harper & Row, 1966).

story. For Bultmann, the story of the resurrection is not a historical fact as much as it is a symbolic story that captures the new life and hope believers have in Christ. He promotes that it is existential faith in the message of the gospel (not belief in the historicity of the gospel) that saves believers from a life of hopelessness and despair.

Paul Tillich

The theologian Paul Tillich (1886-1965), though, finally took existentialism to its logical conclusion – atheism. Like the mysticism of Dionysius, the existentialism of Tillich claimed that God (in Himself) is unknowable. In his assessment of Tillich's theology, Carl Armbruster claimed that the "most fundamental statement Tillich makes about God is that he is being-itself."[21] Armbruster, nevertheless, went on to say, "Negatively, this means that God is not *a* being, not even the highest being, alongside other beings....He is beyond essence and existence because as being-itself he does not participate in nonbeing and finitude. He does not exist." That is, God goes beyond every possible conception about God.

Though Tillich did not believe that God existed as an independent reality, the term *God* is still useful. It is useful not because the term *God* communicates something real about this ultimate, unknowable being, but that it symbolizes our *ultimate concern*. "God is the fundamental symbol for what concerns us ultimately."[22] In other words, the term *God* does not speak of some external reality, but rather symbolizes that which internally controls us *subjectively*. If we don't like the term *God*, then Tillich said we are free to exchange that term with any other term that expresses the depth of heart or the ultimate concern of our life:

[21] Carl Armbruster, *The Vision of Paul Tillich* (New York: Sheed And Ward, 1967), 136.
[22] Ibid., 53.

The name of this infinite and inexhaustible depth and ground of all being is *God*. That depth is what the word *God* means. And if that word has not much meaning for you, translate it, and speak of the depths of your life, of what you take seriously without any reservation. Perhaps, in order to do so, you must forget everything traditional that you have learned about God, perhaps even that word itself. For if you know that God means depth, you know much about Him. You cannot then call yourself an atheist or unbeliever.[23]

Therefore, as this quote above indicates, Tillich did not believe in atheists, for even atheists have some concern that is ultimate for them. Faith in God consists of this ultimate concern. This ultimate concern is not based on the reality of the existence of God, but on the fact that all men have an ultimate concern.

Because our God is our ultimate concern, God has no ontological existence. He only exists within our *subjective* thoughts. "'God' is the name for man's ultimate concern. However, this is not to say that there is first a supreme being who then obliges man to render the homage of ultimate concern."[24] But according to Tillich, "It means that whatever concerns a man ultimately becomes god for him, and conversely, it means that man can be concerned ultimately only about that which is god for him."[25]

In other words, God does not demand faith, but our faith, according to Tillich, "is a total and centered act of the personal self, the act of unconditional, infinite, and ultimate concern."[26] In the end, religion exists only because man exists. Therefore, even though Tillich argued against atheism, he did not believe in a God that existed outside of the human mind.

[23] Paul Tillich, "The Depth of Existence," in *The Shaking of the Foundations* (New York: Charles Scribner's Sons, 1948), 57.

[24] Ibid., 136.

[25] Ibid., 136.

[26] Cited in Ibid., 47.

In this sense, David Hume (1711-1776) was right when he said: "Or how do you MYSTICS, [and I would add existentialists] who maintain the absolute incomprehensibility of Deity, differ from sceptics or atheists, who assert, that the first cause of ALL is unknown and unintelligible?"[27]

Gordon Kaufman

The professor of divinity at Harvard Divinity School, Gordon Kaufman (1925-2011), weirdly enough agreed with Hume:

> The central problem of theological discourse, not shared with any other "language game," is the meaning of the term "God." "God" raises special problems of meaning because it is a noun which by definition refers to a reality transcendent of, and thus not locatable within, experience. A new convert may wish to refer to the "warm feeling" in the heart to God, but God is hardly to be identified with this emotion; the biblicists may regard the Bible as God's Word; the moralist may believe God speaks through men's consciences; the churchman may believe God is present among his people – but each of these would agree that God himself transcends the locus referred to. As the Creator or Source of all that is, God is not to be identified with any particular finite reality; as the proper object of ultimate loyalty or faith, God is to be distinguished from every proximate or penultimate value or being. But if absolutely nothing within our experience can be directly identified as that to which the term "God" properly refers, what meaning does or can the word have?[28]

It is amazing that there are theologians who don't believe in God. Alvin Plantinga, former president of the American Philosophical Association, spoke of his own bewilderment

---

[27] David Hume, *Dialogues Concerning Natural Religion* (Indianapolis: The Bobbs – Merrill Company, 1947), 158. Words in bracket are present author.

[28] Cited in Alvin Plantinga, *Warranted Christian Belief* (New York: Oxford University Press, 2000), 32.

concerning this phenomenon when he said that "a theologian who does not believe in God is like a mountaineer for whom it is an open question whether there are any mountains or a plumber agnostic about pipes: a beguiling spectacle, but hard to take seriously."[29] Atheism, nevertheless, is the logical conclusion of existentialism. If there is no *objective* and external reality for belief to attach itself to, then there ceases to be any concrete warrant for belief.

Conclusion

In all this, we see the various attempts to separate *faith* from *reality*. Though there may not be any *objective* evidence for the existence of God, this is definitely not a problem for those who think that a *subjective* experience is all you need. "I don't need evidence to believe," so they say. "And if you ask me why I believe in Christ, I would answer with the words of the hymn *I Serve a Risen Savior.* I believe because 'He lives within my heart.'"[30] In this subjectivity, it is only a religious experience that can bring faith – a religious experience that, unfortunately, can simply not be understood by those who do not believe. As Blaise Pascal claims: "The heart has its reasons, which reason does not know."[31]

Although Kierkegaard, Barth, Bultmann, and others have sought to divide, to at least some degree, faith from reason, this is not what the Bible seeks to do. As we will see in the next chapter, faith and reason are not at war with each other; faith in Christ Jesus is not detached from the logical truth claims of the Bible. Rather, it is rooted in these objective and historical certainties.

---

[29] Ibid., 39.

[30] Written by Alfred H. Ackley (b. Spring Hill, PA, 1887; d. Whittier, CA, 1960), both text and tune were published in the Rodeheaver hymnal *Triumphant Service Songs* (1933).

[31] Blaise Pascal, *Pensées*, 277.

3

Faith is
Not Irrational

Scripture never separates faith from reality. Faith may believe in spiritual realities that transcend our empirical senses, but God is not asking us to suspend logic or for us to believe in something that is either irrational or unsubstantiated. He is not asking us to take a leap of faith into the darkness. If anything, we are called to run to the light and build our life on the most solid foundation possible – His Word.

Faith is Not Irrational

Moreover, faith in Christ is not blind and irrational. We should not believe because it is absurd. Faith is not a mixture of certainty and doubt. Faith is also not merely an existential and subjective experience of the Divine.

The renowned French atheist François-Marie Arouet (1694-1778), better known as Voltaire, was mistaken when he said, "Faith consists in believing not what seems true, but what seems false."[1] And he was also wrong when he claimed, "Faith consists in believing what reason does not believe."[2] Faith is not, as Friedrich Nietzsche (1844-1900) claimed, a desire "to avoid

---

[1] Voltaire, *The Works of Voltaire: A Contemporary Version*, 21 Vols. A Critique and Biography by John Morley, notes by Tobias Smollett, trans. William F. Fleming (New York: E.R. DuMont, 1901)., 4:327.
[2] Ibid., 5:253.

knowing what is true."³ Richard Robinson (1902-1996) in *An Atheist's Values* incorrectly described faith as "belief reckless of evidence and probability."⁴ And George H. Smith could not have been more wrong when he bifurcated reason and faith in his bestselling book *Atheism: The Case Against God*:

> The conflict between reason and faith may be viewed as a struggle to control *spheres of influence*. Since reason and faith cannot simultaneously reside over any given sphere, the dominance of one requires the exclusion of the other. Once we see that a sphere for faith can be manufactured only at the expense of reason, we can appreciate why the "unknowable" is a central tenant of theism and why Christianity has found it necessary to declare war on reason.⁵

Though Voltaire, Nietzsche, Robinson, and Smith have declared war on faith, Christianity does not declare war on reason. In fact, according to the Scriptures, to reject the God of Bible is an act of irrationality and absurdity (Ps. 14:1). Faith is the *only* reasonable response to the truth. For instance, the Apostle Paul asked for prayer to be protected from the irrationality of those who opposed the gospel, "Finally, brethren, pray for us ... that we may be delivered from unreasonable (ἀτόπων, *átópōn*)⁶ and wicked men." And the reason for their irrational behavior, Paul explains, is their lack of faith in Christ, "for all *men* have not faith" (2 Thess. 3:1-2, KJV).

---

³ Friedrich Nietzsche, *Anti-christ*. Trans. H.L. Mencken (New York: Cosimo Classics, 2005), 57.

⁴ Cited in John Hick, *Faith and Knowledge* (Ithaca, NY: Carnell University Press, 1966), 27.

⁵ Smith, George H., *Atheism: The Case Against God* (Amherst, NY: Prometheus Books, 1989), 125.

⁶ Technically speaking, the word ἀτόπος speaks of something that is morally wrong or ethically out of place. However, the Bible does not disjoin unethical behavior from irrational thinking (See Eph. 4:17-18).

We are called to think rationally about the promises of God: "Come now, let us *reason* together, says the LORD: though your sins are like scarlet, they shall be as white as snow; though they are red like crimson, they shall become like wool" (Isa. 1:18).[7] Rather than telling others that it is impossible for them to know God until they take a leap of faith into the darkness, we are called to give a rational defense to those who ask for a reason for the hope we have in Christ (1 Pet. 3:15). The object of faith, according to Paul, is objectively "true and rational" (Acts 26:25).

It is true that we are often irrational. And because of the awareness of our own fallibility, we should never elevate our human reason above divine revelation. The grounds of belief is not fallible reason but God's infallible Word. But even so, revealed truth is not and cannot be illogical.

Because faith is reasonable, the Reformed scholastic theologian Francis Turretin (1623-1687) explained, though reason is not the "principle upon which faith rests," it is "the instrument of faith." [8] Princeton theologian Charles Hodge (1797-1878) rightly stated: "The assumption that reason and faith are incompatible; that we must become irrational in order to become believers is, however it may be intended, the language of infidelity; for faith in the irrational is of necessity itself irrational."[9]

Faith Trusts God

Though faith is not illogical, it trusts God even when it cannot fully make sense of all the data at hand. When we seek the wisdom and expertise of a physician, it is not necessary for the doctor to explain all the scientific details behind his diagnosis.

---

[7] Emphasis is mine.

[8] Francis Turretin, *Institutes of Elenctic Theology*, Vol. 1, trans. George Musgrave Giger (Phillipsburg: P&R, 1992), 24.

[9] Charles Hodge, *Systematic Theology*, Vol. 3, (Grand Rapids: Eerdmans, 1981), 83.

Though an abbreviated explanation can be helpful, we're usually satisfied to take the physician's word for it. In this case, faith is not a leap into the darkness, but a confidence in the wisdom and expertise of the physician. It is true that doctors are occasionally wrong and second opinions are often warranted because the best of doctors are just mere men; yet, if it is evident that God is God (perfect, all-knowing, all-wise, and all-powerful), then it would be foolish and illogical for us not to trust His Word.

If we have faith in certain people, it is because we trust their wisdom and character. There are certain people in my life that I trust – my wife being one of them. I trust her. I don't need her to provide evidence for everything she says; her proven fidelity is enough for me to trust her.

In the same way, God has given ample evidence for His faithfulness. In fact, if the evidence is overwhelming, it becomes foolish on our part to continue to question Him. In this way, it was not a blind leap of faith for Abraham and Sarah to believe God over the empirical evidence that they were too old to have children. They trusted God's Word because they were "fully convinced that God was able to do what he had promised" (Rom. 4:21). God had already sufficiently proven Himself to them. Yes, humanly speaking, it was impossible. Yet, the One who made the promise was God. And God, by definition, is able to suspend the laws of nature.

In the same way, "By faith," the Bible says, "we understand that the universe was created by the word of God, so that what is seen was not made out of things that are visible" (Heb. 11:3). Again, if there is good reason to believe the God of the Bible, then it is reasonable to believe that He created the universe out of nothing. In fact, as I hope to show in this book, a personal God creating everything out of nothing is the *only* logical and self-consistent explanation of the origins of the universe.

If God is God, and if the Bible is His Word, then trusting the Bible is the only reasonable thing to do. Trusting God's Word is trusting in the veracity and trustworthiness of God. I, personally, have never trusted in green leprechauns or in their silly promises. Not only is there no evidence of their existence, I have no reason to believe, even if they did exist, that they would be trustworthy. Conversely, if the evidence is overwhelming that the Bible is God's Word and that God is fully trustworthy, as this book will seek to demonstrate, then those who trust God will never be disappointed (Rom. 10:11).

Trusting God is the essence of saving faith. I have proven myself fallible. Since it's common for me to have errors in judgment, why then would I trust my own judgment over and above the judgment of God? If God has proven Himself to be God, it is absurd for me not to trust Him.

It is self-verifying that every man-made philosophy has its origin in fallible and finite men. Because of this faulty foundation, the philosophies of men cannot help but be inconsistent and ever-changing. Moreover, as we shall see, the various explanations that man has sought to give for the origin, nature, and purpose of the universe do not hold up under their own weight. Only God's Word does not contradict itself. As the following chapters will show, it is the only self-verifying testimony that is cohesively consistent with itself. Why then would I trust in the wisdom of men over the wisdom of God? If God's Word proves itself faithful over and over, and if it provides us with the *only* consistent and cohesive system of thought, then it is only rational to trust the God of the Bible.

Conclusion

Though Dionysius and Kierkegaard have (to one degree or another) separated faith from reason (as we saw in chapters 1 and 2), the Bible never disjoins these two things. If rationality is impossible without the truth claims of Christianity, then we must submit ourselves to them, or otherwise we are the ones who become irrational. As we shall see, the Christian worldview is the only worldview that is rationally consistent with itself. Unbelief, in all of its forms, is what is irrational.

All truth, if worked out to its logical end, leads to the God of the Bible. Though this sounds like a huge leap of logic, its not. Something as seemingly simple as mathematics even, can only be cohesively reasoned with presupposing the God of the Bible. In fact, all truth, wherever it's found, only makes sense in the Christian worldview. Only the Christian worldview can make sense of logic, mathematics, ethical values, and our sensory experiences. Therefore, as I seek to show in this book, if we do not believe and submit ourselves to the God of the Bible, then we will be knowingly and foolishly rejecting the truth in order to hang onto a life of selfishness and the foolish notion of our own self-autonomy.

PART 2

What Shapes Beliefs

When a man's folly brings his way to ruin,
his heart rages against the LORD.
Proverbs 19:3

4

Shaped by Self-Interest

"Let's buy it, dad!" These words darted out of my mouth as soon as I saw the yellow truck with its custom rims and ground effects. Immediately I could proudly see myself driving it to school. Not only was it cool, but I couldn't believe it was in my price range. This could be mine, or so I thought.

My father responded with the dreaded but predictable words, "We need to test drive it first." Though this sounds only reasonable, you must realize that I was young and poor. My parents promised to help me buy my first vehicle by doubling all the money I earned over the summer. I worked hard, but only saved $900.00. And even back in the early nineties, you could not expect much for $1,800.00. The last thing I wanted was some grandma wagon.

So when I saw this customized truck, I was ready to pull the trigger without any investigation. In fact, I didn't want to test drive it, for deep down I knew it was too good to be true. If we happened to discover its mechanical problems, I knew my father would stand in the way of me being cool.

You see, I thought if we bought it before we learned it needed repairs, though more money would be needed to get the thing running, the most important thing would be accomplished – I would have a respectable looking ride to show off to all my friends.

The truth is, I didn't want to know the truth, for I assumed the truth would stand in the way of my happiness.

As you can imagine, when we opened the hood, it was missing half of its engine. Yep, too good to be true. I ended up with my dad's old, brown, farm truck – dependable but no ground effects.

I realize now that I was willing to overlook all the glaring red flags and knowingly do something foolish because of my imprudent pride. My emotions, my pride, and my inverted values hindered my judgment. I was not objective or rational because I did not want to be objective or rational.

Foolishness is living in opposition to what we know to be true. I am afraid this irrational condition and manner of thinking is universally prevalent in all of us. We are not merely irrational every now and then. Without God, we live in a state of irrationality.

Only irrational fools would consistently and practically deny that $2 + 2 = 4$. Not only is the answer to this equation a part of common sense, it is easily demonstrable and highly useful. If a postmodern thinker practically rejects the absolute and universal principles of mathematics, he may applaud himself for being consistent with his relativistic worldview, but in the process, his checkbook will be a total mess. Regardless of what we claim we believe about the laws of math, we cannot live practically without consistently submitting ourselves to them. For this and many other reasons, it is intellectually difficult to deny the absolute and universal nature of mathematics.

The same is true concerning the truth of Scripture. Scripture does not merely provide a few isolated, unrelated, and discounted truths; it gives us the *only* complete and cohesive worldview that provides meaning and rationale to the universe. As this book seeks to demonstrate in PART 5, only by presupposing the God of the Bible is ultimate truth possible.

Postmodern thinkers question $2 + 2 = 4$. This is because without presupposing the God of the Bible, there is no *basis* for universal or absolute truth. $2 + 2 = 4$ is only true (universally and absolutely) because God *is* true and has convincingly revealed Himself to all of us. Without the knowledge of God, which we all have, we have *no warrant* for knowledge at all, such as $2 + 2 = 4$. God is ultimate reality, and God is ultimate truth. Because God is ultimate, rather than seeking to justify knowledge based merely on human reason or human experiences, we must have knowledge of God to justify knowledge of everything else. Without knowledge of God, knowledge itself is impossible. In other words, without the God of the Bible, nothing makes sense in the grand scheme of things. As the Psalmist says, "In your light we see light" (Ps. 36:9).

If the Bible provides us with the only cohesive system of thought that allows us to properly interpret all of reality, why is it so hated and rejected by so many? If the truth claims of the Bible are logically demonstrable, why is it so despised and ridiculed by some of the brightest and smartest minds? The truth is, that if people loved the truth, they wouldn't reject the truth. Or, as British historian Malcolm Muggeridge famously said: "People do not believe lies because they have to, but because they want to." The problem is not that the truth is irrational; the problem is that fallen man is not without his personal biases and foolish pride. As we shall see in this chapter, people are self-centered by nature, and their self-centeredness is *the* controlling influence in how they feel, think, and behave (Rom. 1:18, 25).

Man is Not Neutral

The Bible describes this as depravity. Depravity is an inner heart condition that prevents us from loving any truth that is in opposition to our internal desire to be independent, free, and self-governing. Because we are born depraved, with a fallen nature, we hate the God of the Bible. We can, though, love a god of our own imagination – a god we can control. If we want to go to heaven, then we can work our way there. If we want to go to hell and hang out with our drinking buddies, then that is fine too. But to lovingly submit every detail of our lives, including our aspirations, thoughts, and beliefs to the absolute, sovereign God is not enticing in the least.

The Bible claims, however, that the entire universe and every individual person within it are made for the glory of God. This design not only determines our intended purpose, but it demands how we should think, feel, and live. In other words, we are not made for ourselves. Yet, we do not naturally want to be confined to such a sacrificial lifestyle, and even less do we want our sin, shame, and guilt to be fully exposed. This is what the Bible does, however. The Bible defines our lives and exposes our sin and guilt. This personal rebuke and criticism is too much to accept by those of us who love ourselves. Those of us who desire to cover up our sins to establish our own purpose and control our own dreams will reject any truth that endangers these objectives. It is not that we are incapable of understanding the truth; without the grace of God, we simply do not appreciate it.

For this reason, it is a false notion to think that our beliefs, opinions, and judgments are determined merely by the facts. When the facts oppose us, we will oppose the facts. Absolute objectivity is impossible for sinful and self-loving individuals. Only computers and machines are completely neutral. This is because computers do not care one way or another about the truth. As much as I like my new iMac, it could care less about me. As "smart" as it may be, it is void of any emotions and feelings. If I do a web search for Adolf Hitler or for Jesus Christ, my computer remains indifferent. It simply does not have a judgment or opinion on such things.

This is not true, however, with emotional people. People have an opinion on almost everything, especially on those things that relate to and affect their personal lives. Most people could care less about the fact that George Washington was the first President of the United States of America. Most people will accept this historical fact with little to no evidence. "Who cares, for how does that affect my day to day life?" Yet, when something touches us directly or indirectly, all of a sudden we will show great interest and concern. Bring up religion, politics, gun control, abortion, sexual orientation, George Bush, Obama, and other such heated topics, and all of a sudden people get testy. If there is one subject we all have a heavy and emotional investment in, it would be the grand subject of 'me, myself, and I.'

Just as we naturally seek to avoid physical pain and gravitate towards physical pleasure, we all hate to be criticized, rebuked, and shamed. We love to be recognized, praised, and honored. This tendency makes it easier to embrace that which is personally beneficial and harder to accept that which is personally detrimental. If you tell me I am brilliant, I will not put up an argument, even if there is no supporting evidence. But if you tell me I am not the sharpest tool in the woodshed, I will become angry, even if it is evident to all.

Richard Swinburne, emeritus professor of philosophy at the University of Oxford, recognizes that "humans," such as ourselves, "are creatures of limited intelligence and notoriously liable to hide from themselves conclusions which seem to stare them in the face when those conclusions are unwelcome."[1]

I have sadly seen this first hand. In High School, one of my friends committed suicide. No one saw this coming, especially the boy's mother. I knew *denial* was one of the steps of grieving, but I didn't realize how strong this emotion could be. At the graveside, the mother of this boy threw herself on top of the casket and began to shake it rapidly while crying out, "*Wake up,*

[1] Richard Swinburne, *Is There a God?* (New York: Oxford, 1996), 123.

wake up, wake up!" Everyone else stood silent. Reality was bitter, and in that moment it was too hard for this mother to accept. She, for the time being, would not allow herself to believe her only child was about to be buried. Though the evidence was overwhelming, it was not enough to convince her of something she did not want to believe. Because she loved her son, she did not love the truth. In this way, none of us are neutral.

Man's Nature Controls His Values

We cannot help but have something we love the most. And whatever we love the most will, in turn, determine what we hate and loathe. If we love darkness, then we will hate the light. If we love pleasure, then we will hate pain. If we love ourselves, then we will hate our enemies. This dichotomy is unavoidable. With this in mind, everything falls into a sliding scale from the object of our greatest affection to the object of our deepest hatred, with everything else in between. This scale is our value system. The things we appreciate and love form our values, and this value system determines our morals and ethical behavior.

This is because the object we love the most becomes our god – what we serve and worship. Whatever we love the most will control our thinking, emotions, and behavior. It will control us, and we will willingly bow down to it. For instance, let's say you loved baseball more than life itself. Your love for baseball would not only shape your opinion about baseball, it would control your life. If baseball was your greatest love, then it would shape how you spent your time and money, it would influence your friendships, and it would shape almost everything else in your life. This does not mean you wouldn't enjoy other things unrelated to baseball, but it does mean those unrelated things would be subjugated to your principle concern – baseball. Your love for baseball would be the ruling principle behind everything you thought and did. No doubt it would be a willing enslavement, but an enslavement it would be.

Man's Nature Controls His Behavior

With this in mind, as I have already pointed out, the Bible authoritatively teaches that which is clearly evident from our own personal observation and inward experience, namely that our chief object of affection is self. Without God's grace, we make ourselves the center of our thoughts and activities.

It is hard to deny that human nature is selfish. Infants are born not thinking about their mothers but themselves. Children do not have to be taught to covet and fight over toys. The history of the world is full of strife, bloodshed, and exploitation. Man may give himself to various pleasures and hobbies (such as baseball), materialism, and the pursuit of power and fame, but all these things are rooted in a love for self. When laws, restraints, oversight, and accountability are removed, ours hearts do not naturally move upward. As dumbbells naturally fall to the ground, we also naturally place our own needs and happiness above the needs and happiness of others.

Thankfully, not all of us want to be as bad as Hitler, but without the power of God, none of us will love God more than we love ourselves. We may have a desire to be good, but this love of self will always control the motive behind our seemingly good actions. We may have a love for God, but not a love for God that is greater than our love for ourselves. And whatever appears to be good, if done for selfish reasons, falls short of the glory of God and is classified as sinful.

Thus, selfishness is the controlling influence behind man's behavior. In other words, the problem behind sinful behavior and irrational thinking is man's depraved, selfish heart. As the Scripture claims: Because of "the futility of their minds. They are darkened in their understanding, alienated from the life of God because of the ignorance that is in them, due to their hardness of heart" (Eph. 4:17-18). As a result, the sinful heart is the heart of man's problem.

Man's Nature Controls His Emotions

This sinful heart also controls fallen man's emotions. It is a false but common notion to think that we are not responsible for our emotions. We often speak as if our emotions are alien creatures that attack us from the outside, as if they are outside of our control. "I can't help the way I feel." "You would feel the same way if this had happened to you." "I couldn't help that I fell in love with her." "You can't help who you love." "How could my emotions not be affected if I learn something bad had happened to my mother, or if I hear that my rich uncle was about to give me a million dollars?" "Of course my emotional ups and downs are a result of factors outside of my control." "I am a victim of my own emotions." "I am a victim of my circumstances." "I am an emotional person. I can't help it." With such common statements as these, people would have us believe their emotions are not derived from within themselves but from their external circumstances.

Such excuses eliminate the responsibility to control our emotions. Emotional problems are not like cancer; they are not diseases that attack us without our permission. We are not innocent victims of our own emotions. Emotions are not alien forces that are caused by our ever-changing circumstances. Rather, we are responsible for our emotions. We are responsible for loving that which is good and hating that which is bad. Jesus Christ made it clear in the Sermon on the Mount that we are not only responsible for how we outwardly behave, but also for how we inwardly feel.

It is true that our emotions are *connected* to our circumstances. It is not true, however, that our emotions are *controlled* by our circumstances. Rather, our emotions are controlled by our values (i.e., the things that we love and hate). Because I love my mom, it would deeply sadden me if I learned something bad had happened to her. How distressed would I feel? It all depends on the level and degree of love that I have for my mother. Because I value money, I would naturally rejoice to learn that my rich uncle was going to endow me with a million dollars. It is not that our emotions are controlled by the uncontrolled changes in our environment, but rather it is our pre-established values that control how we emotionally respond to the uncontrolled changes in our circumstances. This means our ever-changing circumstances expose our true nature and our personal values.

If we have emotional problems − and all of fallen humanity does − it is because we have our priorities and values out of place. Emotional problems are a direct result of a heart problem. As a bad tree always produces bad fruit, so a wicked heart will always produce wicked thoughts, feelings, and behavior. A selfish lifestyle that is consumed with satisfying felt needs and gratifying moment-to-moment expectations will no doubt result in an unstable emotional life. Our emotions are a reflection of our values and of our nature.

Man's Nature Controls His Beliefs

This heart problem, which produces various emotional problems, is the reason why sinners do not believe the truth. It is not that the Bible lacks credibility or is incomprehensible; it is that man values himself more than he values the Word of God. That is, fallen man has a fallen and inverted value system. Rather than God being man's chief affection, fallen man has placed himself in that spot. To believe the truth, man must warmly embrace the truth, and this requires submitting to God. Submitting to God is hard because it requires the dethroning of self. But this brings us back to the heart of the problem − man is willingly enslaved to his own selfishness.

Selfishness is blinding. What people do not love, people will not willingly embrace. If they do not have ears to hear, it is because they do not want to hear. By nature, unbelievers are enslaved to their own fleshly passions. Because of this, unbelievers love darkness rather than the light (John 3:19). They will naturally resist and suppress the truth in unrighteousness (Rom. 1:18) because they take "pleasure in unrighteousness" (2 Thess. 2:12).

Thus, the knowledge of God is viewed as a threat to their desire to live for themselves. As R. C. Sproul, the chairman of Ligonier Ministries, remarked: "God manifests a threat to man's moral standards, a threat to his quest for autonomy, and a threat to his desire for concealment."[2]

A lack of faith does not come from a lack of rational and credible evidence, it comes from a fallen heart that is enslaved to its own selfish desires. The French mathematician Blaise Pascal (1623-1662) understood this when he stated: "Those who do not love the truth take as a pretext that it is disputed, and that a multitude deny it. And so their error arises only from this, that they do not love either truth or charity."[3]

Man's Nature Must Change or Beliefs Will Not Change

For this reason, neither logic nor evidence can change our hearts. Denial and hatred of God's Word will cause even the most intellectual and brilliant people to become fools. As the Scriptures say, "For although they knew God, they did not honor him as God or give thanks to him, but they became futile in their thinking, and their foolish hearts were darkened. Claiming to be wise, they became fools (Rom. 1:21-22). And the "fool has said in his heart, there is no God" (Ps. 53:1).

It is not as if unbelievers need more empirical evidence to convince them of the truth, for even if they saw a man raised

[2] R. C. Sproul, *If There's a God, Why are there Atheists?* (Wheaton, IL: Tyndale House Publishers, 1988), 73.

[3] *Pensées*, 261.

from the dead, the Bible says they would still stubbornly hold on to their sins and reject the truth (Luke 16:31). The only thing that can produce faith in Christ is a heart transplant. Sinners must be born again. They must have the love of God poured into their dead hearts before they will willingly repent of their sins and run to Christ Jesus for forgiveness. Sin must be hated and Christ must be loved before sinners will embrace the gospel. Pascal understood this as well:

> Do not wonder to see simple people believe without reasoning. God imparts to them love of Him and hatred of self. He inclines their hearts to believe. Men will never believe with a saving and real faith, unless God inclines their heart; and they will believe as soon as He inclines it.[4]

Though faith in Christ is not blind, illogical, or without empirical evidences, it does go against one's self-centeredness. You must bow in submission to accept Christ as Lord (Rom. 14:11); and this is the difficulty. Your rejection and denial of the truth is not because you lack evidence, it is because you love yourselves and your sins more than you love the Christ who came to die for sinners such as you.

[4] *Pensées*, 284.

5

Shaped by
Self-Evident Truths

Why did Esau sell his birthright for a bowl of soup? What a foolish thing to do. Esau's father, Isaac, was likely the richest man alive, and as his firstborn, Esau was in line to inherit everything. The problem, however, was Esau had become hungry – very hungry. Starved after a long day of hunting, he reasoned that his inheritance would be useless if he happened to die of hunger. "I must eat or I will die," so he thought to himself. He was willing to give up everything for a bowl of beans. His present appetite was more important than his future glory. Of course, afterwards, this foolish transaction eventually led Esau to weep bitterly with a guilty conscience (Heb. 12:16).

We have all been guilty of trading in future benefits for a few moments of pleasure. Who has not made mistakes? To err is human, right?

I remember being willing to sell my soul for a game of freeze-tag. I look back and think to myself, 'What was I thinking?' When I was around 12, I felt inwardly convicted when I heard the gospel of Christ. As a preacher's kid, it was not the first time I heard the gospel, but it was one of the few times the gospel brought conviction on me. I was reminded of the good news that God was willing to forgive my sins. I had the answer to my guilt. Though I knew Christ was the only answer, there was something more important to me than my eternal welfare – a silly game. In the midst of contemplating my sins, guilt, shame, and the free offer of the gospel, a few friends approached and invited me to come join them in a game of freeze-tag. I remember feeling conflicted as I wanted to be saved from my sins, but I did not want to disappoint my friends. Sadly, I thought to myself, "salvation can wait." I was not willing to surrender control of my life to God. I loved the pleasures of this world more than I loved Christ. I hated my sins but not enough to forsake them. It was evident that I feared man more than I feared God. All it took for me to forfeit eternal life was a silly game of freeze-tag. It is one thing when our irresponsibility affects this present life, but quite another to turn our backs on Christ and forfeit our souls for eternity.

As with Esau, my foolishness only added to my already guilty conscience. Shame, of course, comes from doing something we know is foolish and irrational. Because we have all acted irrationally, we all know what guilt feels like. Conversely, because we all experience a guilty conscience, it is evident that we all know the difference between right and wrong. Yet, sin is irrational. It is contrary to what is reasonable and good. Because we know better, a guilty conscience is unavoidable.

Fair Play is Self-Evident

If you have forgotten what guilt feels like, just take a few moments to remember all the shameful things you have done in your past. If you have ever tried covering up something that you have done, you have known guilt. Open the closet and look at all those ugly skeletons. Be honest. Would you want all those memories broadcasted on national television? The fact that we try to lock those disgraceful moments up with the chains of a million excuses and seek to forget them is evidence that we have a guilty conscience.

Stop reading for a moment and pull up that one ugly memory that embarrasses you. You may have to dig a bit because we have an uncanny way of covering up, suppressing, and justifying our shame. Got it? Now ask yourself, "Why does this make me feel so dirty and guilty? Why do I want to keep this hidden from others? Where does this guilt come from?"

A guilty conscience is a hard thing to overcome. We all have one, but where did it come from? Why do we so often feel guilty? Can guilt be caused merely by an abstract code of morality? Is guilt just a byproduct of social constructs, political correctness, and parental instruction? Was Edward O. Wilson, professor of entomology at Harvard, right when he claimed: "Human emotional responses and the more general ethical practices based on them have been programmed to a substantial degree by natural selection over thousands of generations"?[1] Did morality evolve? Is the knowledge of right and wrong only relative?

C. S. Lewis, a former atheist, argued against such a notion. According to Lewis, because we judge people, cultures, and ourselves, we believe that there is a universal law of fair play. He said this higher court is evident when two people quarrel:

> Quarreling means trying to show that the other man is in the wrong. And there would be no sense in trying to do that unless you and he had some sort of agreement as to what Right and Wrong are; just as there would be no sense in saying that a footballer had committed a foul unless there was some agreement about the rules of football.[2]

By saying, "That's not fair," we are not merely saying that the offense we are complaining about does not please me. We are saying that the offense is contrary to the universal rule of fair play. We are saying that the other person is wrong because he

---

[1] Edward O. Wilson, *On Human Nature* (Cambridge: Harvard University Press, 2004), 6.
[2] C. S. Lewis, *Mere Christianity* (New York, NY: Touchstone, 1980), 18.

knows better. It is one thing when someone takes the seat you wanted at the theater because he got there first, but it is quite another thing when returning from the restroom, you discover your jacket has been relocated and that a stranger is sitting in the seat that you had reserved for yourself. The first incident is inconvenient. The second incident clearly goes against fair play. But why is someone stealing your seat not fair? Who says that this "seat-thief" should know better?

When people are confronted with violating the standard of fair play, most often, Lewis says, they do not argue against the standard. They don't typically say, "Who says I can't be selfish and exploit others for my own personal benefit?" Can you imagine anyone ever sincerely saying, "The golden rule (do unto others as you would have them do to you) is wrong?" Rather than denying the objective and binding nature of the universal law of fair play, violators often claim that they did not go against the standard. If not that, they construct some special excuse or circumstance that happens to exempt them from the moral obligation to follow the rule of fair play. In other words, people caught in a transgression typically do not argue against the law but deny, justify, or excuse themselves.

Moreover, if we say that the law of fair play is only a cultural construct, then we have no right to judge or criticize other cultures for their crimes against humanity. This is evident, says Lewis,

> The moment you say that one set of moral ideas can be better than another, you are, in fact, measuring them both by a standard, saying that one of them conforms to that standard more nearly than the other. But the standard that measures two things is something different from either. You are, in fact, comparing them both with some Real Morality, admitting that there is such a thing as real Right, independent of what people think, and some people's ideas get nearer to that real Right than others. Or put it this way. If your moral ideas can

be truer, and those of the Nazis less true, there must be something – some Real Morality – for them to be true about.[3]

He went on to state that, although other civilizations in different ages might have had subtle differences in cultural expectations, no civilization has ever believed that selfishness is honorable:

Think of a country where people were admired for running away in battle, or where a man felt proud of double-crossing all the people who had been kindest to him. You might just as well try to imagine a country where two and two made five. Men have differed as regards to what people you ought to be unselfish to – whether it was only your own family, or your fellow countrymen, or everyone. But they have always agreed that you ought not to put yourself first. Selfishness has never been admired.[4]

Self-centeredness is the heart of all sinful behavior. The moral law prohibits selfishness. Each of the Ten Commandments prohibit a different expression of selfishness and can be summed up with the one word that is antithetical to selfishness – *love* (Rom. 13:9-10). According to Scripture, love is patient, kind, sacrificially giving, and does not seek its own interest (1 Cor. 13:4-5). We know intuitively that we ought to love others and restrain from selfishness. At least it is intuitive that we don't want others to exploit us for their own advantages. For this reason, guilt does not come from breaking some abstract principle of living, but from injuring another individual.

According to the Bible, we know right from wrong because the law of God is written on our hearts (Rom. 2:15). If we did not instinctively know right from wrong, we would not constantly be justifying, condemning, or excusing ourselves in the things we think, feel, and do (Rom. 2:14-15). There is no reason to make

---

[3] *Mere Christianity*, 25.
[4] Ibid., 19.

excuses if there is no such thing as the standard of fair play or if that standard was not rooted in a personal God. We are either condemning or justifying ourselves in the things that we do (Rom. 2:15). It is self-evident that we all know right from wrong because we are either proud or disappointed with ourselves. If there was not a standard of fair play, we would neither feel guilty nor proud. But, because we know better, our irrationality is inexcusable.

In addition, we all stand in approval of the standard of fair play. I have not met a sane person who knowingly or willfully wants to be mistreated, taken advantage of, or exploited. With few exceptions, people agree that love is better than selfishness. The problem is not that there is a standard, but that we do not fulfill its requirements.

Selfish behavior has introduced us to self-condemnation. Thus, guilt is part of the human condition. If we deny this, we only incur more guilt because we know that we are lying to ourselves. That is, if we are honest with ourselves, we cannot deny our shame and guilt. Though there is no empirical proof for ethical distinctions, we cannot rid ourselves of the external standard. By showing how we *ought* to behave, the law reveals how often we fall short of its obligations.

Some truths, such as the law of fair play, are self-evident, which means that some truths are accepted without proof. In fact, none of us, including atheists, can prove everything that we believe. There are certain truths that we all naturally take for granted.

For instance, it is nonsensical to think we only believe ideas that can be proven true. If everything had to be proven through reason or experience, then nothing could be proven. If evidence were needed for every proposition that we believed, then we would need to believe infinitely more propositions. Even if we had enough time to answer an infinite regression[5] of questions, we would be forced to admit that our inability to find any ultimate truth leaves us without warrant for any of our beliefs. Even the committed evidentialist Antony Flew conceded that every "system of explanation must start somewhere....So inevitably, all such systems include at least some fundamentals that are not themselves explained."[6]

Thankfully, there are such things as self-evident truths. Self-evident truths testify of their truthfulness without needing any extra confirmation, demonstration, or proof. '2 + 2 = 4' and 'no man is both married and unmarried' are examples of self-evident truths. We don't have to travel to the end of a bottomless pit and answer an infinite regression of questions, for we can construct and anchor our knowledge on self-evident truths.

We call these self-evident truths, such as the law of fair play, axioms. An axiom is a premise or starting point that is taken for granted before acquiring any additional knowledge. Axioms are self-evident beliefs that anchor the rest our beliefs.

Logic is Self-Evident

Another axiom is the law of non-contradiction. For instance, the law of non-contradiction cannot be proven one way or the other. It states that something cannot be entirely true and entirely false at the same time and in the same sense. That is, an elephant painted entirely pink cannot also be at the same time be painted entirely blue. This would be a contradiction. Though we all know this to be true, we cannot prove it. Using logic to prove the law would be a form of circular reasoning, since we would have to assume that which we want to prove. The law of non-contradiction also cannot be proven by sense experience seeing

---

[5] An infinite regression is an unending series of propositions that would be necessary if every single proposition required demonstration.

[6] *There Is a God*, 134.

that immaterial laws, such as the laws of logic, cannot be examined or tested by the scientific method. Yet, without the use of the law of non-contradiction, both deductive reasoning and inductive scientific experiments are impossible. So, if you believe in the law of non-contradiction, then you believe in something that cannot be proven to be true. This self-evident axiom must be taken for granted before any other knowledge can be obtained.

Moreover, those who are foolish enough to try and deny the law of non-contradiction end up contradicting themselves in the process. Without the law of non-contradiction, a positive or negative statement can be entirely true and entirely false at the same time and in the same sense. If that were the case, words and propositional statements would mean nothing. Furthermore, to deny the laws of logic is to use a logic that is irrational. Thus, to deny the laws of logic is to argue in a self-referentially absurd manner.

Those who intellectually reject the absolute and universal nature of logic declare themselves fools from the very start. Thankfully, these absurd thinkers do not carry out their beliefs in the real world. They still drive on the right side of the road as they seek to avoid on-coming traffic. Those who intellectually deny the laws of logic prove themselves either ridiculously absurd or blatant liars. If you happen to meet such a person, who stubbornly refuses to play by the rules, the prudent thing to do is simply walk away.

God is Self-Evident

Self-evident truths, such as the law of fair play and the law of non-contradiction, must be accepted before we can rationally believe anything else. With this in mind, the biblical worldview offers three basic truths that are necessary to a cohesive system of thought. These truths are logic, moral distinctions, and God.[7] These things are inherent because they are necessary conditions preprogrammed within our thinking so that we can construct meaningful thought and cognitive beliefs as we interact with the external world.[8]

Yes, the knowledge of God is an inherent belief.[9] Inwardly, we all know this to be true. "All that is meant," by the word *inherent*, according to Charles Hodge, "is that the mind is so constituted that it perceives certain things to be true without proof and without instruction."[10] As John Calvin cleverly worded it: "Whence we infer, that this is not a doctrine which is first learned at school, but one as to which every man is, from the womb, his own master; one which nature herself allows no individual to forget, though many, with all their might, strive to do so."[11]

Therefore, Calvin unapologetically stated: "There is within the human mind and indeed by natural instinct, an awareness of divinity."[12] Awareness of divinity, otherwise known as *sensus divinitatis*, according to Alvin Plantinga, "is a disposition or set of dispositions to form theistic beliefs in various circumstances, in

[7] I believe there are other basic beliefs and inherent truths, such as the general trustworthiness of sense perception, the law of causality, and the belief in other minds.

[8] Charles Hodge was not comfortable with the word innate, but sought to explain the knowledge of God as a preconditioned or inherent faculty that makes the knowledge of God inescapable: "I do not say that men are born with some innate knowledge of God – they have none – but I do say that they are born with the faculty of knowing God" (*Systemic Theology*, Vol. 1. 192).

[9] The nineteenth-century Dutch theologian Herman Bavinck agreed: "We are fully convinced – prior to any argumentation – of our own existence, the existence of the world around us, the laws of logic and morality, simply as a result of the indelible impressions all these things make on our consciousness. We accept that existence – without constraint or coercion – spontaneously and instinctively. And the same is true of God's existence" (*Reformed Dogmatics*. trans. John Vriend. Grand Rapids: Baker, 2004., Vol. 2. 90).

[10] *Systemic Theology*, Vol. 1. 192.

[11] *Institutes*, 1.3.3.

[12] *Institutes*, 1.3.1.

response to the sorts of conditions or stimuli that trigger the working of this sense of divinity."[13]

It may be true, as indicated by Plantinga, that experience (that is, the perception of general revelation) is needed for these intuitive dispositions or beliefs to become activated, but, even so, without these intuitive beliefs we could not make sense of self-consciousness and the world around us.[14] Experience could not be interpreted without these intuitive dispositions or basic beliefs. This means, as we shall see, that knowledge of certain truths (such as God) must be presupposed before either reason or experience can function properly.

In fact, the knowledge of a personal God is a necessary condition for *all* knowledge (as Part 5 will show). According to Westminster Seminary professor, K. Scott Oliphint, "it is a knowledge that is presupposed by any (perhaps all) other knowledge."[15] None of us, according to Cornelius Van Til (1895-1987), former professor emeritus of apologetics at Westminster Theological Seminary, could "utter a single syllable, whether in *negation* or *affirmation,* unless it were for God's existence."[16]

As we shall see in chapter 12, though an atheist may rightly know who won the 1976 World Series, an atheist cannot explain the origin of the immaterial laws of physics or the origin of human consciousness. And both the laws of physics and consciousness are a vital part of the game of baseball. But, more importantly, since an atheist cannot provide an all-encompassing rational system based on a cohesive worldview (i.e., a grand metanarrative), as I hope to demonstrate in chapter 14, skepticism cannot help but creep into the cracks of its own

[13] *Warranted Christian Belief,* 173.

[14] Calvin, however, claimed that we do not need to go outside ourselves to process the knowledge of God (*Institutes,* 1.4.4).

[15] *Covenantal Apologetics,* 103.

[16] Cited in Don Collett, "Van Til and Transcendental Argument" in *Revelation and Reason,* ed. K. Scott Oliphint and Lane G. Tipton (Phillipsburg, NJ: P&R, 2007), 269.

mislaid foundation, inevitably destroying the flooring and revealing the level below – nihilism. In other words, if followed through to its logical end, atheism leads to nihilism, in which historical events, such as the 1976 World Series, are questionable. If the knowledge of God (which presupposes logic and moral distinctions) were not pre-supplied, the construction of a cohesive worldview would be impossible.

Specifically, how do we know that these three truths (God, logic, and moral distinctions) are inherent within us all? We know it not only because these beliefs are confirmed by the inward testimony of our consciences, but also because without these concepts, as we shall see, nothing makes sense. We need God, logic, and morality to formulate a cohesive worldview that can be lived out in our everyday lives. To suppress or eliminate knowledge of these truths leads to absurdity.

These inherent beliefs (God, logic, and moral distinctions), are not wholly independent from each other though. Since these beliefs are foundational to who God is – for He is a God of rationality (logic) and righteousness (moral distinctions) – to have an inherent knowledge of God is to have an inherent knowledge of logical and ethical absolutes. This is to say, God is the foundation and source of logical and ethical absolutes.

The law written on man's conscience is not an abstract idea of justice that exists outside of God. The law is God's moral character. God is righteous. God is logically consistent with His own nature. He cannot contradict His character. God cannot be non-God. The laws of ethical living (morality) and the laws of thinking (logic) are not social constructs or abstract principles independent of God. God is not underneath the law. He is the law. That is, the law is a reflection of His moral essence. The laws of logic and morality only exist because God exists.

Conclusion

So what this all shows is that of these three truths, the greatest is God. The *sensus divinitatis* includes the knowledge of logic and moral distinctions because these truths are grounded in the knowledge of God. Without God, laws of behavior and thinking would be non-existent. To put it another way, our guilty consciences, which stem from our knowledge of the laws of logic and morality, presuppose God. The converse is true as well. Our knowledge of God presupposes the laws of morality and logic.[17] We cannot have knowledge of the laws of morality and logic without having the knowledge of God.[18] Because these beliefs are inherent, incorrigible, and necessary, the Bible does not seek to prove these things but accepts them as irrefutable realities. All truth must be built on the knowledge of God, or, as we shall see, there is no ground for knowledge at all.

[17] According to Richard Muller, "Calvin had distinguished between three kinds of 'reasons': 'reason naturally implanted' in human beings by God, which 'cannot be condemned without insulting God'; a vitiated reason, occurring in 'corrupt nature' which sinfully warps God's revelation; and 'reason...derived from the Word of God'" (*Post-Reformation Reformed Dogmatics*, Vol. 1., 275).

[18] Meredith Kline is helpful in the manner in which he links our knowledge of ethics with being made in the likeness of God: "Likeness to God is signified by both image of God and son of God. Man's likeness to God is a demand to be like God; the indicative here has the force of an imperative. Formed in the image of God, man is informed by a sense of deity by which he knows what God is like, not merely that God is (Rom. 1:19ff.). And knowledge of what one's Father-God is, is knowledge of what, in creaturely semblance, one must be himself. With the sense of deity comes conscience, the sense of deity in the imperative mode. The basic and general covenantal norm of the imitation of God was thus written on the tables of man's heart (Rom. 1:32; 2:14f.)." (*Kingdom Prologue: Genesis Foundations for a Covenantal Worldview*. Eugene, OR: Wipf & Stock, 2006, 62).

6

Shaped by Conscience

Since God is the ultimate truth, He must also be the source of all truth.[1] All truth comes from God and points back to God. Without God's self-revelation, truth is impossible. "God's existence," says Don Collett, professor of Old Testament at Trinity School of Ministry, "is the basis for all predication, such that one cannot predicate truly or falsely about anything unless God exists."[2]

Why Knowledge is Possible

Yet, how do we know the truth? How is the knowledge of God possible? How is revelation possible? As we have seen, Pseudo-Dionysius claimed that because of God's infinite transcendence, God cannot reveal Himself to man. Immanuel Kant, on the other hand, claimed that the knowledge of God is impossible because of the epistemological limitations of finite man. Either way, the gap between an infinite God and finite man is too vast

---

[1] The English Puritan John Owen claimed: "It is necessary to the unlimited self-sufficiency of God that He Himself alone may know Himself perfectly. His understanding is perfect and has no limits. Therefore, as that attribute of God by which He comprehends Himself and all of His perfections is an infinite attribute, it can be entered into by no other being. God Himself alone is all-knowing and all-wise and, therefore, knowledge in its true fullness can rest only in God Himself" (*Biblical Theology*, 15).

[2] Don Collett, "Van Til and Transcendental Argument" in *Revelation and Reason*, ed. K. Scott Oliphint and Lane G. Tipton (Phillipsburg, NJ: P&R, 2007), 266.

for either God or man to cross. According to the Bible, however, God is not only able to reveal Himself, He *has* revealed Himself to us through His Son – Jesus Christ. Jesus is the Word of God (John 1:1). Jesus is the wisdom of God (1 Cor. 1:24). Jesus is the light (John 1:4). Jesus is the truth (John 14:6). All truth is derived from the mind of God, and Christ Jesus, as the express image of God, is the conduit through which the mind of God is communicated to man.[3]

The knowledge of God, of self, and of the universe reveals the glory of God, and this glory has been communicated to us through Christ Jesus. As Carl Henry (1913-2003), founder of the popular Christian magazine, *Christianity Today*, stated: "The logos [the second person of the Trinity] of God – preincarnate, incarnate, and now glorified – is the mediating agent of all divine disclosure. He is the unique and sole mediator of the revelation of the Living God."[4]

As any piece of art or engineering marvel reveals the wisdom and creativity of the artist or engineer, creation reveals the wisdom and power of God. "The heavens declare the glory of God; the skies proclaim the works of his hands" (Ps. 19:1). The "whole earth is full of His glory" (Isa. 6:3). "For since the creation of the world God's invisible qualities – his eternal power and divine nature – have been clearly seen, being understood from what has been made, so that people are without excuse" (Rom. 1:20). George Park Fisher (1827-1909), emeritus professor of divinity at Yale, stated: "A dog sees on a printed page only meaningless marks on a white ground. To us they contain and convey ideas, and bring us into communion with the mind of the

---

[3] See Ronald Nash, *The Word of God and the Mind of Man* (Phillipsburg, NJ: P&R Publishing, 1982), 59-69.

[4] Carl Henry, *God, Revelation and Authority* (Waco: Word Books, 1979), Vol. 3., 203. Words in bracket are present author.

author. So it is with Nature."[5] He went on to say: "To ignore God as the author of Nature as well as the mind is as absurd as to make 'the anthem the offspring of unconscious sound.'"[6]

Yet, the knowledge of God's invisible attributes, which are clearly manifest in creation, has come to us through Christ. As it is written, "In the beginning was the Word, and the Word was with God, and the Word was God. He was in the beginning with God. All things were made through him, and without him was not any thing made that was made" (John 1:1-3). As the instrument through which God created all things, knowledge derived from the universe comes to us by the immanent power of Christ Jesus.

Christ is not only the medium of general revelation but also the mediator of special revelation. Not only do we learn about the works of God through Christ, we discover the nature of God through Christ. How can we see the invisible God? By looking at Christ. Christ is the "image of the invisible God" (Col. 1:15). God manifested Himself in His humanity. He came near by becoming one of us. "And the Word became flesh and dwelt among us, and we have seen his glory, glory as of the only Son from the Father, full of grace and truth" (John 1:14). Though no one has ever seen God, Christ has made Him known (John 1:18).

The holiness, righteousness, mercy, love, and the very nature of God have been manifested in this world through the person and work of Jesus Christ. For instance, if we want to learn about the justice and mercy of God, all we have to do is look at the cross. As the Scriptures say: "[God] has spoken to us by his Son...through whom also he created the world. He is the radiance of the glory of God and the exact imprint of his nature, and he upholds the universe by the word of his power" (Heb.

[5] George Park Fisher, *The Grounds of Theistic and Christian Belief* (New York: Charles Scribner's Sons, 1915), 34.
[6] Ibid.

1:2-3). Though God is transcendent and separate from man, He is also immanent. In Christ, He is never far from us. Truly, Jesus is the way, the truth, and the life. There is no other way to God but through Him (John 14:6).

As the perfect reflection of God, Christ is capable of revealing the infinite mind of God to the minds of men. But, how is the finite capable of grasping the infinite? Even through the mediation of Christ, how is man the proper receptor of natural and supernatural revelation?

Though there is an immense gap between Divinity and humanity, this gap is not immeasurable. Knowledge of anything requires some form of similarity or analogous relationship. Some point of connection is required between God and man for communication to be possible. And this is exactly what we find in Genesis 1. As God, in Christ, created all things to reveal the glory of God, He created man in His own image and likeness.

Because man is made in the image of God (known as the *Imago Dei*) he is not identical with God, but he is also not entirely different. This analogous relationship between God and man is what makes man capable of receiving and understanding divine revelation (Gen. 1:26). As we shall see, the *Imago Dei* equips us with an innate and incorrigible knowledge of God and ourselves and provides us with the apparatus to properly understand the world around us.

Man is a part of natural revelation because God created him. Along with the rest of creation, mankind reveals the glory and wisdom of God. Man reveals God because he is a part of God's creation, but more importantly, man reveals God for he was created after the very likeness of God. Because man cannot help but know himself, he cannot help but immediately know God.

These basic truths are part of the *Imago Dei* and supply man with an immediate knowledge of God through the knowledge of himself. John Calvin was so convinced of this that he began his *magnum opus*, *The Institutes of the Christian Religion*, with these words:

> Nearly all the wisdom we possess, that is to say, true and sound wisdom, consists of two parts: the knowledge of God and of ourselves. But, while joined by many bonds, which one precedes and brings forth the other is not easy to discern. In the first place, no one can look upon himself without immediately turning his thoughts to the contemplation of God, in whom he lives and moves. . . Again, it is certain that man never achieves a clear knowledge of himself unless he has first looked upon God's face, and then descends from contemplating Him to scrutinize himself.[7]

We cannot know ourselves without knowing God because we are made in God's image.[8] Because we cannot help but know ourselves, the knowledge of God is innate. Our life, as God has breathed life into us, gives us enough light to see God (Ps. 56:13). In seeing ourselves, we see a reflection of God. Having a life that is analogous to the life of God gives us knowledge of God, or as Van Til would say: "For man, self-consciousness presupposes God-consciousness."[9]

Fisher likewise understood that belief "in the personality of man, and belief in the personality of God, stand or fall together."[10] Our awareness of God (*sensus divinitatis*) is the result of being made in the image of God. Oliphint claims, "by virtue of. . . being created in the image of God, always and everywhere [we] carry the knowledge of God with [us]."[11] "This knowledge does not come by the proper and diligent exercise of our

---

[7] *Institutes* 1.1.2., 1.1.1.

[8] In line with the thoughts of Calvin, John Frame stated, "Neither knowledge of God nor knowledge of self is possible without knowledge of the other" (*The Doctrine of the Knowledge of God*, 65).

[9] Cornelius Van Til, *The Defense of the Faith* (Philipsburg, NJ: R&R, 1967), 90.

[10] George Park Fisher, *The Grounds of Theistic and Christian Belief* (New York: Charles Scribner's Sons, 1915), 1.

[11] K. Scott Oliphint, *Reasons for Faith* (Philipsburg, NJ: P&R, 2006), 139.

cognitive, emotive, or volitional capacities; it rather comes by God's own revelatory activity within us."[12]

This means that the knowledge of God is intuitive. The knowledge of God "is immediate," according to Oliphint, "because it is not gained by way of inference. There is nothing that we do – no demonstration, no syllogism – that is the ground for the acquisition of this knowledge."[13] "It is *implanted* (or inserted) knowledge of God."[14] Oliphint went on to say that it is, "given to us, through the things that are made, by God himself."[15] As Fisher said many years prior: "The ultimate source of the belief in God is not in processes of argument. His presence is more immediately manifest[ed]."[16]

The knowledge of God is what some philosophers call a properly basic belief. Plantinga says basic beliefs are "not accepted on the evidential basis of other propositions."[17] Basic beliefs are similar to memory or perceptual beliefs. They are not inferred or deduced. We do not need evidence or rational argumentation to believe in God any more than we need evidence or argumentation to believe in memories.

According to Plantinga, "The *sensus divinitatis* is a belief-producing faculty (or power, or mechanism) that under the right conditions produces belief that isn't evidentially based on other beliefs."[18] "This capacity for knowledge of God," says Plantinga, "is part of our original cognitive equipment, part of the fundamental epistemic establishment with which we have been created by God."[19]

---

[12] *Covenantal Apologetics*, 103.
[13] *Reasons for Faith*, 155.
[14] Ibid.
[15] Ibid.
[16] *The Grounds of Theistic and Christian Belief*, 24.
[17] *Warranted Christian Belief*, 175.
[18] Ibid., 179
[19] Ibid., 180.

The *Imago Dei* endows us with the capacity to know God, but it does more than that – it provides us with an inherent knowledge of God (*sensus divinitatis*). It furnishes us with moral and logical distinctions. Though this may not seem immediately clear, we must realize that the knowledge of God that is implanted in us is not simply a knowledge of an abstract being (which we call God), but it is a knowledge of a personal, moral, and rational being.

This means that the laws of logic and morality are essential to God's essence and have been stamped on us because we are made in the likeness of this God. Being created in the image of God furnishes us with a rational mind and an ethical standard that ensures knowledge of God, of the world around us, and of ourselves.[20] We know right from wrong. We understand that 'A' cannot be both 'A' and 'non-A' in the same sense and at the same time because we are made in the image of God.

We were designed to know God because we were made in His image and have been given the cognitive tools necessary to see God as we observe ourselves and the world around us. We know God because we were made to be rational and ethical beings.

Consequently, being made in the image of God means that our own self-consciousness is a part of God's general revelation. This implies that God's general revelation of Himself is both internal (within our own self-consciousness) and external (in the physical universe that surrounds us). And this internal revelation (*sensus divinitatis*) endows us with the capacity to properly interpret the message of God's external revelation.

More specifically, being made in the image of God gives us the apparatus to see the likeness of God within ourselves as well

---

[20] Cornelius Van Til claimed: "Thus the knowledge of God is inherent in man. It is there by virtue of his creation in the image of God" (*Defense of the Faith*, 172.), cited in Greg Bahnsen, *Van Til's Apologetic* (Phillipsburg, NJ: P&R Publishing, 1998), 221.

as the glory of God in creation. As Greg Bahnsen (1948-1995), former scholar in residence for the Southern California Center for Christian Studies, remarked: "Man is created in the image of God to engage in the world in a rational way. Not only is man's mind analogical to God's, but it is compatible with the God-created universe because of God's designing us and our environment."[21] The universe, according to Calvin, is "a mirror in which we are to behold God."[22] Calvin said, "men cannot open their eyes without being compelled to see him." [23] He went on to state, "wherever you cast your eyes, there is no spot in the universe wherein you cannot discern at least some sparks of his glory."[24] For this reason, John Murray (1898-1975), professor of theology at Princeton and then Westminster, affirmed:

> It was of his sovereign will that God created the universe and made us men in his image. But since creation is the product of his will and power the imprint of his glory is necessarily impressed upon his handiwork, and since we are created in his image we cannot but be confronted with the display of that glory.[25]

This is echoed by John Frame, one of the leading interpreters of the philosophy of Cornelius Van Til, who says that "we know God by means of the world. All of God's revelation comes through creaturely means...Thus we cannot know anything about God without knowing something about the world at the same time...We cannot know the world without knowing God."[26]

---

[21] Greg Bahnsen went on to state: "Rather, we are saying that the laws of logic reflect His nature, the way He is in Himself. They are, therefore, eternal expressions of the unchanging character of God" (*Pushing the Antithesis*, 210-211).

[22] John Calvin, *Calvin's Commentaries*, Vol. 1, trans. John King (reprint, Grand Rapids: Baker, 2003), 58-62.

[23] *Institutes* 1.5.1

[24] Ibid.

[25] *Collected Writings of John Murray*, Vol. 4, 1.

[26] *The Doctrine of the Knowledge of God*, 64.

Plantinga explains how creation reveals the knowledge of God to us:

> It isn't that one beholds the night sky, notes that it is grand, and concludes that there must be such a person as God; an argument like that would be ridiculously weak...It is rather that, upon the perception of the night sky or the mountain vista or the tiny flower, these beliefs just arise within us. They are *occasioned* by the circumstances; they are not conclusions from them.[27]

The *sensus divinitatis* ensures that the knowledge of God is always present within us. Even if all our memories were erased, we would not lose sight of God. "Ever renewing its memory," Calvin remarked, "he repeatedly sheds fresh drops....Men of sound judgment will always be sure that a sense of divinity which can never be effaced is engraved upon men's minds."[28] As we interact with the world around us, our very lives cannot help but continually reveal God to us. Natural revelation speaks to us even when we do not want to hear its message. It is a constant voice that cannot be silenced. Oliphint claims that it is "a knowledge that God infuses into his human creatures, and continues to infuse into them, even as they continue to live out their days denying or ignoring him."[29]

In addition to the *Imago Dei* stamping, reproducing, and duplicating within us the knowledge of God, when it is renewed in Christ and functioning properly, it equips us with the necessary properties to experientially know God. God made us in His own image because He made us to be rational and morally upright (Ecc. 7:29).

Before the likeness of God in man was defaced by the fall, it consisted of the rational knowledge of God as well as the moral

[27] Ibid., 175
[28] *Institutes* 1.3.1, 1.3.3.
[29] *Reasons for Faith*, 140.

uprightness to love and obey God. Calvin went on to say, "For we know that men have this unique quality above the other animals, that they bear the distinction between right and wrong engraved in their conscience. Thus there is no man to whom some awareness of the eternal light does not penetrate." [30] Humanity bore this mark because we were created to have more than an intellectual conception of God. We were made in God's likeness so that we could enjoy and glorify God in our lives. We were created to have a personal relationship with God. Before the image of God was marred by sin in the fall, man was equipped, according to Martin Luther, "to love God, to believe God, to know God."[31] In a word, being created in God's likeness makes it possible for us to live in a mutually loving relationship with our Creator.[32]

We were designed and efficiently equipped to enjoy a loving and a covenantal relationship with God. Yet, our guilt is evidence that this covenant relationship has been broken. Even without instruction from another, because we are made in the image of God, we cannot help but immediately and irresistibly conclude that our failure is a failure against a personal God. Failure to live in accordance with the laws of right thinking and the laws of right behavior is a failure not only of our own nature, but also a failure against a personal God who made us in the likeness of His nature.

Guilt testifies of the fact that our relationship with the Creator is broken. For a God that is both rational and righteous is not merely a supernatural, impersonal force, but a living, thinking, emotional, and righteous Person – One who has the right and power to tell us how to live. By knowing ourselves in this manner, we cannot help but understand this reality. We immediately

---

[30] *Calvin's Commentaries*, cited in Greg Bahnsen, *Always Ready*, 39.
[31] Cited in Herman Bavinck, *In the Beginning* (Edinburgh: Banner of Truth Trust, 1979), 179.
[32] *Reasons for Faith*, 155.

comprehend by the testimony of our lives and the world around us that we are in some analogous relationship with a personal and holy God.

At War with God and Ourselves

Being made in the image of God may have originally equipped us to have a personal relationship with God, but sin damaged that relationship long ago. Like a painting that has been washed out by exposure to the sun, the likeness of God is still present within us. However, it is no longer a pure representation as the *Imago Dei* no longer functions according to its original design.

Consequently, as we noticed in chapter 4, being driven by self-interest, we can no longer think or live in a manner that perfectly reflects the glory of God's image. Our thoughts, affections, and lives are no longer a pure representation of God's likeness. Rather than being drawn to the knowledge of God that remains stamped on our consciences, we are at war with this knowledge. The knowledge of God remains, but a love for God has been supplanted with self-love. Though the knowledge of right and wrong still speaks within our consciences, the desire to love God and one's neighbor above ourselves is no longer present in our hearts. Yet, though the rational laws of the mind (logic) are still stamped on our thinking, apart from God's grace, the intellectual and practical consistency to live congruently with these laws is missing. Sin is irrational, for it warps, contorts, and distorts a sound mind and leads to additional foolish and sinful behavior.

As a result, our guilty consciences demonstrate both our knowledge of God and also our rejection of this knowledge. This guilt makes God's holiness terrifying. As Adam and Eve hid from God after they disobeyed Him, we seek to suppress the knowledge of God in unrighteousness (Rom. 1:18). This is our way of hiding from God. This takes place every time we fail to give thanks to God (Rom. 1:21). Ceasing to acknowledge God is the first step towards practical atheism. Most of us do not intellectually deny God's existence. We simply live as if He does not exist or as if He is not watching us. Once we think we have pushed God's holy gaze away from our lives, we feel that we are no longer accountable for our actions. Then comes a whole host of sinful practices which harden our minds and hearts even more towards God (Heb. 3:13). As Jonah fled from God, we too seek to flee from the knowledge of God and find refuge in the cold darkness.

How far are we willing to travel away from God? Though all of us are born with the knowledge of God, we want to live and die as practical atheists. In order to justify our irrational behavior, we devise contradictory and unreasonable systems of thought that eliminate God from the equation. Because we naturally place our own interests above the interests of God, we would like to think that we are intellectually self-sufficient. We do not need to submit to divine revelation. In the same way we suppress guilt, we seek to stomp out our awareness of God. The *sensus divinitatis* must be rooted out. We want to determine what is right and wrong, and what is true and false, for ourselves rather than acknowledge that all knowledge comes from God. This happened when Eve questioned God in the Garden (Gen. 3:4-6). And ever since then, we have tried to make ourselves the source of our own beliefs.

We are at war with God and ourselves. We hate God but we cannot fully eliminate the stamp of God within our own consciousness. We struggle against the reality that we are made in the image of God. As Oliphint rightly claimed: "It is this image of God that is the presupposition behind everything else that we are."[33] Thus, we are tormented and seek to run from God because we carry the knowledge and reflection of God with

[33] K. Scott Oliphint, *Covenantal Apologetics* (Wheaton, IL: Crossway, 2013), 93.

us wherever we go. We are tormented because we carry the knowledge of God in ourselves.

We would like to free ourselves not only from the knowledge of God, but also from the laws of logic and morality engraved on our hearts. Laws are binding and point to a lawgiver. Ethical standards only serve to reinforce our guilty hearts. No matter how hard we try, we cannot live without the laws of logic and morality that come from the knowledge of God, because without the knowledge of God, all knowledge is impossible.

The postmodern thinker may attempt to live without any absolutes, but everywhere he turns he crashes into an unmovable logical fence that binds him. "Man," says Van Til, "constantly throws water on a fire that he cannot quench."[34] Man may suppress the truth, but the truth will not die. It cannot die. Understanding this, Calvin stated:

> Finally, they entangle themselves in such a huge mass of errors that blind wickedness stifles and finally extinguishes those sparks which once flashed forth to show them God's glory. Yet that seed remains which can in no wise be uprooted: that there is some sort of divinity; but this seed is so corrupted that by itself it produces only the worst fruits.[35]

To what extent will depraved men go to deface the remaining image of God that is stamped on their nature? As we shall see in the next few chapters, they will go so far as to deny the universal nature of the laws of logic and moral absolutes. If rational sanity demands submission to God, man has proven that he is more willing to embrace intellectual absurdity than to succumb to the knowledge of the truth.

Because sin damaged men would rather accept a lie than submit to the truth, they stand in front of a mirror scratching,

[34] *The Defense of the Faith*, 92.
[35] *Institutes*, 1.4.4.

picking, and clawing at their faces in order to remove the image of God that is staring back at them. They are eager to erect a god fashioned in their own human likeness rather than to submit to the God who made them in His own divine likeness. They would rather worship an illogical idol in order to obtain intellectual independence than submit to the God of all wisdom. In so doing, they are willing to sell their souls for a bowl of soup. Absurdity and a guilty conscience, however, are things that mankind will never shake until they turn to Christ and bow the knee to His eternal lordship.

Conclusion

Without submitting to these three innate and ineradicable truths (logic, morality, and God), we cannot think or live coherently. These basic truths are necessary conditions for knowledge. In other words, to deny the existence of God (which includes the denial of the laws of logic and moral distinctions) leads to absurdity in one's thinking and behavior. Without God, all things fall apart.

Yet, I will take it one step further in the following chapters. For any of us to have a holistic worldview that is capable of answering life's deepest questions, not just any God will do. The triune God of the Bible is needed. Though not all the truth claims of the Bible are innate, they consist of the only logical and cohesive framework that is in perfect agreement with the inherent knowledge of logic, morality, and God. The biblical worldview is the only coherent system of thought. Only when we submit ourselves to God's authority may we escape our own incoherent and dysfunctional thinking. Until then, a guilty conscience and irrational thinking and behavior will continue.

7

Shaped by Our Worldview

Not only is our perception of reality controlled by the affections of our heart, our perception is controlled by our thinking. This sounds obvious, but we must realize our cognitive thoughts are not neutral anymore than our heart is neutral. How we think about any particular subject cannot help but be shaped by our thoughts about God, knowledge, and morality. Our thoughts about these core beliefs are the foundation behind our worldview, and our worldview shapes our thinking.

A worldview, or what the Germans call a *Weltanschauung*, is like a pair of glasses that allows us to observe the world. If our glasses are green tinted, we will have a hard time seeing the true color of the sun. If our glasses are red tinted, we will have a hard time identifying the true color of the grass. It is not until we see through clear lenses that reality will appear as it truly is in-itself. The *sensus divinitatis*, which includes the laws of logic and ethical distinctions, is the inherent set of glasses that God has given us to perceive reality. Because of our fallen nature, however, these glasses have fallen into bushes full of thistles and thorns. What was once perfectly transparent has been deeply scratched. Our vision is now blurry. Though we can dimly make out the image of God and the laws of logic and morality from within our own nature, we no longer appreciate the true beauty of the knowledge, power, and glory of God that is clearly stamped on every blade of grass and every darting ray of the sun.

In the same way that light and power are self-verifying, even so logic, morality, and God are self-verifying. By what light do we see light? We see light by its own light. How does power prove itself to be powerful? It proves itself by its own power to effect change. How does logic prove itself to be true? Because without it, we cannot know anything. How does morality prove itself to be innate within us all? Because we get mad when others wrong us and hate movies that end badly – with the good guys not properly vindicated. How do we know God? Because without a knowledge of God, nothing makes sense. As the rest of the book seeks to explain, without the God of the Bible, absurdity is all that remains.

The existence of God, logic, and morality are core realities that make knowledge possible. They are the pillars behind the biblical worldview. That is, the biblical worldview is not only built on our innate knowledge of God, logic, and morality, but the biblical worldview also reinforces those three pillars by providing us with the only cohesive and self-defendable system of thought that corresponds with these core presuppositions.

As we shall see, all other worldviews fail to be consistent with themselves. This inconsistency takes place in two ways. Either a worldview starts off by denying the innate knowledge of God, logic, and morality, and thus fails to be consistent from the get-go. Or, if a worldview happens to accept the innate knowledge of God, logic, and morality as basic premises, it will quickly deny these premises by constructing a system of thought that is inconsistent with the knowledge of God, logic, and morality.

Everyone Has a Worldview

To understand this, we first need to understand that we all have a worldview. Our worldview may be incoherent, or we may live inconsistently with what we believe, but we cannot help to formulate, even if it is unconsciously, a conceptual system of thought that incorporates our most basic beliefs.

Ronald Nash (1936-2006), philosophy professor of Reformed Theological Seminary, defines a worldview as "a set of beliefs about the most important issues in life.[1] Our worldview consists of our most basic beliefs about God, the universe, and ourselves. Nash went on to state:

> Implicit in all this is the additional point that these beliefs must cohere in some way and form a system. A fancy term that can be useful here is *conceptual scheme*, by which I mean a pattern or arrangement of concepts (ideas). A worldview, then, is a conceptual scheme by which we consciously or unconsciously place or fit everything we believe and by which we interpret and judge reality.[2]

Greg Bahnsen was a little more pointed in his description of a worldview: "A worldview is a network of presuppositions which are not tested by natural science and in terms of which all experience is related and interpreted."[3] This clear definition succinctly states all the major components of a worldview. A worldview is a set of correlating presuppositions that are not derived by sense experiences but are necessary to interpret sense experiences.

James Sire, a worldview scholar, reminds us that a worldview is more than just a set of presuppositions or a conceptual scheme that exists only in the mind. A worldview also consists of the fundamental commitment of the heart. What we love the most, which has to do with our ethical values, has more to do with our worldview than with the answers we will give to strange philosophical questions. What we love the most will determine

---

[1] Ronald Nash, *Worldviews in Conflict* (Grand Rapids: Zondervan, 1992), 16.
[2] Ibid.
[3] Greg L. Bahnsen, *Pushing the Antithesis* (Powder Springs, GA: American Vision, 2007), 42.

how we feel about everything, how we make decisions, and how we behave. "Would it not be better," Sire asks, "to consider a worldview as the *story* we live by?"[4] Does not the manner in which we live (or seek to live) speak more about what we believe than what we say that we believe? Sire explains the practicality of this:

> I wake up in the morning, not asking myself who I am or where I am. I am immediately aware of a whole host of perceptions that my mind orders into the recognition that it's morning: I'm home, I'm crawling out of bed. In this immediate awareness I do not consciously ask or answer, *What is the really real?* or, *How do I know I am home?* or, *How can I tell the difference between right and wrong?* Rather, my unconscious mind is using a network of presumptions about how to interpret for the conscious mind what is going on. In some way all the basic worldview questions are being answered by the way I am acting and behaving.[5]

With this concern in mind, Sire provides an expanded definition of a worldview:

> A worldview is a commitment, a fundamental orientation of the heart, that can be expressed as a story or in a set of presuppositions (assumptions which may be true, partially true, or entirely false) which we hold (consciously or subconsciously, consistently or inconsistently) about the basic constitution of reality, and that provides the foundation on which we live and move and have our being.[6]

According to Sire, a worldview cannot be separated from a "world-and-life-view." And for this reason, a worldview must not only pass the coherency test, but also it must pass the test of life. Can we consistently live out our worldview in the real world?

---

[4] James W. Sire, *Naming the Elephant: Worldview as A Concept* (Downers Grove, IL: IVP, 2004), 101.

[5] Ibid., 107-108.

[6] Ibid., 122.

Beliefs are Interconnected

Because a worldview is a fundamental commitment of the heart and a cognitive framework that we use to understand everything else we believe, constructing a worldview, even if we are not fully conscious of it, is unavoidable for all of us.

We all have presuppositions. Also, we cannot help but compare and contrast what we are learning with what we are convinced that we already know.

As already stated, the law of non-contradiction cannot be proven by logic or science, but both logic and science are built on its foundation. Without the law of non-contradiction, nothing makes sense. Logic is a necessary condition for us to process data and rationally formulate knowledge. Thus, whether we like it or not, we all consciously or unconsciously utilize the law of non-contradiction as we process and assimilate new data.

For instance, my five-year-old son, Martyn, is learning the rules of the road. If he had no innate concept of the law of non-contradiction, then he would not have yelled at me when I took a right turn at a red light. He shrieked, "Stop! The light is *red*!" Who told him red traffic lights *always* means stop? Why was he so scared when I turned right? He was scared because a red light cannot mean stop and go at the same time. Who taught him this basic logical principle? The fact that it is an innate concept allows him to process new information and sensations with what he already processed in the past. The new data only makes sense when it is compared with the old data already stored in his memory. In this case, he rejected the new information because it did not comport with what he thought he already knew. After explaining that this was an exception to the rule, he was able to readjust his thinking and format a more complex system of thought.

Conclusion

We all do this because a single belief never stands in isolation from other beliefs. What we believe about *this* will consequently affect how and what we believe about *that*. Truth is not disjointed from other truths. Everything in the universe (as the word *uni*verse implies) is interconnected. Because of the law of non-contradiction, we cannot help but seek to formulate a cohesive system of thought with mutually supporting propositions. If there is a contradiction in our understanding of the rules of the road or a contradiction in our understanding of the complexities of the universe, we know something is flawed in our thinking.

8

Shaped by Three Ultimate Questions

Because every single belief correlates with every other belief, it is impossible not to systematize our knowledge into different categories of thought. Like a big dresser full of drawers, we take what we know (or think we know) about religion and throw that information into one drawer, we take what we know about science and throw it into another drawer, and so on. Eventually, as our database grows, we install dividers in those drawers and begin to make subcategories of subcategories. Without our minds seeking coherency, all this would be impossible. But because our minds do this automatically, it is also unavoidable.

Every System is Shaped by Three Fundamental Questions

The collective, systematic arrangement of all our beliefs can be reduced to a few core presuppositions. We no doubt possess countless categories of thought, but all the diverse categories and subcategories of thought can be condensed to three major divisions: (1.) objective reality, (2.) subjective knowledge, and (3.) practical morality. That is, the three basic and ultimate questions of life are: (1.) *What exists outside of our minds?* (2.) *What exists inside of our minds?*, and (3.) *How do we feel about it?*

Because the knowledge of (1.) God, (2.) logic, and (3.) ethics are innate within us all, every cognitive thought will naturally fall into one of those three overarching categories or presuppositional starting points. Interestingly enough these three categories of thought correspond nicely with the three main branches of philosophy: (1.) *metaphysics*, (2.) *epistemology*, and (3.) *ethics*.[1]

Though these philosophical categories (*metaphysics*, *epistemology*, and *ethics*) sound complex, we all have metaphysical, epistemological, and ethical beliefs. For instance, even "scientists," claimed Nash, "make important epistemological, metaphysical, and ethical assumptions."[2] Cleverly, Nash went on to explain:

> They assume, for example, that knowledge is possible and that sense experience is reliable (epistemology), that the universe is regular (metaphysics), and that scientists should be honest (ethics). Without these assumptions that scientists cannot justify within the limits of their methodology, scientific inquiry would soon collapse.[3]

For this reason, Bahnsen concluded: "Worldviews are systems of inter-locking presuppositions. As systems they include metaphysics and epistemology and ethics all bound up together in a mutually self-supporting system."[4]

---

[1] James Sire lists the presuppositions behind every worldview as the answers we give to these 7 questions: (1.) "What is prime reality – the really real?" (2.) What is the nature of external reality, that is, the world around us?" (3.) "What is a human being?" (4.) "What happens to persons at death?" (5.) Why is it possible to know anything at all?" (6.) How do we know what is right and wrong?" (7.) "What is the meaning of human history?" (Ibid., 94). I agree with this list of questions by Sire; however, it appears to me that these questions can be reduced to metaphysics, epistemology, or ethics.

[2] *Faith and Reason*, 27.

[3] Ibid.

[4] *Pushing the Antithesis*, 118.

1. What is Real?

The German philosopher Martin Heidegger (1889-1976) asked the question, "Why is there something rather than nothing?" This question has been viewed as one of the most important questions in all of philosophy. It comes from inquiring did the universe create itself, or has it always been here? Is there a God who created the universe? Where do we come from? Did Divine Intelligence (i.e., God) create matter, or is human consciousness derived from an undirected material process? In other words, which came first, mind or matter? If there is a God, what is our relationship to Him? What is our relationship to the universe? What is the relationship between God and the universe? Is God the ultimate being, or is the universe all there is? Are God and the universe one and the same, or are they distinct? Ultimately, all these questions can be condensed to this: Is there a God, and if so, is He the cause of there being "something rather than nothing?"

There is an entire division of philosophy that is devoted to answering this question known as metaphysics.[5] Though the many complexities of the vast amount of different philosophies and religious constructs have a way of making things confusing, there are only three possible answers to the God question – *naturalism, impersonal-supernaturalism,* and *personal-supernaturalism.* Besides these three options, there are no other possible answers.

A. *Naturalism*

Naturalism is the belief that *if* there is a God, He is entirely unknowable and practically irrelevant. Thus, naturalists believe the universe is a self-contained, closed system. That the origin and function of the universe are explained by natural or physical causes, such as the theory of evolution, and that everything that is real can be reduced to the physical world.

[5] Technically, by metaphysics, I am referring to *ontology* – the nature of being.

According to the Christian mathematician John Byl, "The main underlying theme of naturalism is that nature is self-sufficient. Nature, it is alleged, exists by itself, deriving all meaning and purpose from itself. It needs nothing outside of itself to explain it."[6] In the famous words of the astrophysicist Carl Sagan (1934-1996), "The Cosmos is all there is, or ever was, or ever will be."[7] Nature must be able to explain itself. Those within this group include atheists, agnostics, and deists.[8]

B. Impersonal-supernaturalism

Those in this group include Yoda and his followers, pantheists, panentheists, polytheists, liberal christians, animists, monists, and dualists. These are those who believe that *Ultimate Reality* is a divine force that is impersonal and entirely imminent (in one way or another) throughout the universe. Although polytheists and liberal christians believe in a *personal* deity/deities, they are included in this category because as a whole, they believe in an *impersonal* Ultimate Reality – that either God or Morality is ultimately behind are capability of knowing.

C. Personal-supernaturalism

Personal-supernaturalism is the belief in an all-powerful and transcendent, yet personal God who both created and imminently governs the universe. Though He is transcendent, He is omnipresent. God created and governs the universe, but He remains independent and separate from the universe. This group includes the three major monotheistic world religions – Judaism, Christianity, and Islam.

---

[6] John Byl, *The Divine Challenge* (Edinburgh: Banner of Truth Trust, 2004), 33.

[7] Carl Sagan, *Cosmos* (New York: Random House, 2002), 4.

[8] Deists do not properly fit into this camp. After they explain the origins of the universe by looking to a supernatural cause, they depart and hold hands with naturalists by making this supernatural cause useless for life.

These three different metaphysical answers (A. *naturalism*, B. *impersonal-supernaturalism*, and C. *personal-supernaturalism*) can be understood and distinguished from each other by the way they seek to explain the relationship between material and immaterial substances (i.e., consciousness). In other words, which came first, mind or matter?

A. *Naturalism* = Matter Comes before Mind

B. *Impersonal-supernaturalism* = Mind & Matter Come Together

C. *Personal-supernaturalism* = Mind Comes before Matter

To simplify further that which I have already oversimplified, these three overarching categories can be reduced to two – naturalism and personal-supernaturalism. Though impersonal-supernaturalists differ from naturalists in that they are not materialists or empiricists (for they believe in the existence of a spiritual, invisible dimension to the universe that is not detectable by the empirical senses), they, for all practical purposes, do not believe in a supernatural power that can be truly known. Because they do not believe in a distinct and personal God, their God is unknowable. Either the supernatural force is entirely transcendent, or entirely imminent, but either way it is unknowable – at least unknowable as a personal being.

And, if the supernatural side of the universe is beyond the transcendental wall, then all that is left for rational and empirical inquiry is the physical and material side of things. If the supernatural cannot think, or feel—or simply doesn't make that knowledge or emotion available to us for whatever reason—then it cannot be a proper subject of knowledge. So, in a somewhat less precise way of thinking, naturalism and impersonal-supernaturalism can be grouped together in the same broad category, because in both, man is left to discover all the answers for himself.

Since the liberal christian worldview believes in a God who is ultimately unknowable, they would fit into the Naturalism category for all practical purposes. This is because even though liberal christianity says that God is personal *emotionally*, He is also at the same time distant *doctrinally*. In other words, they are ethically and epistemologically naturalists, but they still latch onto the doctrine of Jesus Christ for the sake of emotional encouragement. For them, God's main purpose is to uplift, build up, and encourage us when our self-esteem gets too low, and so God is in this way personal. But when it comes to understanding doctrine or morality in this day and age, God becomes completely beyond our reach. They interpret moral instruction found in the New Testament as cultural and subjective, and thus, they have created an entirely new worldview, with a God whose mind is transcendentally padlocked from our knowing, but at the same time is deeply and personally involved with boosting our confidence and keeping us comforted emotionally. Even though liberal christianity says there are logical and ethical absolutes found within the mind of God, they believe that since the bible is a cultural relic, God's absolute knowledge was never transmitted and thus, like naturalists, they are forced to live a life in ambiguity of what is right and what is wrong.

So the ultimate metaphysical question comes down to this: Does the universe have all the answers to its own origins and design? In other words, are we, as finite beings, self-sufficient and capable of unraveling all the mysteries of the universe? Was Protagoras right when he said, "man is the measure of all things?" Does the presupposition of a closed universe supply us with a cohesive worldview? Or, do we need a supernatural and personal God to prevent us from becoming irrational and absurd in our thinking? In short, do we need a supernatural, personal and self-revelatory God to answer our ultimate questions about reality, or is science and human reason alone sufficient?

2. How Do We Know?

This naturally leads us to the second branch of philosophy, which is *epistemology*. Epistemology is concerned with knowledge. Is knowledge possible, and if so, how do we know what we know? How do we know if there is a God or not? How do we know if science is sufficient to answer all the questions? How do we know what our relationship is with ultimate reality, God, and the universe? How do we know what the relationship is between mind and matter? Though the question of how we know what we know is a difficult one to answer, there are three major answers that have been suggested historically: *rationalism*, *empiricism*, and *existentialism*.

A. Rationalism

Rationalists, for the most part, are those who believe ultimate reality (i.e., God) consists of something that is non-material, such as ideas, mind, rational thought, or an ultimate spiritual being. If (the cosmic) mind comes before matter, then knowledge is principally derived deductively through the proper use of reason. Rationalism is the idea that man is capable of ascertaining true knowledge through unaided (or pure *a priori*) reason alone, without the assistance of general or special revelation.

The French mathematician René Descartes (1596-1650) is considered the quintessential rationalist. He began his epistemological inquiry by questioning everything. Though he doubted the existence of everything, he could not doubt that he doubted. Because doubting was the one thing he was certain of, he concluded that by doubting/thinking, he must exist as a self-conscious being. Thus, he is known for the phrase "*I think, therefore I am.*"[9]

---

[9] René Descartes, *Discourse on Method and Meditations on First Philosophy* (Indianapolis/Cambridge: Hackett Publishing Company, 3rd ed., 1993), 19.

Because he could not be sure his body existed, he concluded his existence lay in thinking rather than in any physical substance.[10] By doubting, He also deduced that he could not be perfect, "for I saw clearly that it is a greater perfection to know than to doubt."[11] Because he was able to conceptualize that which is entirely perfect, he determined that the idea of that which is perfect could not have arisen within himself any more than it is logical for that which is lesser to produce that which is greater. "Hence it follows," he argued, "that something cannot come into being out of nothing, and also that what is more perfect cannot come into being from what is less perfect."[12]

Accordingly, since Descartes saw that he was able to perceive not only a more perfect thing, but the most perfect thing, he reasoned that this conception of the most perfect thing could not have proceeded or originated out of anything other than God Himself. In this fashion, Descartes logically deduced that God also existed, and on this rational foundation (based on *pure* reason), he went on to deduce the rest of his worldview.[13]

---

[10] "From this," Descartes said, "I knew that I was a substance the whole essence or nature of which was merely to think, and which, in order to exist, needed no place and depended on no material thing" (Ibid.).

[11] Ibid.

[12] Ibid.

[13] Rather than interpreting Descartes as a pure rationalist, a case could be made that he foresaw the presuppositional argument for the existence of God. For the *Cogito, ergo sum* syllogism to function, the knowledge of God must be presupposed. Commenting on this, Jean-Marie Beyssade explained that this "proof cannot succeed, or even get off the ground, 'if one has no idea, i.e. perception, which corresponds to the meaning of the word 'God'" ("The Idea of God and Proofs of His Existence" in *The Cambridge Companion to Descartes*. ed. John Cottingham. Cambridge: Cambridge University Press, 1995., 176). Beyssade went on to state: "The *à priori* proof of God starts from the supposed fact, which is taken for granted, that all perfections are united in a single nature which is called 'God'" (Ibid.,178). Because we all know that God exists as the most perfect being, we can conclude by observing our own imperfection that we could not have arrived at this presupposition of the most perfect being on our own, but it must have been implanted there by God Himself.

B. Empiricism

Unlike rationalists, empiricists, strictly speaking, believe that all knowledge is derived from the senses. Even though the English philosophers Francis Bacon (1561-1626) and John Locke (1632-1704) were empiricists who believed in God, most empiricists believe that reality consists of only that which is physical or material. They tend to be naturalists, for they answer the God question by saying that the universe is a closed system. Therefore, if matter comes before mind (consciousness), knowledge originates through experience and experience through the physical senses alone. Empiricism, which is also unbiblical, is the notion that there are no innate presuppositions or basic beliefs within our precognitive minds to assist us in the processing and categorizing of all the multiple sensations that are flowing into our thoughts through life's experiences.

For instance, John Locke rejected the rationalism of René Descartes. Where did those ideas, which Descartes doubted, originate? Descartes did not come to his conclusions when he was a newborn; he was a grown man with a life full of experiences. The only thing that connects the mind with the external universe is the five senses. Therefore, according to Locke, it is only through experience that ideas can get into the thought process from the outside. Locke believed man was born with no innate knowledge.

> Let us then suppose the mind to be, as we say, white paper, void of all characters, without any ideas; how comes it by that vast store which the busy and boundless fancy of man has painted on it with an almost endless variety? Whence has it all the materials of reason and knowledge? To this I answer in one word, from experience; in that all our knowledge is founded, and from that it ultimately derives itself.[14]

---

[14] Cited in Gordon Clark, *Thales To Dewey* (Jefferson, MD: The Trinity Foundation, 2nd ed., 1989), 360.

For Locke, our minds are born as a blank slate (i.e., *tabula rasa*). Knowledge is limited to what is physical and can be discerned by the senses. Because God does not exist as a part of the observable universe, if He exists at all, He is not an object of knowledge seeing that He cannot be detected by the empirical senses.

C. Existentialism

Existentialism is the third major theory of knowledge. It, at least in its secular form, is rooted in naturalism. The universe is a closed system, which means that knowledge is limited to sense experiences and that God does not exist, or that He is unknowable and thus irrelevant. Thus, existentialism is finite man's attempt to dig his own way out of his finiteness in his endeavor to establish meaning for life without any objective foundation.

Historically, existentialism came after the philosophies of Locke and Kant. These two philosophers, in different ways, locked the transcendental God behind an impenetrable wall. Yet, existentialists were not happy with the consequences. Naturalism leads to no God, no afterlife, no purpose, no absolute code of morality, and no free will (seeing that our thoughts are merely chemical reactions and electrical impulses within the hard tissue of the brain that are predetermined by fixed laws of nature in the same way the planets circle the sun according to the fixed laws of physics).

With no God, life ends without any ultimate purpose. Life ends in death and annihilation. The resultant meaninglessness of life was rather depressing and unacceptable for existentialists however. Rather than going back and questioning the presuppositions behind naturalism, while existentialists agree that God is unknowable, they turned around and claimed that individual freedom and purpose could still be had. Either by religiously taking an experiential leap of faith into the unknowable transcendental realm or by atheistically creating one's own meaning and purpose in life by an act of the will, man could rescue himself from a life of despair and hopelessness. With the notion that truth is rooted in man's existence, man could create meaning for himself.

3. Who Determines What is Right?

The third major branch of philosophy is *ethics*.[15] How should we live? What should we value the most? What is the ultimate good? These are the questions that this branch of philosophy seeks to answer. How one answers (1.) what is real? and (2.) how do we know? will thus determine how one answers (3.) who determines what is right? For example, those who reject the existence of God, of course, will not look to Him for guidance. The source of our ethical standards can be reduced to two options – ethics are either objective/absolute in nature or they are subjective/relative in nature. That is, we will either submit to God or we will do what is right in our own estimation.

A. Universal and Absolute Ethical Standard

The moral standard is derived not from abstract principles, but from the character of a holy, righteous, trinitarian God because *love* marks the essence of the relationship between the Father, the Son, and the Holy Spirit. Since God made us for His own purpose, He has the right to tell us how to fulfill that intended purpose. Because He made us in His image, we are to mirror His love by loving Him and loving our neighbors. Out of love, He has invited us to share in His love. Loving God with all of our hearts, minds, and souls and loving our neighbor as ourselves is not merely the heart of the universal standard of morality, it is

---

[15] This branch of philosophy also includes *aesthetics*.

the key to fulfilling our purpose and finding personal meaning and fulfillment.

Man was not made to be alone, for man is not self-sufficient. Selfishness is forbidden because it ruins meaningful relationships. Thus, obeying God's law is the key to our own personal fulfillment because it drives us away from self-idolatry into a loving and meaningful relationship with God and other people.

B. Subjective and Relative Ethical Standards

Those who reject the supernatural and personal God are forced, if they desire to remain consistent with their beliefs, to reject any absolute ethical standard. With no transcendent God to know, obey, and love, not only is there no ultimate purpose for life, there is no absolute standard to follow. With the removal of any objective destination, there is no need for any road maps to chart. Relationships are left to be governed by what seems right in the eyes of self-seeking individuals.

From a naturalistic standpoint, ethics are constructed for merely pragmatic purposes. At best, ethics are situational and relative in nature. With no God, there is no universal Lawgiver. If there is no universal and absolute justice and accountability, then this also means evil men, like Adolf Hitler, got off easy. In fact, with no universal standard, who is to say Adolf Hitler was in the wrong?

Conclusion

As you can see, the various answers to these three ultimate questions about *ultimate reality*, about *knowledge*, and about *ethics* are intertwined. How we answer one will heavily influence, if not completely determine, how we answer the other two questions. The answers to these questions determine our worldview, and our worldview cannot help but shape what we believe and how we interpret the world around us.

9

Shaped by Our Presuppositions

John Frame was right when he said, "One's view of reality will determine, to a great extent, his view of knowledge, and vice versa."[1] For instance, if we presuppose a self-sufficient and closed universe, then of course we will lean heavily, if not entirely, on sense perception and science. Special revelation and miracles will be ruled out, if one wishes to maintain naturalism. On the other hand, if we start with the presupposition that there is a God, then our view of knowledge will be determined by our theological position of God's relationship with the universe.

If God is completely transcendent, like the mystics and liberal theologians believe, then we will be prone, if we hang on to religion at all, to become existentialists. If we believe God is completely imminent, as do pantheists, we will more than likely become mystical as well. In both cases it is impossible to know God.

If we believe God is both transcendent (separate from the universe) and imminent (interacts within the universe), then we will look to both God's general revelation (what we learn through nature) and special revelation (what we learn in Holy Scriptures) as valid sources of information. Both point us back to God.

[1] *The Doctrine of the Knowledge of God*, 401.

Science reveals certain truths about God's created order and glory, while Scripture reveals more precisely the identity and nature of this God and how we are to properly worship Him. With this said, Bahnsen concluded: "Clearly then, [our] method of knowing depends on the nature of reality."[2]

The Relationship between God, Knowledge, and Ethics

As I pointed out in chapter 4, our values – the affections of our heart – heavily influence what we choose to believe. For instance, John Stuart Mill's father admitted he became an atheist not because of any epistemological concerns but because of ethical reasons. He rejected the idea of God because he could not appreciate and value a God who would allow so much evil to take place in the world. In the words of his son, John Stuart Mill:

> My father, educated in the creed of Scotch Presbyterianism, had by his own studies and reflections been early led to reject not only the belief in Revelation but the foundations of what is commonly called Natural Religion. My father's rejection of all that is called religious belief was not, as many might suppose, primarily a matter of logic and evidence: the grounds of it were moral, still more than intellectual. He found it impossible to believe that a world so full of evil was the work of an Author combining infinite power with perfect goodness and righteousness. His aversion to religion, in the sense usually attached to the term, was of the same kind with that of Lucretius: he regarded it with the feelings due not to mere mental delusion but to a great moral evil. It would have been wholly inconsistent with my father's ideas of duty to allow me to acquire impressions contrary to his convictions and feelings respecting religion: and he impressed on me from

[2] *Pushing the Antithesis*, 119.

the first that the manner in which the world came into existence was a subject on which nothing was known.[3]

He was not the first person to reject the idea of God out of a hatred for Him. Atheist Thomas Nagel freely admitted his bias against God:

> I speak from experience, being strongly subject to this fear myself: I want atheism to be true and am made uneasy by the fact that some of the most intelligent and well-informed people I know are religious believers. It isn't just that I don't believe in God and, naturally, hope that I'm right in my belief. It's that I hope there is no God! I don't want there to be a God; I don't want the universe to be like that. My guess is that this cosmic authority problem is not a rare condition and that it is responsible for much of the scientism and reductionism of our time.[4]

Another example of this is found in the writings of Christopher Hitchens (1949-2011). The arguments he crafted against God were based on his personal disdain for God. He did not appeal to metaphysics or to epistemology in his argumentation but to ethics; he made a moral case against God. Hitchens claimed not to be an atheist but an antitheist. According to Hitchens, "God is not great."[5] In sum, *why* we should hate God is how Hitchens made his case for atheism. However, despising the concept of hell and citing various cases of religious misconduct does not disprove the existence of God.

Likewise, English physicist Paul Davies confesses that he is not emotionally neutral: "There's no need to invoke anything supernatural in the origins of the universe or of life. I have never

---

[3] Cited in Bertrand Russell, *Why I Am Not a Christian*, 118.

[4] Thomas Nagel, *The Last Word* (Oxford: Oxford University Press, 1997), 130–131.

[5] Christopher Hitchens, *God is Not Great* (New York: Twelve, 2007).

liked the idea of divine tinkering."[6] Davies knows that he is not alone in his sentiments, for he believes that many "scientists who are struggling to construct a fully comprehensive theory of the physical universe openly admit that part of the motivation is to finally get rid of God."[7]

This, however, is not to be taken as something unusual. Quite a few self-proclaimed atheists, so it seems, are motivated to question the existence of God out of their hatred for Him. Having a holy Judge who will hold us accountable for all of our thoughts, emotions, and actions is not an easy thing to embrace. Naturally, none of us want to submit every single area of our lives to a divine authority. Guilt, divine authority, divine surveillance, and divine accountability seem to be where the conflict really lies. Therefore, suppressing the knowledge of God is often easier than facing this knowledge with a guilty conscience.

In this way, if we like it or not, our ethical values (what we like and dislike) have a vital role in shaping our thinking and beliefs. I think it was for this reason that Frame claimed it is "useful to regard epistemology as a branch of ethics."[8]

With this said, how we answer any one of the three ultimate questions of life (God, knowledge, and ethics) will consequently influence how we will answer the other two. Vern Poythress, professor of New Testament interpretation at Westminster Theological Seminary, concludes: "In many respects they presuppose one another. Though we may temporarily focus on only one subdivision within philosophy [metaphysics, epistemology, or ethics], the others lurk in the background."[9]

---

6 Cited in John C. Lennox, *God and Stephen Hawking* (Oxford: Lion Books, 2011), 41.

7 Paul Davies, *The Cosmic Jackpot* (Boston: Houghton Mifflin Company, 2007), 15.

8 *The Doctrine of the Knowledge of God*, 63.

9 Vern Poythress, *Redeeming Philosophy* (Wheaton: Crossway, 2014), 19.

Because every worldview, at its basic level, consists of the answers we give to (1.) the God question, (2.) the knowledge question, and (3.) the ethics question, these three questions are both intrinsically and inextricably interwoven together.

The Necessity of Presuppositions

The answers we give to the metaphysical, epistemological, and ethical questions become the basic presuppositions that determine our worldview. These presuppositions are like axioms, which we must presume to be true before we can go any further. That is, we must take them for granted seeing we have no rational or empirical evidence to support our answers. As Greg Bahnsen stated:

> A "presupposition" is an elementary assumption in one's reasoning or in the process by which opinions are formed....It is not just any assumption in an argument, but a personal commitment that is held at the most basic level of one's network of beliefs. Presuppositions form a wide-ranging, foundational perspective (or starting point) in terms of which everything else is interpreted and evaluated. As such, presuppositions have the greatest authority in one's thinking, being treated as one's least negotiable beliefs and being granted the highest immunity to revision.[10]

Every worldview, including theism, atheism, naturalism, and empiricism, is based on a few core presuppositions. These presuppositions interpret life's experiences but are not derived from life's experiences.

For instance, because there is no evidence supporting the foundation for empiricism, empiricists are forced to make a precommitment to the starting presupposition that *every belief to be justified must be supported by evidence.* This precommitment is a leap

---

[10] Cited in Greg L. Bahnsen, *Pushing the Antithesis* (Powder Springs, GA: American Vision, 2007), 44.

of faith. Though those who take this leap may work hard to prove, explain, argue, and provide evidence for everything else that they believe, the presuppositional foundation for their worldview is simply taken for granted or presumed.

That *nothing exists beyond the natural world* is the core presupposition behind the naturalistic worldview. Naturalists presuppose this belief without any scientific evidence. As John Lennox, professor of mathematics at the University of Oxford, rhetorically queries, "So, is naturalism actually demanded by science? Or is it just conceivable that naturalism is a philosophy that is brought to science, more than something that is entailed by science? Could it even be, dare one ask, more like an expression of faith, akin to religious belief?"[11]

The Hungarian-Swedish biologist George Klein was willing to admit that it was: "I am not an agnostic, I am an atheist. My attitude is not based on science, but rather faith."[12]

Professor Richard Lewontin, a geneticist and one of the worlds leading supporters for evolutionary biology, also confessed that he is committed to materialism even before the investigation gets started:

> We take the side of science *in spite* of the patent absurdity of some of its constructs…in spite of the tolerance of the scientific community for unsubstantiated just-so stories, because *we have a prior commitment* … to materialism. It is not that the methods and institutions of science somehow compel us to accept a material explanation of the phenomenal world, but, on the contrary, that we are forced by our *à priori* adherence to material causes to create an apparatus of investigation and a set of concepts that produce material

---

[11] John Lennox, *God's Undertaker* (Oxford: Lion Books, 2009), 9.
[12] George Klein, *The Atheist in the Holy City* (Cambridge, MA: MIT Press, 1990), 203. Cited in Ibid., 35.

explanations, no matter how counter-intuitive, no matter how mystifying to the uninitiated.[13]

For instance, Richard Dawkins acknowledged that he accepted naturalism as a starting presupposition without any evidence or proof:

When asked by the Edge Foundation, "What do you believe is true even though you cannot prove it?" Dawkins replied: "I believe that all life, all intelligence, all creativity and all 'design' anywhere in the universe, is the direct or indirect product of Darwinian natural selection. It follows that design comes late in the universe, after a period of Darwinian evolution. Design cannot precede evolution and therefore cannot underlie the universe." At the bottom, then, Dawkins's rejection of an ultimate Intelligence is a matter of belief without proof.[14]

Scientists may naïvely think that they do not bring presuppositions into their investigations. They may even claim that they do not believe in any metaphysical realities – seeing that metaphysics transcends the scope of scientific investigation. But, saying you don't believe in metaphysics is a metaphysical statement. Science cannot prove that there are no metaphysical realities, and such an assertion as "I don't believe in metaphysics" would not make any sense without the use of logic and ethics.

Thus, even scientists have presuppositions about God, knowledge, and ethics that they presuppose and bring with them into their laboratories.

It is not that having presuppositions is wrong, for we all have presuppositions. For instance, Christians start by presupposing the God of the Bible, and this presupposition provides a

[13] Cited in *God's Undertaker.*, 35-36.
[14] Roy Abraham Varghese, preface to Antony Flew, *There Is a God* (New York: HarperOne, 2007), xix.

worldview that acknowledge both the existence of supernatural events (such as the miracles and the resurrection of Christ) as well as the revealing power of science.

There is nothing wrong with scientific knowledge. Christians can thank God for an orderly universe that allows them to learn from the past as well as plan for the future. A transcendent and imminent God, whose sovereign rule is perfectly compatible with the laws of physics, provides the Christian with a perfect foundation for all of their empirical and rational knowledge. An orderly universe only makes sense when one has an orderly God. Since all truth comes through general and special revelation, then true scientific and biblical truth cannot be not at odds with each other.

The System Controls the Verdict

Once we have chosen – whether consciously or unconsciously – our presuppositions, such as theism, atheism, naturalism, rationalism, or empiricism, we then use them as a cognitive framework to interpret and understand all of our life's experiences. Presuppositions are like an operating system in a computer – the overarching system that reads/runs all the other programs. Our presuppositional foundation determines not only how we process information, it determines how we answer the questions that we ask. It shapes us in the same way our values shape us, which means our thinking is never neutral. No matter how unbiased we may try to be, how we interpret and process data cannot help but be influenced and shaped by the basic presuppositions behind our worldview.

For this reason, trying to convince someone who has a naturalistic worldview about the validity of miracles is like trying to get on the same page with someone who is reading from a different book. The only sure way a naturalist will be convinced of the validity of the miracles of Christ is if he has a change in his worldview and the basic presuppositions that lie behind it, as John Byl explained:

> If one's worldview reflects one's most basic faith commitments, how can we hope to rationally convince an opponent that any particular belief of theirs is false? To put it another way, if worldviews are like spectacles through which we view the world, how are we to convince someone wearing yellow-tinted spectacles that there are blue flowers? He won't be able to see blue until he exchanges his yellow spectacles for a pair that enables him to see a wider range of colours. But that amounts to a radical conversion, a major switch in faith commitment.[15]

The Controlling Presupposition

Thus, the three basic beliefs or presuppositions that shape every worldview, as we have already mentioned, are the answers we give to (1.) the ultimate reality question, (2.) the knowledge question, and (3.) the ethics question. Between the corresponding metaphysical, epistemological, and ethical presuppositions, which is the central presupposition that controls the other two?

In support of a Christian worldview, Sire emphatically says, "Ontology [what is real] precedes epistemology [what we know]."[16] In other words, what we know does not determine what is real. The method of how we know what we know does not establish the existence or non-existence of anything. This seems obvious. Wishing that unicorns were real does not make it so any more than atheism eliminates God. Rather, what is really real, such as God and the universe, determines what we know. This is what Sire means when he says, "Ontology precedes epistemology."

---

[15] *The Divine Challenge*, 19.
[16] *Naming the Elephant*, 56. Words in brackets are present author.

Sire is right from an ontological perspective. The reality or non-reality of God, either His existence or His non-existence, determines everything else. God's existence is logically primary, as God is ultimate reality. In fact, without the existence of God, knowledge and ethical distinctions are impossible because they logical flow out of ontology and not the other way around.[17] Therefore, we must presuppose God if we are to have a reliable epistemological and ethical standard.

Just because knowledge of God does require the existence of God, though, does not mean that we must always start with the knowledge of God to conclude that He exists. We could start with epistemology or ethics as well, and eventually conclude with the existence of God, because metaphysics, epistemology, and ethics are all inter-dependent. They each cannot be rightly understood without rightly understanding the other.

Thus, of these three core presuppositions, it does not matter if we presuppose God first or not as we set forth our apologetic argument. All that matters is that we remain logically consistent with the presuppositions that we have chosen to embrace as our ultimate starting point, because that is what truly matters – consistency. Thus we must always beg the question, *do we remain consistent with ourselves?*

---

[17] James Sire reminds us that everything is turned upside down when we place epistemology before ontology (the nature of being). This puts man in the place of God, and places subjective opinions above objective reality. Yet, I would suggest that what motivates fallen man to place his own thinking and reasoning powers above objective reality – i.e. above God – is the fallen deposition of his heart. Unregenerate man is depraved. His principle love is self. Ethics (which concerns itself with what we should love and how we should behave) is to flow first from the being of God and second from our knowledge of Him. Fallen man, however, has placed *self* above *God*. Self-love is fallen man's primary commitment, and this self-love (his ethical commitment) shapes his epistemology, which in turn shapes his understanding and acceptance of God (ontology). The proper order of ontology (ultimate reality), epistemology, and ethics (man's primary commitment) has been reversed in the fall.

Conclusion

In conclusion, all of our beliefs are shaped by our individual worldviews, each of which happens to be rooted in a few core presuppositions. We cannot think coherently or learn anything new without filtering information through our conceptual framework that includes our beliefs about God, about knowledge, and about ethics.

If we are going to be coherent thinkers, however, then we must have a worldview that is capable of answering all the ultimate questions of life without contradicting ourselves in the process. Therefore, the ultimate question that we must ask ourselves is this: Are we consistent with ourselves? That is to say, do our presuppositions coherently support our worldview, or better yet, is how we live consistent with how we view life?

The objective of the rest of this book is to show that the biblical worldview is the only coherent and consistent worldview. It is to show that to deny the Christian worldview is to live inconsistently with our conscience (i.e., the necessary conditions of God, knowledge, and ethics) by willingly accepting an absurd and self-defeating system of thought. In the words of the presuppositional apologist Cornelius Van Til: "We as Christians alone have a position that is philosophically defensible."[18]

[18] Cornelius Van Til, *Common Grace and the Gospel* (Phillipsburg, NJ: R&R Publishing, 1972), 8.

PART 3

How to Test Beliefs

…for I will give you a mouth and wisdom,
which none of your adversaries
will be able to withstand or contradict.
Luke 21:15

10

Cohesiveness
is Mandatory

"My father taught me that the question 'Who made me?' cannot be answered, since it immediately suggests the further question 'Who made God?'" Reading this in the *Autobiography of John Stuart Mill* led Bertrand Russell to reject the cosmological argument for the existence of God. In the words of Russell: "If everything must have a cause, then God must have a cause. If there can be anything without a cause, it may just as well be the world as God, so that there cannot be any validity in that argument."[1]

It is true that the cosmological argument only makes sense within the framework of the Christian worldview. But, what Russell does not seem to understand is that *his* critique of the cosmological argument does not make sense in either the Christian or the naturalist's worldview.

In fact, there is no worldview in which his statement makes any logical sense. Russell's statement, "If there can be anything without a cause, *it may just as well be the world* as God," is self-refuting on its own terms. In other words, he is attempting to refute an argument with an irrational statement.

---

[1] Bertrand Russell, *Why I Am Not a Christian* (New York, NY: Simon & Schuster, 1957), 6-7.

For instance, within the Christian worldview, the cosmological argument makes perfect sense. When we presuppose the
God of the Bible, the God who created the universe to operate
with precise regularity, then both science and religion can coexist
in perfect harmony. The Bible teaches us certain things, and
science teaches us certain things. These two sets of things are not
in opposition. Science teaches that everything in motion has a
cause. Since everything in motion must have a cause, then
everything in the universe, which is in motion, must have a
cause. Though science cannot prove or explain the Cause, the
only logical answer is that the Cause is something that is not in
motion – the Unmoved Mover.

Within the framework of the Christian worldview there is a
logical and an innate explanation of who this Unmoved Mover
actually is – God. It may not properly disclose the glory of a
trinitarian God of love, but at least *within* the Christian
worldview the cosmological argument is a rational argument
because the God of the Bible, who created the universe, and who
is unlike the universe, is autonomous, immutable, and self-
existent.

Russell, though, rejected the presupposition that God exists
and instead operated from an atheistic and naturalistic
worldview. Even though he thought of himself as an agnostic, he
was adamant in that God was never allowed to be a valid answer
to any of life's questions.

The presuppositions, or the starting point, for this naturalistic
worldview is *materialism* and *empiricism*. As naturalism seeks to
explain everything as having a naturalistic cause, materialism is
similar in that it says the physical or material is all that exists in
ultimate reality (making it not very ultimate). Mind only exists as
a function of the body. Matter and nature is all that there is.[2] If

---

[2] Materialists believe that our memories, thoughts, and feelings are explained
by the properties of the brain.

this is true, then all knowledge can only be obtained by the *empirical* senses (i.e., sense perception).

Thus, *naturalism, materialism,* and *empiricism* are the basic presuppositions of the atheistic worldview. With this in mind, for Russell to claim that it is possible for the world to be without a cause is completely irrational in an atheistic worldview where knowledge is ascertained and limited to the scientific method. According to the evidence, nothing that has a beginning is autonomous. That is, nothing is self-sufficient and able to move itself without any external assistance. Science teaches in the first, second, and third laws of motion that everything that has a beginning, such as the universe, *must have an external cause.*

In other words, every *effect* must have a *cause.* According to science, there is no such thing as an uncaused effect. To say otherwise is to deny the laws of science, which are core presuppositions of atheism and naturalism. The universe cannot, according to the laws of science, be its own cause anymore than any *effect* can be its own *cause.* The statement: "If there can be anything without a cause, *it may just as well be the world*" makes absolutely no sense at all within the atheistic worldview. In fact, it makes absolutely no sense in any worldview to say it is possible for the universe to be without a cause. More precisely, it makes no sense to presuppose empiricism – that scientific knowledge is the only means for understanding the existence of the world – and then to deny the laws of science in your attempt to explain the origins of the universe.

Russell began his critique of the cosmological argument on the false premise that "everything must have a cause." Yet, the cosmological argument does not state that *everything* must have a cause. It states that every *effect* must have a cause. It states that everything that has a beginning must have a cause. This is a big distinction that Russell conveniently overlooked.

It is nonsensical to say that something can be its own cause. Even God cannot create Himself. This would be a clear contradiction, for God to create Himself He would have to first exist prior to the act of self-creation. So, although God is *self-existent*, He is not *self-created*, for this would be impossible. Either God's existence is in Himself, or He does not exist at all. Either He is eternal, or He is non-existent.

Because the universe is full of effects, there must have been a first cause. Because the universe cannot be its own cause, there must be a self-existent God who created the universe. There must be a non-material, non-contingent, and self-existent being who created the universe. This is the only logical explanation. This is why Jonathan Edwards (1703-1758), one of America's most prominent theologians, said, "Nothing ever comes to pass without a cause. What is self-existent, must be from eternity, and must be unchangeable; but as to all things that *begin to be*, they are not self-existent, and therefore must have some foundation of their existence without themselves."[3]

Though the cosmological argument is not enough to establish the God of the Bible, it is at least a coherent argument within the greater context of the Christian worldview. My purpose, however, in exposing the irrationality of Russell's critique is not to seek to build a case for God's existence on the cosmological argument. Rather, my purpose is to illustrate that Russell operated out of an atheistic worldview (a worldview that consists of naturalism, empiricism, and relativism). And, if Russell wants to prove that the universe does not need God for its existence,[4] he must do so in a way that remains consistent with the basic

---

[3] Jonathan Edwards, *The Freedom of the Will* (Morgan, PA: Soli Deo Gloria, 1996), 48.

[4] Though it is not fair to require atheists to prove the non-existence of God, it is only reasonable to ask for them to produce a worldview that is not self-contradictory.

presuppositions of his own atheistic worldview. This is something neither he, nor any other atheist, can do.

The daunting task for naturalists is that they are forced to answer all the questions of life in a fashion that does not contradict the foundation of their worldview, or otherwise they become irrational and incoherent babblers. That is, naturalists must have a naturalistic explanation for everything, or otherwise they cease to be naturalists. Is evolution a reasonable explanation for logic, mathematics, emotions, willful intent, and ethics? We will seek to answer that question later, but for now it is important to realize that naturalists are obligated to answer all of life's questions from within the confines of their worldview.

This is not only true for atheists; it is true for all of us. Whatever we accept as our starting presuppositions, if we are going to continue to hold onto those presuppositions, we cannot deny these starting presuppositions by borrowing capital from an antithetical worldview. This is cheating, and it exposes an inconsistency in our thinking.

The Veracity of Any System is Cohesiveness

If any system of thought is incoherent, then it cannot be trusted. For instance, when I was a child, one of my older brothers discovered that our parents were hiding our Christmas gifts in a large cardboard box under their bed. You've got to be kidding! For a kid, this was like a treasure chest. Once the secret was out, the temptation seemed too great to resist. We just had to take a peek. With much eagerness, we each took a turn sneaking into this dark hiding place. What started as a one-time endeavor, turned into multiple visits a day; that is, until we were called out for it. My mother discovered that the lid to the box was not properly closed. One of us was careless.

As always, when my mother did not know who was the guilty child, she lined us boys up in the kitchen, from the oldest to the youngest, with me at the end. We were all guilty, but which one of us was going to take the fall? The questioning began with James, my oldest brother. He quickly denied knowing anything about it. As the stern face of my mother turned from James to her middle child, with a voice of certainty, Jason belted out, "It wasn't me, Mommy, *I made sure* I closed the lid every time I looked!"

Though young Jason was truthful, for he was not the reason we got caught, his defense was the reason we all got busted. The inconsistency in this story is easy to spot, but any inconsistency reveals that something is amiss. My brother's self-incriminating confession is a funny memory now, but what if our inconsistency happens to exist in the core beliefs of our worldview?

Minor inconsistencies in peripheral matters may be easily corrected in any system of thought, but inconsistency in the primary and core presuppositional statements of how we view life exposes a real problem with the conceptual system itself. An atheist and a Christian may both be mistaken about who won the World Series in 1976, but this mistake does not, in-and-of-itself, undermine either one of their worldviews. This bit of knowledge is tangential to their overall conceptual system of thought. It is of much greater concern, however, if the presuppositions behind their worldview are faulty. If the foundation is broken, there is no hope for the building to remain standing.

C. Stephen Evans, professor of philosophy at Baylor University, understood that believing in God is not the same thing as believing in the Loch Ness monster: "The Loch Ness monster is merely 'one more thing'… God, however, is not merely 'one more thing.' The person who believes in God and the person who does not believe in God do not merely disagree about God, they disagree about the very character of the universe."[5] It is harmless enough if we happen to be mistaken about who won the 1976 World Series, but if we happen to get the God question wrong, essentially everything else that we believe will be negatively affected.

For instance, logical positivism used to be popular in the early part of the twentieth century. Logical positivists claimed that only two types of propositions were meaningful: analytic statements and synthetic statements that were empirically verifiable. An analytic statement is a proposition that is true by virtue of its meaning. The statement "all bachelors are single" is an example of an analytic statement. It is meaningful because of the impossibility of the contrary. The statement, by the very nature of it own terms, verifies itself. A verifiable synthetic statement, on the other hand, is a proposition that is confirmed by sense experience. "The fire is hot" is a meaningful statement because it is easily demonstrated by the empirical test of putting your hand into the flames. If any proposition was unable to meet these two forms of verification, then it was considered a non-meaningful statement.

Because it is impossible to verify God's existence through empirical examination, logical positivists argued, belief in God is nonsensical. In his book *Language, Truth, and Logic*, professor of logic at Oxford, Alfred J. Ayer (1910-1989), explained:

> There can be no way of proving that the existence of a god, such as the God of Christianity, is even probable. Yet this also is easily shown. For if the existence of such a god were probable, then the proposition that he existed would be an empirical hypothesis. And in that case it would be possible to deduce from it, and other empirical hypotheses, certain experiential propositions which were not deducible from those other hypotheses alone. But in fact this is not

5 Cited in John Blanchard, *Does God Believe in Atheists?* (Darlington, UK: Evangelical Press, 2001), 14.

possible....For to say that "God exists" is to make a
metaphysical utterance which cannot be either true or false.
And by the same criterion, no sentence which purports to
describe the nature of a transcendent god can possess any
literal significance.[6]

Consequently, logical positivists, such as Ayer, took pride in
claiming that metaphysical statements, such as "God exists,"
could not be verified as meaningful, and thus should not be
accepted. Their confidence in their criteria for verification
continued until people turned their own verification principle on
them. "No proposition is meaningful unless it's an analytic or
synthetic statement" is itself a proposition that is neither analytic
nor synthetic. Logical positivists unwittingly undermined their
own foundation by making the metaphysical statement that only
non-metaphysical statements are meaningful. Consequently,
logical positivism self-destructs – it is self-referentially absurd.

The inconsistency within logical positivism is not merely a
peripheral matter, such as who won the 1976 World Series; it is
rather a fatal flaw in the philosophical system itself. Yet, how
about naturalism, empiricism, and rationalism? Do these core
presuppositions uphold a consistent and cohesive worldview?
Can these worldviews support themselves?

We Must All Start Somewhere

We must remember that we all have presuppositions that we
either loosely take for granted or we firmly presuppose.
Consciously or unconsciously, we all start somewhere. Even
evidentialists, who claim that every belief must be supported by
evidence, recognize the impossibility of such a claim. Not only do
they not have any evidence to support the presupposition that
every belief requires evidence, they also understand that each
belief would require infinitely more beliefs. Evidentialists,

[6] A. J. Ayer, *Language, Truth, and Logic* (New York: Dover Books, 1952), 115.

whether they like it or not, build their worldview on the unscientific claim that every justified belief requires evidence. They, like all of us, must start at some given point. Some start with a commitment to naturalism and empiricism, others start with divine revelation and a personal God. Regardless, every philosopher, scientist, skeptic, religious thinker, and soccer mom has a foundation that undergirds all of their beliefs.

What are your presuppositions? What do you think about God, about knowledge, and about ethics? Do you presuppose that there is a God or not? Do you believe that you are self-sufficient to build a trustworthy worldview, or do you believe you need divine revelation to guide you? Do you believe ethics are universal or relative in nature?

Required to Remain Faithful

Though I believe God has written the answers to these questions on our hearts by giving us the innate knowledge of Himself, of logic, and of morality, for the sake of the argument, let's say that you honestly do not know. "I don't know if there is a God or not." "I don't know if ethics are universal." "I don't know if I believe in divine revelation or not." "I am skeptical." If agnosticism is your stance to these all-important questions, then go ahead and answer them in the negative. Go ahead and say that you don't believe in God. Say that you don't believe in divine revelation or in an absolute code of morality. Presuppose naturalism (that there is no God), empiricism (that there is no divine revelation), and relativism (that there is no absolute standard of right and wrong) and then see if you can construct a cohesive and consistent worldview on the foundation you have chosen.

However, no matter what presuppositions you have chosen, you must remain consistent with them until the end. It is logically inconsistent to jump from one presuppositional foundation to the next. We have seen how Bertrand Russell cheated when he critiqued the cosmological argument. He did not stay true to his core epistemological presupposition – empiricism. If you are an atheist, stick to your guns. Follow through with your presuppositions. Don't build on someone else's foundation. Hold strong to what you believe. Take Socrates' advice and "follow the argument wherever it leads."[7] If there is no such thing as a supernatural and personal God, then the consequences must be accepted and embraced. Cheaters cannot be trusted, and this includes ourselves.

Because we have no choice but to accept a few core presuppositions, the only rational thing for us to do is examine the validity of our presuppositions and follow them through to their logical and natural conclusions. If our presuppositions hold up under the weight, then they are worth maintaining. If we discover our worldview is inconsistent with itself, then we are justified in rejecting it and looking for another. As in the words of the presuppositional apologist Gordon Clark (1902-1985):

> If one system can provide plausible solutions to many problems while another leaves too many questions unanswered, if one system tends less to skepticism and gives more meaning to life, if one worldview is consistent while the others are self-contradictory, who can deny us, since we must choose, the right to choose the more promising first principle.[8]

No matter how rational our line of reasoning may be, if our presuppositional foundation is defective, then the system itself should be discarded. After all, as R. C. Sproul explains:

---

[7] In *Plato's Republic*, Socrates instructs his interlocutors that "we must follow the argument wherever, like the wind, it may lead us" (394d: trans. G. M. A. Grube. Indianapolis: Hackett, 1974., 65).

[8] Cited in Ronald Nash, *Worldviews in Conflict*, 54.

A scientist who refuses to acknowledge facts that he knows are true can hardly be expected to arrive at sound conclusions. Any reasoning process that begins with a denial of the known and proceeds on the basis of prejudice can hardly produce light, no matter how lucid and cogent the argument may proceed after the initial error is made.[9]

Cohesiveness, therefore, is necessary for any worldview. If a worldview cannot uphold its own weight, but falls into absurdity under the pressure of its own truth claims, then it is not a worldview worth embracing.

Why would you knowingly build your house on an active fault line? Why then would you want to build your life on a faulty worldview? In fact, to continue to embrace and defend a faulty and incoherent worldview is to prove you are willing to embrace the absurd and willfully blind yourself to the truth.

Conclusion

Does the Christian worldview support itself? Can the naturalistic worldview remain consistent with its basic core beliefs? No philosophical, humanistic or religious system of thought is based on a single line of thought that leads to an eternal regression without a foundation.

Atheism, pantheism, supernaturalism, naturalism or any other worldview has a foundation, an interlinking system of thought based on a core set of presuppositions that are fitted together, whether *consistently* or *inconsistently*. Everyone has presuppositions, and if we want to prove that our presuppositions are worth embracing, then we must construct a *consistent* worldview based on those presuppositions.

---

[9] R. C. Sproul, *If There's a God, Why are there Atheists?* (Wheaton, IL: Tyndale House Publishers, 1988), 65.

Cohesiveness, cohesiveness, cohesiveness, therefore, is the ultimate test behind any worldview. As we shall see, the Christian worldview has the only valid presuppositional foundation, as it is the only conceptual system of thought that successfully passes the all-important test of cohesiveness.

PART 4

The Irrationality of Unbelief

Fools find no pleasure in understanding
but delight in airing their own opinions.
Ecclesiastes 10:3

11

The Irrationality
of Naturalism

The Christian worldview is true because of the impossibility of the contrary. It is not merely the best worldview out of all the other possible worldviews; it is the only coherent worldview. All the conditions that are necessary for knowledge are completely lost without the God of the Bible. Both deductive and inductive knowledge requires divine revelation to be communicated to those who are made in the likeness of a self-revealing, rational, loving, personal, and trinitarian God. If we take the trinitarian and self-revelatory God out of the equation, and leave man to himself, then absolute absurdity is all that remains.

To help demonstrate this, let's take a look at the logical consequences of the most basic presuppositions that lay behind the various non-Christian worldviews: naturalism, impersonal-supernaturalism, and personal-supernaturalism. Are any of these foundations secure enough to hold their own weight?

We begin by examining the cohesiveness of one of the more widely accepted presuppositions in the Western world – *naturalism*. Naturalism is the basic belief that the material universe is all that there is in existence. This means the universe is a closed system, with no supernatural explanation for any of life's questions. This implies (1.) *materialism* – the universe consists of only that which is physical and material. This also implies (2.)

empiricism – knowledge is limited to the senses. (3.) *Determinism* is also implied – man is merely a machine, without a free will, with his thoughts and emotions being determined by the fixed laws of physics that control the motions of all moving things in this materialistic universe. (4.) *Relativism* is also a byproduct of naturalism – without a Divine lawgiver, ethical morality must be situational and relative at best. (5.) *Nihilism*, sadly, comes next – all of world history and every individual life within it are ultimately meaningless.[1] With no design, there is no purpose. In the end, nothing truly makes any sense. Take God out of the picture and this is what we get.

The Irrationality of Materialism

But lets start from the beginning. Naturalism leads to materialism – all that exists is reducible to mass and energy independent of any supernatural influence.

Materialism finds its roots in some of the earliest philosophers of ancient Greece. Thales believed that the basic element of the universe was *water*, while Anaximenes believed that it was *air*. Heraclitus concluded that everything is reducible to *fire*, and Pythagoras, the ancient mathematician, said *number* was the basic element. Though the answers provided by these Presocratic philosophers sound somewhat primitive, they were some of the first attempts to explain the universe without any supernatural element.

What supposedly prevented the Greeks from abandoning belief in the gods was unexplainable, natural phenomena. Any unusual or traumatic occurrences, which appeared to defy the orderly and normal functions of nature, such as earthquakes, tsunamis, and solar and lunar eclipses were viewed as supernatural events. The wrath of the polytheistic gods must be

---

[1] Materialism, empiricism, relativism, etc. are not so much opposing worldviews as they are various facets of a naturalistic worldview.

behind such dreadful things, for what other explanation could there be for such wild and unpredictable disturbances? The supernatural was needed to explain such mysteries.

Thales, however, by the use of scientific observation, explained and predicted a solar eclipse. What was once an act of the gods was now an act of nature. In time, science gave more and more naturalistic explanations to many of the mysteries of the universe.

It was Nicolaus Copernicus (1473-1543), Galileo Galilei (1564-1642), and Isaac Newton (1642-1727) who supposedly dropped the bombshell on religion. Copernicus placed our sun at the center of the universe. Galileo agreed with Copernicus, which did not place him in conflict with the Bible, but with Aristotle and the Catholic Church. Newton provided a scientific explanation for the movements of our planets in his law of gravitation. The mystery of how the earth and other planets suspend themselves in space now had a naturalistic answer. As science seemed to be providing more and more answers, the need for God was slowly being pushed out the back door.

Naturalism was growing stronger, but it was not until Charles Darwin (1809-1882) provided a scientific explanation for the origins of life that, according to Richard Dawkins, it became "possible to be an intellectually fulfilled atheist."[2] A naturalistic understanding of the origins of life was not new to Darwin, but according to law professor Phillip Johnson from the University of California, "Charles Darwin made evolution a scientific concept by showing, or claiming to have shown, that major transformations could occur in very small steps by purely natural means, so that time, chance, and differential survival could take the place of a miracle."[3] The English biologist Julian Huxley

---

[2] Richard Dawkins, *The Blind Watchmaker* (New York: Norton, 1996), 6.

[3] Phillip E. Johnson, *Darwin on Trial* (Downers Grove, IL: IVP, 2 ed. 1993), 12.

(1887-1975) went as far as to say, "In the evolutionary scheme of thought there is no longer either need or room for the supernatural. The earth was not created, it evolved. So did all the animals and plants that inhabit it, including our human selves, mind and soul as well as brain and body."[4]

What Darwin was to biology, Georges Lemaître (1894-1966) and Edwin Hubble (1864-1934) were to astronomy. Lemaître proposed that the universe had a beginning by tweaking the calculations of Einstein, who believed that the universe was in an eternally constant state.[5] By mapping the galaxies and their movements, Hubble verified Lemaître's theory by proving the universe is ever expanding by showing that galaxies are moving further and further away from each other. With the expansion of the universe, it was postulated that everything originated at a single point – a singularity.

With a big bang, from this singularity, the universe exploded into existence out of nothing. Though this sounds like Genesis 1:1, naturalists have sought to explain how the Big Bang could have occurred without God. With evolution and the Big Bang[6] as naturalistic explanations to the origin of the universe, supposedly the physical laws of nature have taken the place of any supernatural explanation.

But certain questions need to be answered. Can any naturalistic/materialistic explanation support the laws of physics? Can materialism support its own foundation? First, we will show the absurdity of a *Big Bang* without God, and then we will show the absurdity of *evolution of the species* through natural selection. Neither one of these theories can give an account for the *laws* that undergird their foundation.

---

[4] Cited in *God's Undertaker*, 87.

[5] See Walter Isaacson, *Einstein: His Life and Universe* (New York: Simon & Schuster, 2007), 254-255.

[6] By *Big Bang* I mean an *unintelligent* cosmic explosion, not that the universe is without a finite beginning point.

The Irrationality of the Big Bang

If a supernatural God is not an option, there are *only* two possible answers to the origin of the universe. Not three of four, but only two answers can be given – the universe either came into existence out of nothing, or it's eternal. Both fly directly in the face of the laws of science.

If you believe that the world came out of nothing, you must truly begin with *nothing*! Christian apologist Francis Schaeffer (1912-1984) explained that if you start with nothing, you couldn't secretly add *something* to the equation: "Now, to hold this view, it must be absolutely nothing. It must be what I call *nothing* nothing. If one is to accept this answer, it must be nothing nothing, which means there must be no energy, no mass, no motion, and no personality."[7] I would also add that there would be no such thing as *time* or *chance*. If nothing exists, then time and chance do not exist either. They do not exist even as concepts without something (such as an intelligence or mass and energy) being in existence first.

So, did nothing create something? Former Cambridge physicist Stephen Hawking and former Oxford chemist Peter Atkins claim that it did. Hawking explains that because "there is a law like gravity, the universe can and will create itself from nothing."[8] Atkins, with less explanation but with more words, concurs:

> In the beginning there was nothing. Absolute void, not merely empty space. There was no space. There was no space; nor was there time, for this was before time. The universe was without form and void.

---

[7] Francis Schaeffer, *Trilogy*, "He is There and He is Not Silent" (Wheaton, IL: Crossway, 1990), 282.

[8] Stephen Hawking and Leonard Mlodinow, *The Grand Design* (New York: Bantam Books, 2010), 180.

By chance there was a fluctuation, and set of points, emerging from nothing and taking their existence from the pattern they formed, defined a time. The chance formation of a pattern resulted in the emergence of time from coalesced opposites, its emergence from nothing. From absolute nothing, absolutely without intervention, there came into being rudimentary existence.[9]

Do Hawking and Atkins not know that they sound ridiculous? For something to come from nothing, then something must have created itself. But self-creation is impossible. As R. C. Sproul explains, "For something to create itself, it must have the ability to be and not be at the same time and in the same relationship."[10] If the law of gravity is an observed property of matter, how did the law of gravity exist when matter did not exist? How can gravity create anything if it does not even exist?

Bewildered by Hawking's statement, John Lennox states: "To presuppose the existence of the universe to account for its existence sounds like something out of *Alice in Wonderland*, not science."[11] But, Atkins' explanation is not any better. Is it not completely absurd to say, "In the beginning there was nothing," and then go on to say, "By chance there was a fluctuation"? How can there be chance when there is nothing to begin with? What is chance in a non-existent universe? It is absurd to think that we can create something when we add nothing to nothing. Nothing, plus chance (which is nothing), plus time (which is also nothing) brought about everything. If time and chance are nothing, it does not matter how much of it there is, it still adds up to nothing. The old maxim of Parmenides' (515-460 BC) principle, *Ex nihilo nihil fit*, still rings true today: nothing can come from nothing.

[9] Peter Atkins, *Creation Revisited* (Oxford: W. H. Freeman & Company, 1992), 149.

[10] R. C. Sproul and Keith Mathison, *Not a Chance: God, Science, and the Revolt against Reason* (Grand Rapids, Baker Books, 2014), 26.

[11] John C. Lennox, *God and Stephen Hawking* (Oxford: Lion Books, 2011). 31.

To say otherwise, as we already pointed out in chapter 10, goes directly against the first, second, and third laws of motion that state every *cause* must have an *effect*. To believe that the universe is an *effect* or a fluctuation that had no *cause* is evidence that we would rather deny the existence of God than remain rationally sane. To say nothing created something is to believe in a divine miracle without believing in God. "What this all goes to show is that nonsense remains," concluded Lennox, "even when talked by world-famous scientists."[12]

Well, maybe it's impossible for nothing to produce something, but that does not mean the universe could not be eternal. The cyclic theory of the universe states that the universe is its own eternal cause. Under this model, from the moment of the Big Bang, the universe will continue to expand outward in all directions until its own gravitational force is so strong that it pulls everything back on itself, causing the universe to collapse into a cosmic black hole, which in return provides the energy needed for another Big Bang. This eternal process of expansion and retraction repeats itself indefinitely.

This, however, only pushes the problem back. Who fired off the first Big Bang to get things started? An infinite regression of effects does not solve anything. It is an attempt to explain the effects by a cause, but never willing to answer the question of who or what caused the first effect. Because self-creation is a logical contradiction, it is impossible for the universe to have gone through multiple self-creations.

Moreover, the second law of thermodynamics states that the total amount of *useable* energy in any isolated system never increases. The design and complexity of a German high-performance vehicle does not improve over time. If you don't believe me, all you have to do is to ask the mechanic who continued to be paid for working on my Audi A4. Though it ran

12 Ibid., 32.

with precision the first few years, before trading it in for a new car, it would not stay out of the garage. But I am not picking on German engineering, for all things in the universe – from automobiles to dying stars – fall apart over time. Because the amount of *useable* energy in any closed system naturally dissipates, the universe is not self-sustainable. Thus, even if the universe went through multiple self-recreations, the process could not sustain itself forever. Ultimately, everything would end in maximum entropy (disorder). Without an external power source, eventually the universe would die with all of its useable energy being fully depleted. And if there is a definite end to the process, then there could not have been an eternal beginning. Thus, it is irrational to think the universe is eternal.

Moreover, explosions do not create complex and wonderfully designed infrastructures no matter how many times they occur. Chance and time will never create the Empire State building with its running water, electricity, elevators, and nicely fitted glass windows by the random explosion of raw materials. The massive energy behind the Big Bang just so happened to throw all of the raw materials of the universe into a precise, mathematical, and uniform framework where it runs with the precision of the immaterial laws of physics. Are we to believe raw matter was randomly and blindly thrown into perfectly and mathematically structured galaxies? Even Big Bang supporter James Trefil, professor of physics at George Mason University, confessed that there "shouldn't be galaxies out there at all, and even if there are galaxies, they shouldn't be grouped together the way they are." He went on to say:

> The problem of explaining the existence of galaxies has proved to be one of the thorniest in cosmology. By all rights, they just shouldn't be there, yet there they sit. It's hard to

convey the depth of the frustration that this simple fact induces among scientists.[13]

The Big Bang did not merely end with lifeless galaxies, but with a perfectly positioned planet that is capable of all the vast amount of complexities that are necessary for life to thrive and flourish – known as the anthropic principle. Intelligent Design advocate Jim Nelson Black summarizes the madness in his book *The Death of Evolution*:

> We also know that the mixture of oxygen and nitrogen in Earth's atmosphere must be exact, within very narrow limits, for us to breathe. In order to sustain life, the planet must be precisely situated in the solar system to remain in the habitable zone around the sun. If the earth were to orbit 5 percent closer to the sun, the seas, rivers, and lakes would evaporate and all carbon-based life would cease to exist. If the planet were 20 percent farther from the sun, the water would freeze.
>
> Relative to the size of the planet, the outer crust of the earth is paper thin. If it were any thicker, the process of plate tectonics, which controls the inner temperature of the earth and the presence of chemical elements essential to life, could not take place. The terrestrial depth also affects the movement of molten elements beneath the surface of the earth, including the iron ore responsible for the magnetic field around our planet. The magnetic field, in turn, shields the planet from dangerous solar winds generated by the sun and keeps the earth in precisely the right orbit with relation to the sun, moon, and neighboring planets.
>
> These are merely a few of the factors that make the earth just right for life. And there are many more . . . The chance of all these factors and the hundreds of others that allow life to exist on earth occurring purely by chance are astronomical – the

---

[13] Cited in Jonathan Sarfati, *Refuting Evolution* (Green Forest, AR: Master Books, 1999), 93.

odds are literally trillions to one. The British mathematician Roger Penrose conducted a study of the probability of a universe capable of sustaining life occurring by chance and found the odds to be 1 in $10^{10^{123}}$ (expressed as 10 to the power of 10 to the power of 123). That is a mind-boggling number. According to probability theory, odds of 1 to 10^{50} represents "Zero Probability." But Dr. Penrose's calculations place the odds of life emerging as Darwin described it at more than a trillion trillion trillion times less than Zero.[14]

Those numbers presuppose that the building blocks to the universe were already in existence. If, however, nothing comes out of nothing, then there is no chance for the Big Bang to have created the universe on its own initiative. Black rightly concluded that holding to the Big Bang theory "demands a complete suspension of belief better suited of the readers of fairy tales."[15] Even the evolutionist Arthur Stanley Eddington (1882-1944) conceded that the scientific evidence behind the origins of the universe, though he thought it was repugnant, pointed to an Intelligent Designer:

> The picture of the world, as drawn in existing physical theories shows arrangements of the individual elements for which the odds are multillions to 1 against an origin by chance. Some people would like to call this non-random feature of the world purpose or design; but I will call it non-committally anti-chance. We are unwilling in physics that anti-chance plays any part in the reactions between the systems of billions of atoms and quanta that we study; and indeed all our experimental evidence goes to show that these are governed by the laws of chance. Accordingly, we sweep anti-chance out of the laws of physics – out of the differential equations. Naturally, therefore, it reappears in the boundary conditions, for it must be got into the scheme somewhere. By

---

[14] *The Death of Evolution*, 31-32.
[15] Ibid., 33.

sweeping it far enough away from the sphere of our current physical problems, we fancy we have got rid of it. It is only when some of us are so misguided as to try to get back billions of years into the past that we find the sweepings all piled up like a high wall and forming a boundary – a beginning of time – which we cannot climb over.[16]

The mathematical odds are too great to overcome for the universe to have been caused by mere chance. After knowing the facts, it takes more blind faith to believe that a random universe blindly created itself than it does to accept an Intelligent Designer.

Moreover, these mathematical odds create another problem for the naturalists. Not merely do the mathematical odds oppose the possibility of the universe being sparked into existence by an unintelligent cosmic explosion, an unintelligent explosion cannot provide any explanation for the existence of the absolute and immaterial laws of math.

The laws of physics operate in accordance to the laws of math. For instance, the acceleration of gravity can be precisely measured by a mathematical equation ($g = 9.81\text{m/s/s}$). The distance a falling object travels increases at the square of the time it travels. According to the inverse square law, the intensity of gravity is inversely proportional to the square of the distance of two bodies. The force of a magnet will diminish with the cube of its distance away from ferromagnetic materials (such as iron). The point is that the laws of physics cannot be separated from mathematics. Seeing this connection caused English astronomer James Jeans (1877-1846) to remark: "The universe appears to have been designed by a pure mathematician."[17]

---

[16] http://www.uncommondescent.com/intelligent-design/arthur-stanley-eddington-darwinists-and-repugnant-notions/

[17] Cited in *The Cosmic Jackpot*, 8.

But where do the immaterial and mathematical laws come from? How can mathematics exist independently of intelligent consciousness? Professor of mathematical sciences at Trinity Western University, John Byl, explains why this is an awkward dilemma for naturalists:

> Naturalism has great difficulty dealing with mathematical objects. Mathematical objects are abstract ideas. How can matter ever evolve into ideas? How can ideas exist, other than in some mind? Naturalism alleges that mind evolved from matter. How, then, did mathematics exist before mind evolved? If the answer is that mathematics did not exist before the appearance of man, how are we to account for the mathematical structure of the laws of physics, which are assumed to have held from the start? If mathematical truths are universal and eternal, this seems to require the existence of a universal, eternal Mind. Yet, if mathematics exists objectively, beyond the human mind and physical world, how can man gain access to it?[18]

This was one of the reasons the long-standing atheist Antony Flew renounced his atheism: "The important point is not merely that there are regularities in nature, but that these regularities are mathematically precise, universal, and 'tied together.'"[19] A self-creating universe is nonsensical because it destroys the foundation that it is seeking to uphold – the laws of nature. Consequently, the Big Bang theory cannot explain why the world is orderly, symmetrically arranged, and abides by the mathematical principles of the laws of physics.

Seeing an Intelligent Mind behind the mathematically precise structure of the universe seems more natural and plausible than thinking that blind chance created and organized the universe out of nothing. Yet, the *New York Times* columnist and science writer George Johnson would have us believe that our minds are

---

[18] *The Divine Challenge*, 59
[19] Antony Flew, *There Is a God* (New York: HarperOne, 2007), 96.

playing tricks on us when we automatically assume that such geometrical organization found throughout the universe was engineered by an Intelligent Mind: "When we see such intricate symmetry, our brains automatically assume there was an inventor."[20] But this apparent design, says Johnson, is merely an illusion. Similarly, evolutionary biologist Richard Lewontin remarked that objects of nature only "appear to have been carefully and artfully designed."[21]

Johnson went on to say that this instinct to see God as the architect must be suppressed if ever we are to make sense of the universe: "Overcoming that instinct took centuries, and it was only then that the living world began to make sense." [22] "Biologists *must constantly keep in mind*," according to Francis Crick, co-discoverer of the structure of DNA, "that what they see was not designed, but rather evolved."[23]

In other words, though it is not natural for us to believe that the universe created itself, we must suppress the knowledge of God that is triggered when observing the universe if we are ever to believe that the world is without design or purpose. And, according to Johnson, it is only when we see the world as without design or purpose that we can "make sense" of a senseless world.

Naturalists, such as Eddington, Lewontin, Crick, and Johnson, would have us believe that if we happened to find a watch in the desert, with all of its interworking pieces collectively operating for a single purpose with mathematical precision, and the watchmaker was not also visibly present, then we should not believe the watch had any intelligent designer. If the watchmaker

---

[20] George Johnson, "Creation, in the Beholder," *The New York Times*, 20 May 2014, D3.

[21] Cited in Stephen C. Meyer, *Signature in the Cell* (New York: HarperOne, 2009), 17-18. Emphasis is Stephen Meyer.

[22] Ibid.

[23] Cited in *Signature in the Cell*, 12.

cannot be observed through scientific observation, then a watchmaker must be ruled out.[24]

However, the universe is a lot more complex and mathematically precise than any watch. If it is only rational to think watches have watchmakers, then it is also irrational to think the cosmic watch of the universe does not have an intelligent designer. Watches are merely an imperfect copy of our solar system. Watches often need resetting, but the earth continues to make a full spin on its axis every 24 hours and completes a full rotation around the sun every 365.25 days. There are far more complexities and mathematical necessities that go into keeping the world ticking than any man-made clock.

Conclusion

A naturalistic explanation of the universe, no matter if it be by a non-supernatural explosion from a singularity or by some other means, cannot account for the laws of nature that are rooted in the immaterial laws of mathematics. If there is a universe without a Divine Mind, why is there order and geometrical structure when chaos is what should be expected?

[24] See William Paley, *Natural Theology* (New York: Oxford, 2008), 1-10.

12

The Irrationality of Evolution

When thinking about evolution, one must not confuse microevolution (the ability of various species to adapt to their surroundings, such as when a strain of the flu becomes immune to certain antibodies over time) with macroevolution (the idea that every species has descended from a common ancestor). It is sloppy science to confuse microevolution with macroevolution. Proving microevolution does not equate to proving macroevolution.

Microevolution is a fact that is easily demonstrated by taking note of the different ethnicities of people that have developed along geographical lines. Macroevolution, on the other hand, is the theory that the complexities of the human race have evolved from non-living matter through the slow process of adaptation. Moreover, once the material world came into existence out of nothing, macroevolution demands that the immaterial (i.e., consciousness, emotions, etc.) arose from the material, that life derived from non-life, and that our emotions, thoughts, and aspirations slowly developed from dead matter.

Darwin did not provide any evidence for macroevolution, but filled his book, *On the Origin of Species*, with multiple examples of microevolution. Daniel Dennett, the great modern day apologist for Darwin's theory of evolution, admitted that Darwin's observations were limited to the study of various adaptations taking place in already existing traits within already existing species:

> Darwin doesn't even purport to offer an explanation of the origin of the first species, or of life itself; he begins in the middle, supposing many different species with many different talents already present, and claims that starting from such a mid-stage point, the process he has described will inevitably hone and diversify the talents of the species already existing.[1]

In other words, after Darwin had observed the ability a particular species has to adapt to its surroundings, he concluded that man evolved from apes from natural selection. Lennox, however, reminds us that the "word 'selection' ought to alert our attention to this: selection is made from already existing entities."[2] Adaptation can take place within traits and entities that already exist. Bird beaks can get longer or shorter, but there is no empirical evidence that beaks turn into snouts. Skin color can change and height can vary from generation to generation depending on who marries whom, but all these subtle changes are only changes in preexisting traits.

It is not as if Darwin observed any instance where there was a creative process or development of new entities where those entities were not in existence in the first place. The *survival* of the fittest is one thing; the *arrival* of the fittest is quite another. Let's not get these two things confused.

Contrary to the Law of Biogenesis

Macroevolution seems silly. A long time ago, a stone, or a stick, or a pile of dirt, or a pool of water reproduced itself. One of these

---

[1] Daniel Dennett, *Darwin's Dangerous Idea* (New York: Touchstone, 1996), 42-43.

[2] *God's Undertaker*, 104.

rocks, or sticks, or dirt piles, or water holes after many more years, became self-conscious. It had feelings. It no longer wanted to be a rock, so it decided to turn into a monkey. This sounds absurd, but how does slowing the process down and adding a million more steps to the process help? How can life arise from dead matter?

Not only does it sound ridiculous, it is unsupported by the evidence. Life evolving from non-life goes against the law of biogenesis. Louis Pasteur (1822-1895) researched the possibility of life mutating from non-life and concluded, "all life comes from the egg" (*Omne vivum ex ovo*). Living beings come only from other living beings. Though there has been no observable exception to this rule, the same naturalists who reject miracles, such as the resurrection of Christ that was verified by more than 500 eyewitnesses, claim that we are to believe in a more radical miracle – that life evolved from non-life – without even a single eyewitness. Which is more unbelievable, the resurrection of Christ or life being birthed from a rock? At least the Christian worldview makes room for miracles and the supernatural.

Contrary to the Reproductive Principle

Supposedly, because of the all-important *reproductive principle* known as *natural selection*, life emerged from non-living matter through slow adaptations. The elements or parts that were not useful for life died out, and those that were useful for life were reproduced. Supposedly a pile of dirt eventually becoming living, thinking matter is not silly or miraculous sounding if we slow the process down to billions of years.

Yet, how does the reproductive system work for that which is not living? Seeing that reproduction is one of the attributes of life, life must first *exist* before it can reproduce itself. *Survival of the fittest* demands that the reproductive system be already functioning before any adaptations can take place. Rocks do not mutate or reproduce themselves. How does natural selection and the reproduction process ever get started? For good reason, Charles Darwin was completely mute on this point.

Contrary to the Irreducibly Complex Principle

To say that lighting struck a warm puddle of water (i.e., a prebiotic soup) and out popped living matter − the simplest cells − is altogether unbelievable and goes against the theory that life evolved from slow and gradual adaptations. Especially seeing how complex and amazing the simplest cell actually is − which includes more than three billion moving parts and complex chemical reactions.

In his book *Refuting Evolution*, Jonathan Sarfati explains the complexity of the simplest cell and cites the work of molecular biologist Michael Denton, who provides this amazing explanation:

Perhaps in no other area of modern biology is the challenge posed by the extreme complexity and ingenuity of biological adaptations more apparent than in the fascinating new molecular world of the cell....To grasp the reality of life as it has been revealed by molecular biology, we must magnify a cell a thousand million times until it is twenty kilometers in diameter and resembles a giant airship large enough to cover a great city like London or New York. What we would then see would be an object of unparalleled complexity and adaptive design. On the surface of the cell we would see millions of openings, like port holes of a vast space ship, opening and closing to allow a continual stream of materials to flow in and out. If we were to enter one of these openings we would find ourselves in a world of supreme technology and bewildering complexity.

Is it really credible that random processes could have constructed a reality, the smallest element of which − a functional protein or gene – is complex beyond our own creative capacities, a reality which is the very antithesis of chance, which excels in every sense anything produced by the intelligence of man? Alongside the level of ingenuity and complexity exhibited by the molecular machinery of life, even our most advanced artifacts appear clumsy.[3]

In addition, the simplest cells host a genetic code that is duplicated in replication. A vast amount of information is copied from DNA to RNA (ribonucleic acid) in transcription. DNA hosts semantic information, like an instruction manual, with chemical subunits that function as alphabetic characters. The genetic language consists of an alphabet (coding system), correct spelling, grammar (proper arrangements of the chemical subunits), meaning (semantics), and intended purpose. This genetic information is translated as it is conveyed to the amino acids, which are assembled into proteins. This process is amazing. Yet, how did this knowledge emerge? Where did this specific and functional information come from? Another important question is how did the simplest cell evolve with the ability to transmit, store, and translate all this information in its replication process?

Human DNA, for instance, contains more than 3.5 billion letters and enough information to fill 12 sets of the 32 volume Encyclopedia Britannica. All empirical evidence and common sense would have us believe that functional information comes from intelligent minds. "DNA," according to the founder of Microsoft, Bill Gates, "is like a computer program but far, far more advanced than any software ever created." Yet, in the same way it seems absurd to think that time and chance could write a complex computer program, it seems absurd to think that blind chance just so happened to write the genetic code of life on strands of DNA. It takes a fair amount of blind faith to believe

---

[3] *Refuting Evolution*, 124.

that chance could construct a marble statue that looks like Abraham Lincoln, but more than blind faith is needed to believe that chance could write a 385 volume instruction manual and have it neatly stacked on Lincoln's lap. Such information simply cannot be explained by the random and blind arrangement of mass and energy.

This, according to Paul Davies, "arguably the most influential contemporary expositor of modern science,"[4] is a major problem for the theory of evolution: "The problem of how meaningful or semantic information can emerge spontaneously from a collection of mindless molecules subject to blind and purposeless forces presents a deep conceptual challenge."[5]

It must be kept in mind that *macro*evolution cannot take place without new genetic information being added to an organism's genetic code. Without an increase of information, it is impossible for the simplest organism to have evolved into something more complex.

Yet, there is not one stand of observable evidence that new genetic information can be created. For instance, *micro*evolution only operates on genetic information that already exists. For proteins to be capable of building new and more complex forms of life, they would need new and more complex instructions to follow. Mutations that alter existing traits (e.g., varieties of corn and fruit flies) is not a formation of new information but the rearrangement of preexisting information. On the molecular level, something was not created but broken in the mutation process.

If not created, then where does genetic information come from? Stephen C. Meyer, co-founder of the Center for Science and Culture of the Discovery Institute, explains why we should not rule out an Intelligent Mind when asking this question:

[4] *There Is a God*, 111.
[5] Cited in *There Is a God*, 129.

Scientists in many fields recognize the connection between intelligence and information and make inferences accordingly. Archaeologists assume that a scribe produces the inscriptions on the Rosetta Stone. Evolutionary anthropologists establish the intelligence of early hominids from chipped flints that are too improbably specified in form and function to have been produced by natural causes. NASA's search for extraterrestrial intelligence (SETI) presupposes that any specified information embedded in electromagnetic signals coming from space would indicate an intelligent source. As yet, radio astronomers have not found any such information-bearing signals. But closer to home, molecular biologists have identified information-rich sequences and systems in the cell, suggesting, by the same logic, the past existence of an intelligent cause for those effects.[6]

All this genetic information and immense complexity supposedly came from non-living matter that magically happened to be able to reproduce itself. Unless you believe in magic without a magician, the engineering marvel of the simplest cell could not have evolved from non-living matter. For life to begin, the simple cell had to spontaneously appear with all it's necessary parts, thrown together in the proper place, creating the semantic information needed for the living cell to reproduce itself.

Biochemist Michael Behe, in his book *Darwin's Black Box,* goes into great detail not only in explaining the complexity of the single cell, but also explaining how this complexity is needed, with all of its diverse parts simultaneously working together, for a single cell to reproduce itself. [7] The cell is a functionally integrated system that only operates when each of its components (processors, power supplies, and switches) function together.

---

[6] *Signature in the Cell,* 343-344.
[7] M. J. Behe, *Darwin's Black Box* (New York: The Free Press, 1996).

That is, the simplest cell is *irreducibly complex*. Behe illustrated this by observing the components of an old-fashion mousetrap. A mousetrap has six components – a platform, a spring, a wire, a hammer, a catch, and a holding bar. For the mousetrap to work, all of its components must be present and in their proper place, or otherwise it cannot function. Remove just one of its parts, such as the spring, and the trap is completely useless. All the different components of the simplest cell likewise are needed for it to be able to reproduce itself. The cell is *irreducibly complex*. So, if the unnecessary parts are discarded in the evolutionary process, the simplest cell had to come together simultaneously. Yet, the coming together of all these components in a mere spontaneous moment goes against the theory that things slowly adapt to survive. This means the single cell could not have evolved by reproduction, for it either came fully intact or it did not come at all.

Darwin assumed that the simplest living cell would consist of a single component (a blob of protoplasm),[8] but we have learned that it is more like a complex factory with a mass telecommunications network. Understanding this, Dean Kenyon, professor emeritus of biology at San Francisco State University, states: "We have not the slightest chance of a chemical evolutionary origin for even the simplest of cells."[9] This was another reason Flew turned his back on atheism, for he concluded that the "origin of life cannot be explained if you start with matter alone."[10] Christopher Williams, professor of bio-chemistry at Ohio State University, echoed this same conclusion:

[8] The Protoplasmic Theory falsely assumed that the protoplasm was the basic building block of life and that, just as two chemicals such as hydrogen and oxygen from water when combined, two chemical ingredients could combine under the right environmental circumstances and create protoplasm.

[9] Cited in Jim Nelson Black, *The Death of Evolution* (Grand Rapids: Zondervan, 2010), 2.

[10] *There Is a God*, 90.

Few people outside of genetics or biochemistry realize that evolutionists still can provide no substantive details at all about the origin of life, and particularly the origin of genetic information in the first self-replicating organism. What genes did it require – or did it even have genes? How much DNA and RNA did it have – or did it even have nucleic acids? How did huge information-rich molecules arise before natural selection? Exactly how did the genetic code linking nucleic acids to amino acids sequence originate? Clearly the origin of life – the foundation of evolution – is still virtually all speculation, and little or no fact.[11]

What can be said of the simplest cell can be said of many things, such as sight. Sight could not have evolved from non-sight because the eye needs all of its working components to function. Even Darwin admitted: "To suppose that the eye, with all its inimitable contrivances for adjusting the focus to different distances, for admitting different amounts of light, and for the correction of spherical and chromatic aberration, could have been formed by natural selection, seems, I freely confess, absurd in the highest possible degree."[12]

If the eye must come intact for it to function, what good is 5 percent of an eye in the early process of the adaptation of the eye? Richard Dawkins seems foolish when he tries to explain:

An ancient animal with 5 per cent of an eye might indeed have used it for something other than sight, but it seems to me as likely that it used it for 5 per cent vision...So 1 per cent is better than blindness. And 6 per cent is better than 5, 7 per cent better than 6, and so on up the gradual, continuous series.[13]

Dawkins seems to be missing the point. With only 5 percent of the eye, there is absolutely *no* vision. 5 percent, 10 percent, and

[11] Cited in *The Death of Evolution*, 142.
[12] Cited in Ibid., 110.
[13] Cited in *Darwin on Trial*, 34.

even 50 percent of the eye equals zero percent eyesight. Vision is impossible without *all* of its necessary components, and this indicates that it is impossible for the eye to have slowly evolved. Because evolution is blind, it cannot create parts that will possibly be needed thousands of years in the future. Supposedly, the evolutionary process eliminates that which is non-useful for survival – such as 5% of a non-functioning eye. For this reason, eyesight either comes intact, or it does not come at all.

One of the most cited chemists in the world, James M. Tour, who is also professor of mechanical engineering and materials science at Rice University, argued that no scientist is able to explain macroevolution:

> Does anyone understand the chemical details behind macroevolution? If so, I would like to sit with that person and be taught, so I invite them to meet with me. Lunch will be my treat. Until then, I will maintain that no chemist understands, hence we are collectively bewildered. And I have not even addressed origin of first life issues. For me, that is even more scientifically mysterious than evolution. Darwin never addressed origin of life, and I can see why he did not; he was far too smart for that. Present day scientists that expose their thoughts on this become ever so timid when they talk with me privately. I simply cannot understand the source of their confidence when addressing their positions publicly.[14]

In a speech given at Georgia Tech, Tour defended his critique of macroevolution:

> I will tell you as a scientist and a synthetic chemist: if anybody should be able to understand evolution, it is me, because I make molecules for a living, and I don't just buy a kit, and mix *this* and mix *this*, and get *that*. I mean, *ab initio*, I make molecules. I understand how hard it is to make molecules. I

14   http://www.jmtour.com/personal-topics/the-scientist-and-his-"theory"-and-the-christian-creationist-and-his-"science"

understand that if I take Nature's tool kit, it could be much easier, because all the tools are already there, and I just mix it in the proportions, and I do it under these conditions, but *ab initio* is very, very hard.

I don't understand evolution, and I will confess that to you. Is that OK, for me to say, "I don't understand this"? Is that all right? I know that there's a lot of people out there that don't understand anything about organic synthesis, but they understand evolution. I understand *a lot* about making molecules; I don't understand evolution.

Let me tell you what goes on in the back rooms of science – with National Academy members, with Nobel Prize winners. I have sat with them, and when I get them alone, not in public – because it's a scary thing, if you say what I just said – I say, "Do you understand all of this, where all of this came from, and how this happens?" *Every time* that I have sat with people who are synthetic chemists, who understand this, they go "Uh-uh. Nope." These people are just so far off, on how to believe this stuff came together. I've sat with National Academy members, with Nobel Prize winners. Sometimes I will say, "Do you understand this?" And if they're afraid to say, "Yes," they say nothing. They just stare at me, because they can't sincerely do it.

I was once brought in by the Dean of the Department, many years ago, and he was a chemist. He was kind of concerned about some things. I said, "Let me ask you something. You're a chemist. Do you understand this? How do you get DNA without a cell membrane? And how do you get a cell membrane without a DNA? And how does all this come together from this piece of jelly?" We have no idea, we have no idea. I said, "Isn't it interesting that you, the Dean of science, and I, the chemistry professor, can talk about this quietly in your office, but we can't go out there and talk about this?"

But about seven or eight years ago I posted on my Web site that I don't understand. And I said, "I will buy lunch for anyone that will sit with me and explain to me evolution, and *I won't argue with you until I don't understand something* – I will ask you to clarify. But you can't wave by and say, "This enzyme does that." You've got to get down in the details of where molecules are built, for me. *Nobody* has come forward.

The Atheist Society contacted me. They said that *they* will buy the lunch, and they challenged the Atheist Society, "Go down to Houston and have lunch with this guy, and talk to him." *Nobody has come!* Now remember, because I'm just going to ask, when I stop understanding what you're talking about, I will ask. So I sincerely *want* to know. I would *like* to believe it. But I just *can't*.[15]

Cannot Give Account for Consciousness

Not only is the theory of evolution unable to explain the origins of life from dead matter, it has no explanation for the origins of consciousness. Where did consciousness come from? In *The Cosmic Jackpot*, evolutionist Paul Davies claims: "Mindless, blundering atoms have conspired to make not just life, not just mind, but understanding."[16] Yet, a few pages later he admitted that "scientists don't know how life began, and they are almost totally baffled by consciousness."[17] This is because consciousness, which includes self-awareness and willful intent, cannot be reduced to merely physical properties.

Because of this, Thomas Nagel, though he denies the existence of any divine intelligence, says that natural evolution alone cannot explain the origins of consciousness:

---

[15]   https://www.youtube.com/watch?v=PZrxTH-UUdI&feature=youtu.be (52:00 to 56:44) June, 2014.

[16] Paul Davies, *The Cosmic Jackpot* (Boston: Houghton Mifflin Company, 2007), 5.

[17] Ibid., 14.

If evolutionary theory is a purely physical theory, then it might in principle provide the framework for a physical explanation of the appearance of behaviorally complex animal organisms with central nervous systems. But subjective consciousness, if it is not reducible to something physical, would not be part of this story; it would be left completely unexplained by physical evolution – even if the physical evolution of such organisms is in fact a causally necessary and sufficient condition for consciousness.[18]

Not Supported by the Fossil Records

Moreover, where are these blind transitional species with only 5 percent of a non-functioning eyeball? Where are the fossil records? Where are the missing links? Did Java Man disappear? What happened to Lucy? Where is Piltdown Man when you need him? What about Nebraska Man? All these supposed missing links that gave undeniable proof for the evolutionary process of the species have turned out to be either frauds or blatant errors in judgment. Is there not just one missing link that can be found? Colin Patterson, who was the senior paleontologist of the British Museum of Natural History, in his book *Evolution* explained, when questioned, why he did not include any pictures or illustrations of transitional forms:

> I fully agree with your comments about the lack of direct illustration of evolutionary transitions in my book. If I knew of any, fossil or living, I would certainly have included them.... I will lay it on the line – there is not one such fossil for which one could make a watertight argument.[19]

In fact, according to paleontologist David Raup of the Field Museum of Natural History, the fossil records have done nothing to assist Darwin's theory of evolution:

---

[18] Thomas Nagel, *Mind and Cosmos* (New York: Oxford, 2012), 44-45.
[19] Cited in Jonathan Sarfati *Refuting Evolution* (Green Forest, AR: Master Books, 1999), 48.

We are now about 120 years after Darwin and the knowledge of the fossil record has been greatly expanded. We now have a quarter of a million fossil species, but the situation hasn't changed much. The record of evolution is still surprisingly jerky and, ironically, we have even fewer examples of evolutionary transitions than we had in Darwin's time.[20]

Niles Eldredge of the American Museum of Natural History was even bolder when he admitted: "We paleontologists have said that the history of life supports [the story of gradual adaptive change] knowing all the while it does not."[21]

Rather than working in favor of evolution, according to Stephen Meyer, the fossil records provide evidence for Intelligent Design. He cites Darwin's admission that "If numerous species, belonging to the same genera or families, have really started into life all at once, that fact would be fatal to the theory of descent with slow modification through natural selection."[22]

Yet, paleontologists around the world have discovered a sudden explosion of fossil records in Cambrian strata in the sedimentary rock layers without any "transitional intermediate fossils connecting the Cambrian animals to simpler Precambrian forms."[23] Moreover, within the Cambrian layer there is "a startling array of completely novel animal forms with novel body plans; and a pattern in which radical differences in form in the fossil record arise before more minor, small-scale diversification and variations."[24] "This," according to Meyer, "turns on its head the Darwinian expectation of small incremental change only gradually resulting in larger and larger differences in form."[25]

---

[20] Cited in *God's Undertaker*, 113-114.
[21] Cited in Ibid., 114. Words in brackets are Lennox's.
[22] Stephen C. Meyer, *Darwin's Doubt* (New York: HarperOne, 2013), 17.
[23] Ibid., 34.
[24] Ibid.
[25] Ibid.

Such facts as these caused David Berlinski, a senior fellow at the Discovery Institute, to claim:

> The greater part of the debate over Darwin's theory is not in service to the facts. Nor to the theory. The facts are what they have always been: They are unforthcoming. Among evolutionary biologists, these matters are well known. In the privacy of the Susan B. Anthony faculty lounge, they often tell one another with relief that it is a very good thing the public has no idea what the research literature *really* suggests.
>
> "Darwin?" a Nobel laureate in biology once remarked to me over his bifocals. "That's just the party line."[26]

Evolution is Based in a Naturalistic Worldview, Not Science

The theory of evolution is riddled with problems, but according to Lewontin, these problems are easier to embrace than admitting that there is a God:

> We take the side of science *in spite* of the patent absurdity of some of its constructs, *in spite* of its failure to fulfill many of its extravagant promises of health and life, *in spite* of the tolerance of the scientific community for unsubstantiated just-so stories, because we have *a prior* commitment, a commitment to materialism. It is not that the methods and institutions of science somehow compel us to accept a material explanation of the phenomenal world, but, on the contrary, that we are forced by our *à priori* adherence to material causes to create an apparatus of investigation and a set of concepts that produce material explanations, no matter how counter-intuitive, no matter how mystifying to the uninitiated. Moreover, that materialism is an absolute, for we cannot allow a Divine Foot in the door.[27]

---

[26] David Berlinski, *The Devil's Delusion: Atheism and Its Scientific Pretensions* (New York: Basic Books, 2009), 191-192.

[27] Cited in *Refuting Evolution.*, 17-18.

As the quote above suggests, quite a few scientists are convinced of macroevolution not because of the evidence, but because it is a logical conclusion of naturalism. Thus, macroevolution is more of a philosophical conclusion than a scientific finding. Lewontin confessed that he, as with other scientists, had an *a prior commitment to naturalism* – which is a philosophical worldview. Dennett was right when he claimed that "there is no such thing as philosophy-free science; there is only science whose philosophical baggage is taken on board without examination."[28] If we presuppose and remain committed to naturalism, then macroevolution must be embraced regardless of the evidence. As we have seen, scientists, such as Dawkins and Lewontin, continue to embrace naturalism even when they are presented with opposing evidence. Because God is unacceptable, macroevolution, even with all of its inconsistencies, must be maintained.

Naturalism is the framework that these scientists accept by faith and utilize to understand and interpret their observations and experimentations. They are convinced naturalists even before the investigation gets started. For instance, after Dennett recapped the thrust of Darwin's argument in *The Origin of the Species*, without providing any empirical evidence for *macro*evolution, concludes: "Levelheaded readers of the book simply could no longer doubt that species had evolved over the eons, as Darwin said they had."[29]

Though Darwin only observed slight adaptations taking place in preexisting entities within preexisting species, Dennett believes that this was enough evidence to logically deduce that all species (including human consciousness) have evolved from dead matter by natural selection.

[28] Daniel Dennett, *Darwin's Dangerous Idea* (New York: Touchstone, 1991), 21.
[29] Ibid., 46.

Darwin may have produced a large volume full of examples of *micro*evolution, but even if he included a billion more examples of how bird beaks slowly grow longer or shorter under the right circumstances, it would not prove that birds have evolved from flying fish. Evidence for microevolution does not prove macroevolution. Darwin presented no evidence for macro-evolution, but this did not hinder him from concluding that men have evolved from apes.

Dennett not only believes Darwin convincingly proved his case, he went as far as to say: "To put it bluntly but fairly, any one today who doubts that the variety of life on this planet was produced by a process of evolution is simply ignorant – inexcusably ignorant."[30] It is amazing that such bold confidence and fundamentalist like fervor can come without any credible evidence.

Dennett's confidence, however, seems to be more heavily rooted in his naturalism than in evolution. He intentionally or unintentionally revealed his primary commitment when he said: "Even if Darwin's relatively modest idea about the origin of species came to be rejected by science – yes, utterly discredited and replaced by some vastly more powerful vision – it would still have irremediably sapped conviction in any reflective defender of the [old] tradition"[31] that there is a Intelligent Design. In other words, even if Darwin was wrong, Darwin was right in removing God from any possible explanation. And this, my dear friends, is the chief concern and commitment for naturalists.

You see, evolution is not one of many possible naturalistic explanations for the origins of the species; it is the only naturalistic explanation. For this reason, so it seems, naturalists are deeply committed to evolution. As the Nobel Prize-winning physiologist George Wald (1906-1997), professor emeritus of

30 Ibid.
31 Ibid. 83.

biology at the University at Harvard, admitted: "We choose to believe the impossible: that life arose spontaneously by chance."[32] Likewise, after the Scottish anatomist and anthropologist Arthur Keith (1866-1955) said that macroevolution was "unproved and unprovable," he confessed, "We believe it only because the alternative is special creation."[33]

To abandon belief in evolution would require naturalists to abandon their faith-commitment in naturalism. No matter how ridiculous the theory may seem, no matter what evidence is lacking, no matter what kind of internal problems are created, naturalists seem to refuse to give up on evolution because it appears that the only alternative answer to the origin of life is completely unacceptable – "for we cannot allow a Divine Foot in the door." As Wolfgang Smith, a physicist who helped solve the re-entry problem for space flight, explained:

> I am convinced...that Darwinism, in whatever form, is not in fact a scientific theory, but a pseudo-metaphysical hypothesis decked out in scientific garb. In reality the theory derives its support not from empirical data or logical deductions of a scientific kind but from the circumstance that it happens to be the only doctrine of biological origins that can be conceived with the constricted worldview to which a majority of scientists no doubt subscribe.[34]

Wald not only conceded that he chose to believe in the impossible, but he also explained his motive in doing so:

> There are only two possibilities as to how life arose. One is spontaneous generation arising to evolution; the other is a supernatural creative act of God. There is no third possibility. Spontaneous generation, that life arose from non-living matter was scientifically disproved 120 years ago by Louis

[32] Cited in *There Is a God*, 131.

[33] Cited in John Blanchard, *Is Anybody There* (Darlington: Evangelical Press, 2006), 18.

[34] Cited in *Death to Evolution*, 3.

Pasteur and others. That leaves us with the only possible conclusion that life arose as a supernatural creative act of God. I will not accept that philosophically because I do not want to believe in God. Therefore, I choose to believe in that which I know is scientifically impossible; spontaneous generation arising to evolution.[35]

At least Wald was honest in his atheism. Consequently, Thomas Nagel is right when he questions the foundation behind the naturalistic worldview:

> Physico-chemical reductionism in biology [i.e., naturalism] is the orthodox view, and any resistance to it is regarded as not only scientifically but politically incorrect.... But it seems to me that, as it is usually presented, the current orthodoxy about the cosmic order is the product of governing assumptions [presuppositions] that are unsupported, and that it flies in the face of common sense.[36]

Nagel went on to remind us that the naturalism that undergirds the theory of evolution "cannot be regarded as unassailable. It is an assumption governing the scientific project rather than a well-confirmed scientific hypothesis."[37] I believe it is for this reason that Nagel went on to say, "I find the confidence among the scientific establishment that the whole scenario will yield to a purely chemical [physical] explanation hard to understand, except as a manifestation of an axiomatic commitment to reductive materialism."[38]

This axiomatic commitment to the naturalistic worldview, however, takes a blind and irrational leap of faith. Though 'show me the evidence' may be the slogan for naturalists, naturalists

---

[35] George Wald, "Innovation and Biology," *Scientific American*, Vol. 199, Sept. 1958, 100.

[36] Thomas Nagel, *Mind and Cosmos* (New York: Oxford, 2012), 5. The words in the brackets are present author.

[37] Ibid., 11.

[38] Ibid., 49.

prove that they are willing to embrace a worldview that runs contrary to the evidence. For this reason, the Dutch theologian Herman Bavinck (1854-1921) concluded that these "materialist explanations of the universe are not scientific in character but are rather religious worldviews masquerading as science."[39]

Conclusion

Naturalism is a worldview that shapes how its adherents interpret the evidence, but it's an inconsistent worldview. As we have seen, naturalism is not only a worldview that fails to be supported by the evidence, it is a worldview that fails to provide answers for the existence of the immaterial laws of science – the very foundation on which naturalism is ostensibly built. So, ironically, naturalism purports to be based on the laws of science alone, but in reality it is forced to deny the laws of science in its explanation of a self-creating universe. It cannot explain how *nothing* plus *nothing* created the universe that is mathematically structured and miraculously fine-tuned to host life on earth. This inconsistency is not a gap in scientific knowledge. Rather, it's a blatant absurdity.

Moreover, naturalism cannot explain the origins of the semantic and functional language that is written on DNA, or how the complexity of life (even the simplest living cell) emerged from dead matter. This is not to mention the problem of consciousness. In the end, naturalism is a godless attempt at explaining everything, but it cannot even explain itself. Thus, naturalism (with all of its postulations of the origins of mass and energy and life and consciousness) ends in absurdity. To say belief in God takes a leap of faith sounds ridiculous when we compare it with *the absurdity of unbelief*.

[39] Herman Bavinck, *In the Beginning* (Edinburgh: Banner of Truth Trust, 1979), 23.

13

The Irrationality of Empiricism & Determinism

"Every absurdity," says Oliver Goldsmith, "has a champion to defend it." These champions include renowned scientists, philosophers, and theologians. Because experts often disagree with each other, appealing to their expertise is not enough to settle an argument.

The battle between worldviews, therefore, is won not by counting the noses of fallible men. Each worldview must stand up under its own weight. We have already seen how naturalism, though supported by many eminent thinkers, is internally inconsistent with itself. Here, this inconsistency will be shown to be manifested within naturalism's kin as well: empiricism, determinism, relativism, and nihilism.

The Irrationality of Empiricism

Materialism breeds empiricism, for if everything is reducible to mass and energy, then knowledge is *limited* to sense perception. Though most worldviews, including the biblical worldview, accept the basic reliability of sense experience, empiricism states that *all* knowledge is reducible to sense experience. Without empirical evidence, there is no justification for belief in anything.

Empiricism, however, is inconsistent with itself. For instance, those who have dogmatically put their foot down and devotedly claimed that they will not believe anything without empirical evidence have themselves presupposed (without any evidence or proof) empiricism – that knowledge *only* comes through the five senses. As William Clifford (1845-1870) unabashedly declared: "It is wrong always, everywhere, and for anyone, to believe anything upon insufficient evidence."[1] Bertrand Russell fell into this same trap in his reply when asked what he would say to God if he happened to face Him on judgment day: "Not enough evidence, God! Not enough evidence!" Like Clifford, Russell was convinced that there was no justification for any belief without sufficient evidence. "Whatever knowledge is attainable," Russell speciously stated without a shred of scientific evidence, "must be attained by scientific methods; and what science cannot discover, mankind cannot know."[2]

Yet, the deaf person has no right to deny the existence of sound just because he cannot hear. Likewise, because scientific knowledge is limited to the study of the cosmos, it is insufficient to make the claim that only the cosmos exists. That is, science has no grounds to deny the existence of things that transcend and go beyond the reach of science. It would be ridiculous for the deaf person to demand audio evidence before he believed in the existence of sound. It is equally as ridiculous for empiricists to demand empirical evidence before they will believe in an invisible and immaterial God who has communicated to us.

Unless you are willing to believe by faith that all knowledge is limited to scientific knowledge and to embrace the awful consequences, then it is hypocritical to say, 'Science has killed God.' If science has killed God, then science has killed mathematics and the laws of morality along with Him. If

---

[1] W. K. Clifford, "The Ethics of Belief," in *Philosophy of Religion*, ed. Charles Taliaferro and Paul J. Griffiths (Oxford: Blackwell, 2003), 199.

[2] Bertrand Russell, *Religion and Science* (New York: Oxford, 1997), 243.

scientific knowledge is all that there is, then science has killed logic as well. And once logic is dead, frankly, we have no reason to believe in anything. For science to be trustworthy, it requires logic and ethics to remain alive and well. Since it is self-evident that truth is not limited to scientific knowledge, then it is impossible for science to kill God.

Looking for empirical and material evidence for a spiritual and invisible God in a physical and material universe is like looking for the builder of a house in the parts of the house itself. Just because the builder is not made out of wood, brick, or mortar, and he is not found in the staircase, the doorframe, or any other part of the house, does not mean there is no builder.[3] The design and structure of the building clearly cries out that there is indeed a builder. If God is a transcendent spirit, then we should not expect to discover Him through our sensory organs of seeing, tasting, smelling, hearing, and touching.

Of course, an invisible and transcendent God is not an object of scientific experimentation. But that does not rule Him out, as empiricists would have us believe. If we assume that personal experience is the only way to prove anything, then we will not believe houses have builders unless we meet those builders in person. If empiricism is our starting presupposition, then we would also have to suspend belief in logic, in mathematics, and in other minds,[4] for no amount of sense experience can verify these realities.

[3] See *Mere Christianity*, 33.
[4] See Alvin Plantinga, *God and Other Minds* (Ithaca: Cornell University Press, 1990). Yet, prior to Plantinga making this comparison, George Park Fisher linked the grounds for belief in other minds with the grounds for belief in God when he said: "We infer the existence of an intelligent Deity, as we infer the existence of intelligence in our fellow-men, and on grounds not less reasonable…My senses take no cognizance of the minds of other men…What proof is there of the consciousness in the friend at my side? How can I be assured that he is not a mere automation, totally unconscious of its own movements? The warrant for the contrary inference lies in the fact, that being possessed of consciousness, and acquainted with its effects in myself, I regard

Science has its limits. It seeks to discover the reason why things work in the universe but cannot explain the reason why the universe exists in the first place. John Lennox provides us with an insightful illustration of this:

> It is conceivable that someone from a remote part of the world, who was seeing [a Ford motor car] for the first time and who knew nothing about modern engineering, might imagine that there is a god (Mr Ford) inside the engine, making it go. He might further imagine that when the engine ran sweetly it was because Mr Ford inside the engine liked him, and when it refused to go it was because Mr Ford did not like him. Of course, if he were subsequently to study engineering and take the engine to pieces, he would discover that there is no Mr Ford inside it. Neither would it take much intelligence for him to see that he did not need to introduce Mr Ford as an explanation for its working. His grasp of the impersonal principles of internal combustion would be altogether enough to explain how the engine works. So far, so good. But if he then decided that his understanding of the principles of how the engine works made it impossible to believe in the existence of Mr Ford who designed the engine in the first place, this would be patently false – in philosophical terminology he would be committing a category mistake. Had there never been a Mr Ford to design the mechanisms, none would exist for him to understand.[5]

Moreover, and most importantly, what empirical evidence do empiricists, such as Clifford and Russell, have to support their belief in empiricism? Seeing that there is no evidence to substantiate the belief that every belief must be supported by evidence, Clifford and Russell unwittingly hold to a

---

like effects as evidence of the same principle in others. But in this inference I transcend the limits of sense and physical experiment. In truth, by admitting the reality of consciousness in myself, I take a step which no physical observation can justify" (*The Grounds of Theistic and Christian Belief*, 43).

[5] *God's Undertaker*, 45.

contradictory presupposition. "A wise man," said David Hume, "proportions his belief to the evidence." But an even wiser man understands that this is a foolish statement. Because Hume had *no evidence* to support this claim in the first place, his statement is self-refuting.

In the same way materialism cannot give an account for the laws of physics and the laws of morality, empiricism cannot give an account for why the senses are the *only* means of ascertaining knowledge. Thus, empiricism is self-referentially absurd.

The Irrationality of Determinism

If everything can be reduced to the properties of matter, as determinists suggests, then the laws of physics must determine all events, including human actions. This would mean that at the moment when everything, including time and space, was blasted forth from the Big Bang, the chain reaction that determines the course of everything was then determined – from the location and movements of the galaxies to the exact tilt of the axis of the earth. The laws of nature are non-negotiable; they determine the course of everything.

Consequently, if the laws of nature determine everything, such as the orbit of the planets, they also determine the chemical reactions within the brain. If physical matter is all that there is, then our memories, thoughts, and emotions are merely the byproduct of these chemical reactions. As Dawkins freely admitted: "Human thoughts and emotions *emerge* from exceedingly complex interconnections of physical entities within the brain."[6] With less elegance, the French physiologist Pierre Jean Georges Cabanis (1757-1808) stated: "The brain secretes thought as the liver secretes bile."[7]

---

[6] Richard Dawkins, *The God Delusion* (Boston: Mariner Books, 2006), 34.
[7] Cited in James Sire, *The Universe Next Door* (Downers Grove, IL: IVP Academic, 2009), 72.

If this is the case, then we do not have a free will, but all of our thoughts are merely the predetermined results of the laws of physics. The impersonal laws of nature determine and govern all of our lives, thoughts, and emotions. At least, this was the opinion of the English molecular biologist Francis Crick (1916-2004), who co-discovered along with James Watson the double helix structure of the DNA molecule. The notion that causes us to feel like we have free will, according to Crick, is merely an impression of the brain. [8] Crick introduces *The Astonishing Hypothesis: The Scientific Search for the Soul* with these astonishing words: "You, your joys and your sorrows, your memories and ambitions, your sense of personal identity and free will, are in fact *no more than* the behaviour of a vast assembly of nerve cells and their associated molecules."[9]

Crick was an impressive scientist, but a poor philosopher. Crick was right when he linked our mental activity with the nerve cells and molecules in our brain, but once he added the philosophical words "*no more than*" to his explanation of human joy, sorrow, memories, ambitions, personal identity, and free will, he stepped out of the realm of science and entered into the arena of philosophy and theology. Yet, it seems (either by the laws of chemistry or by his own volition) that Crick had his mind made up even before he got started; he admits that one of his principle assumptions about consciousness is that it "is something that requires a scientific explanation." [10] But, is he right in making such an assumption? Was Carl Sagan right when he said, "The Cosmos is all that is or was or ever will be"?

It is beyond the scope and capacity of science to explain metaphysical realities. No amount of scientific evidence can prove that there is *nothing more* to human experiences than

---

[8] Francis Crick, *The Astonishing Hypothesis: The Scientific Search for the Soul* (New York: Touchstone, 1994), 266. Words in italics are present author.

[9] Ibid., 3.

[10] Ibid. 19.

chemical reactions. How is it possible for science to prove that there is *nothing more* to the soul than physical properties interacting with one another? Some realities go beyond the realm of science. For instance, scientists must utilize *ethics, logic,* and their *free will* in their scientific experimentations, but they cannot place these metaphysical realities (*ethics, logic,* and *free will*) in any laboratory test-tube. In fact, in order for scientists, such as Dawkins, Crick, and Saga to deny the existence of metaphysical realities (such as *logic, ethics,* and *free will*), they must temporarily leave the scientific field and enter into the metaphysical arena. But this is self-refuting. It is not wrong for scientists to be philosophers and visa versa, but once scientists push philosophical and metaphysical realities out the door, they do not have the right to turn around and make philosophical and metaphysical statements. If science alone can explain everything, as they say it can, then it should not have to continually rely on philosophical and metaphysical categories in the process.[11]

Determinism, however, is not something proven by science, but is rather a philosophical worldview deduced when naturalism is presupposed. Yet, like naturalism, determinism is a worldview that collapses under its own weight. If mind evolved from matter by the laws of physics, then not only does this undermine any absolute and universal standard for right and wrong, it also undermines mathematics, for mathematics, as with ethics, are

---

[11] Speaking about metaphysical questions, Stephen Hawking claimed: "Traditionally these are questions for philosophy, but philosophy is dead. It has not kept up with modern developments in science, particularly in physics. As a result scientists have become the bearers of the torch of discovery in our quest for knowledge." Commenting on this statement, Lennox remarked: "The very first thing I notice is that Hawking's statement about philosophy is itself a philosophical statement. It is manifestly not a statement of science: it is a metaphysical statement about science. Therefore, his statement that philosophy is dead contradicts itself. It is a classic example of logical incoherence" (*God and Stephen Hawking*. Oxford: Lion, 2011., 18). Lennox went on to say, "For any scientist, let alone a science superstar, to disparage philosophy on the one hand, and then at once to adopt a self-contradictory philosophical stance on the other, is not the wisest thing to do" (Ibid., 19).

rooted in universal absolutes that exist independent of the brain. But once the objective and universal nature of mathematics is undermined, then the laws of physics, which are rooted in mathematics, are undermined as well. Supposedly, the immaterial laws of physics are the legs upon which evolutionary biology stands. To put it more concisely, determinism is rooted in naturalism, which is rooted in the laws of physics, which is rooted in mathematics, which is rooted in logic, which is rooted in absolutes, which is rooted in the immaterial, which undermines naturalism and determinism.

This leads to another inconsistency. If determinism is right, we are not free to accept or reject the argument for determinism. Why try to convince people of the validity of determinism if our beliefs are determined not by rational arguments but by heredity, environment, and what we happened to have eaten for breakfast. If the laws of nature determine our beliefs for us, then we have no basis for holding any of our beliefs as true or false — and this includes the belief in determinism. C. S. Lewis saw the irrationality of such an argument:

> If the solar system was brought about by an accidental collision, then the appearance of organic life on this planet was also an accident, and the whole evolution of Man was an accident too. If so, then all our thought processes are mere accidents — the accidental by-product of the movement of atoms. And this holds for the materialists' and astronomers' as well as for anyone else's. But if their thoughts — i.e., of Materialism and Astronomy — are merely accidental by-products, why should we believe them to be true? I see no reason for believing that one accident should be able to give a correct account of all the other accidents.[12]

Determinists ask us to do something that we do not have the freedom to accept any more than they have the freedom to

---

[12] C. S. Lewis, *God in the Dock* (Grand Rapids: Eerdmans, 1970), 52-53.

reject. According to British philosopher J. R. Lucas, "Determinism, therefore, cannot be true, because if it was, we should not take the determinists' arguments as being really arguments, but as being only conditioned reflexes."[13]

Moreover, Lewis saw another contradiction with determinism, which he described in his book *Miracles: A Preliminary Study*. If our thoughts are controlled by the fixed laws of nature, then "there is no guarantee or even reason to believe that any given thought will truly correspond to a reality outside of the thinker."[14] We cannot be certain that we know anything as it truly is, including the laws of physics that supposedly control our thinking. Thus, for determinists to argue for determinism is self-stultifying.

If we are what we are, we will do what we will do, and we will become what we will become by the fixed laws of the universe. So, when a determinist complains about anything, such as the weather or a moral injustice, he is protesting against the worldview that he is so eager to embrace and to defend. But, then again, I guess it's the laws of physics that force him to complain.

Conclusion

In short, science explains a lot of things, but it cannot explain everything. When science tries to explain everything, it destroys itself by undermining the objective and universal nature of the laws of physics, in which science is fundamentally rooted.

---

[13] Cited in Ronald Nash, *Faith and Reason*, 53.
[14] Thomas Morris, *Francis Schaeffer's Apologetics* (Grand Rapids: Baker Books, 1987), 42.

The Irrationality of Relativism & Nihilism

Relativism is the consequence of naturalism. If naturalism is right in saying that there is no God, then there must be no Lawgiver, and without a divine Lawgiver, we are left to ourselves. But this is not the only problem for the naturalistic approach. If nature is all there is, our thoughts and our ethical judgments are merely the byproduct of the laws of nature – evolutionary ethics.

The Irrationality of Relativism

Bertrand Russell (1872-1970) understood the logical conse- quence of naturalism – man is a mere machine. Man is simply an evolved, mechanical animal that is controlled by the fixed laws of physics. Russell attempted to explain:

> Materialists used the laws of physics to show, or attempt to show, that the movements of human bodies are mechanically determined, and that consequently everything that we say and every change of position that we effect fall outside the sphere of any possible free will. If this be so, whatever may be left for our unfettered volitions is of little value. If, when a man writes a poem or commits a murder, the bodily movements involved in his act result solely from physical

causes, it would seem absurd to put a statue to him in the one case and to hang him in the other case.[1]

According to Russell, these misbehaved machines do not need to be shamed or punished; they need to be fixed and treated medically:

> No man treats a motorcar as foolishly as he treats another human being. When the car will not go, he does not attribute its annoying behavior to sin; he does not say, "You are a wicked motorcar, and I shall not give you any more petrol until you go." He attempts to find out what is wrong and to set it right. An analogous way of treating human beings is, however, considered to be contrary to the truths of our holy religion.[2]

This of course removes all culpability and responsibility from criminal acts. As Russell went on to explain:

> It is evident that a man with a propensity to crime must be stopped, but so must a man who has hydrophobia and wants to bite people, although nobody considers him morally responsible. A man who is suffering from a plague has to be imprisoned until he is cured, although nobody thinks him wicked. The same thing should be done with a man who suffers from a propensity to commit forgery; but there should be no more idea of guilt in the one case than in the other.[3]

In other words, criminals, such as Adolf Hitler, should not be held accountable, judged, punished, or blamed for their selfish and immoral behavior because they are simply victims of natural consequences outside of their control. They should be pitied not punished.

Yet, the laws of physics could care less about moral distinctions. Evolution does not care if it produces a loving

[1] *Why I Am Not a Christian*, 37-38.
[2] Ibid., 40.
[3] Ibid., 41.

mother or a cruel Hitler. The laws of physics have no opinion about life or death, pleasure or pain, health or sickness, and good or evil. Thus, naturalism not only destroys human freedom and moral responsibility, it also eliminates ethical distinctions and morality altogether. This is what we get when we reduce everything down to science.

To save the world from complete anarchy, Russell claimed that pragmatism should govern our behavior. Morality is not a transcendental moral code given to us from above, but is a matter of convenience and practical usefulness. Of course, this is wildly inconsistent with naturalism's denial of free will, but it appears that some could care less about being rational as long as they are free to do what they want with their lives.

The British philosopher Jeremy Bentham (1748-1832) and his disciple John Stuart Mill (1806-1873) also sought to rescue mankind from complete immorality by proposing *utilitarianism*. While trying to promote "moral goodness," utilitarianism aims to bring the most happiness to the most amount of people. As Mill stated in his famous little book on the subject:

> The creed which accepts as the foundation of morals "utility" or the "greatest happiness principle" holds that actions are right in proportion as they tend to promote happiness; wrong as they tend to produce the reverse of happiness. By happiness is intended pleasure and the absence of pain.[4]

Likewise, the American philosopher and psychologist William James (1842-1910), based ethics on expediency. He writes, in his work *Pragmatism*, "The true, to put it very briefly, is only the expedient in the way of our thinking, just as the right is only the expedient in the way of our behaving."[5] Following this path of

---

[4] John Stuart Mill, *Utilitarianism* (Indianapolis: Hackett Publishing Company, 1979), 7.

[5] William James, "Pragmatism" in *Pragmatism in Other Writings* (New York: Penguin Books, 2000), 97-98.

reasoning, Joseph Fletcher (1905-1991), an Episcopal priest turned atheist, became famous for his book *Situation Ethics*. Applying the pragmatism of James to challenging situations, Fletcher became one of the leading advocates for abortion, eugenics, and euthanasia. According to the publisher's description of *Situation Ethics*, "...lying, premarital sex, abortion, adultery, and murder – could be right, depending on the circumstances."[6]

In *Animal Liberation*, Peter Singer, professor of bioethics at Princeton University, applied *evolutionary ethics* to animals. Where as Fletcher uses evolutionary ethics to advocate the murder of the unborn, the handicap, and the elderly, Singer uses evolutionary ethics to advocate the protection of even the simplest of animals.

If man is evolved from animals, what makes man special? According to Peter, man is slightly more evolved than an ape, while an ape is much more advanced than an oyster. Apes and oysters are grouped together as animals while humans stand in a class of their own. But why? Singer argued that any such boundary separating man from animal is entirely arbitrary. If we claim that man's intelligence separates him from beast, then what about people with Down Syndrome? He calls those who give preferential treatment to humans as "speciesists." According to Singer, we should not do anything to animals that we would not do to other humans: "Just as most human beings are speciesists in their readiness to cause pain to animals when they would not cause a similar pain to humans for the same reason, so most human beings are speciesists in their readiness to kill other animals when they would not kill human beings."[7] From this line of argument, Singer went on to condemn chicken farms and the mass slaughtering of animals and then ended by presenting a case for the ethical value of vegetarianism.

---

[6] See the back cover of James Fletcher, *Situation Ethics* (Philadelphia: Westminster Press, 1966).

[7] Peter Singer, *Animal Liberation* (New York: HarperCollins, 2002), 17.

Moral relativists, such as Fletcher and Singer, often place a greater value on eagle eggs than on unborn babies. Placing the rights of animals on par with human rights sounds absurd, but if man is merely an evolved animal rather than a being created in the likeness of God, then who is to say that animals should not be eaten? But then again, if there is no God, who is to say that we shouldn't eat them? If there is no God, who is to say Jeffrey Dahmer, the Milwaukee cannibal, was in the wrong for his crimes against humanity?

If there is no God, then who gets to make the rules? Does the person carrying the biggest stick in the playground get to tell the children how to behave, even a person such as Hitler? Is it okay for parents to abuse their children? Does *might* make *right*? As Wolf Larsen told Hump in the novel *Sea-Wolf*: "Might is right, and that is all there is to it. Weakness is wrong. Which is a very poor way of saying that it is good for oneself to be strong, and evil for oneself to be weak."[8] If Hitler is breathing down my neck, do I have the right to kill innocent Jews? Am I obligated to disobey my superior if he asks me to steal, exploit people, or commit fraud? If there is no transcendent code of morality, who is to say?

Does the majority rule? If so, who determines the boundaries or scope of who is included in the census? Is it right for the majority of High School students to pick on the weirdo at school? Is the majority always in the right? Or, should government be given to a few elite people (oligarchy)? If there is no absolute standard that governs all people alike, who is to say?

If there is no transcendent Lawgiver who stands above humanity, then humanity is left to itself to argue and fight over who is in charge. In the end, everything is relative, and relativism, no matter what form it takes (i.e., utilitarianism,

---

[8] Jack London, *The Sea-Wolf* (New York: Tom Doherty Associates Books, 1993), 65.

pragmatism, and situational ethics), is self-referentially absurd. To say that "there are no absolutes" is to make an absolute statement. Moral relativism has no foundation in a purely naturalistic worldview. Why should we listen to Russell, Mill, James, Fletcher, or Singer? Who put them in charge? Why do they get to write the rules for the rest of us?

If there is no God, why not live lives of rank selfishness? Why not do what we want no matter who gets hurt?

This sounds like freedom. But is it?

If we are going to accept the freedom that supposedly comes with relativism and deny the existence of absolute truth, then we had better understand the consequences. Relativism not only destroys the truths we find inconvenient (such as the existence of God), it destroys all truth. Truth, by its very nature, demands concreteness. Ultimately, something either exists or it does not exist. Something is either true or false. If something is objectively true, our opinions, feelings, and wishes have nothing to do with it. If truth cannot be firmly established, however, then we have no right to say that truth exists at all.

Relativism is not the archer placing his target on a slippery slope, for this implies that the target, though moving, is still there to aim at. Relativism is removing the target altogether. The target has slipped off the cliff and is nowhere to be found.

Relativism cannot be satisfied, as a system of thought, until full-blown nihilism has its tentacles wrapped around every grain of truth. If it encourages us at all, relativism encourages us to aim at nothing. We get to choose what is true for ourselves. The target merely exists subjectively in our mind. Seeing that there is nothing objective and external to aim at, just pull back the bowstring and release the arrow in any random direction you may happen to like.

This supposedly gives us freedom to choose to live however we please. The handcuffs of restraints and the laws that shackle us are forever removed. We are free to smash store windows, loot, set cars on fire, and run chaotically through the streets as we see fit.

We are free, but so is everyone else. With all these aimless arrows flying around, however, someone is bound to get hurt. Let us not be surprised or upset if we find a few of these arrows flying towards us.

The Irrationality of Nihilism

Meaninglessness is the high cost of seeking to live in opposition to the truth. Dawkins understands that naturalism does not provide us with an optimistic worldview: "This is not a recipe for happiness. So long as DNA is passed on, it does not matter who or what gets hurt in the process."[9] He went on to say: "Nature is neither kind nor unkind. She is neither against suffering nor for it. Nature is not interested one way or another in suffering, unless it affects the survival of DNA."[10] Such a cold and depressing understanding of the world led Dawkins to conclude that life itself is meaningless: "This is one of the hardest lessons for humans to learn. We cannot admit that things might be neither good nor evil, neither cruel nor kind, but simply callous – indifferent to all suffering, lacking all purpose." [11] Cornell University historian, William Provine agreed with Dawkins on the absurdity of life:

> The implications of modern science, however, are clearly inconsistent with most religious traditions. No purposive principles exist in nature. Organic evolution has occurred by various combinations of random genetic drift, natural

[9] Richard Dawkins, *River Out of Eden* (New York: Basic Books, 1995), 131.
[10] Ibid.
[11] Ibid.

selection, Mendelian heredity, and many other purposeless mechanisms. Humans are complex organic machines that die completely with no survival of soul or psyche. Humans and other animals make choices frequently, but these are determined by the interaction of heredity and environment and are not the result of free will. No inherent moral or ethical laws exist, nor are there absolute guiding principles for human society. The universe cares nothing for us and we have no ultimate meaning in life.[12]

Jim Black concluded: "Darwinism is an anti-God philosophy offering no hope, no comfort, no happiness, and no ultimate meaning. It offers nothing but a cold, mechanistic existence in which man's only purpose is to live as long as he can before he vanishes into everlasting oblivion."[13]

Such conclusions led behaviorist C. F. Skinner to write *Beyond Freedom and Dignity* where he essentially compared man to a brute beast and brute beast to a machine.[14] Though Skinner agreed that human behavior was less than desirable, he thought that the key for mankind to reach their full potential would not come by embracing the delusional ideas that they are dignified and personally free, but by seeking to reshape the physical and social environments in which they live. Regardless, man is neither free nor dignified. The problem is not in man, but in the laws of physics, and this is where *evolutionary ethics* brings us.

This is *nihilism* – there is no meaning, no purpose, and no ultimate truth. Jean Baudrillard (1929-2007), Jacques Derrida (1930-2004), and Jean-François Lyotard (1924-1998) were all renowned French nihilists who oddly enough constructed their respective nihilistic worldviews in their attempt to deconstruct all

---

12 Ibid., 128

13 Jim Nelson Black, *The Death of Evolution* (Grand Rapids: Zondervan, 2010), 12.

14 C. F. Skinner, *Beyond Freedom and Dignity* (Indianapolis: Hackett Publishing Company, 1971).

other worldviews.[15] Yet, it does not take a genius to see the inconsistency in such a position. As James Sire remarked: "Nihilism...does not stop intellectuals from writing, only from making sense."[16] If there is no meaning, then nothing can be trusted. If nothing can be trusted, then the presuppositions behind *nihilism* cannot be trusted either. Like all forms of relativism, nihilism is inconsistent with itself.

Furthermore, no nihilist really *lives* according to his or her worldview. Schaeffer was right when he said, "no one can hold consistently that everything is chaotic and irrational and that there are no basic answers. It can be held theoretically, but it cannot be held in practice that everything is absolute chaos."[17] Some may claim there are no absolutes and that *meaning* is only a fancy word that has no meaning itself, but once the professor leaves the lecture hall and places his key into the ignition of his Toyota Prius, he conveniently forgets everything he just taught as he happily submits himself to the absolute laws that surround him. The modern artist may paint pictures as if there is no up and down or right and wrong, but she, too, hopes that when she walks out of the studio that the law of gravity holds true and that she doesn't go flying into outer space.

The behaviorist may claim that genetics and the environment are the root cause behind adultery, but that does not prevent him from getting mad when his spouse of twenty years is caught in an affair with his best friend. For some reason, he forgets to take out his anger on the laws of nature but instead places the blame on his wife and friend. "No one," according to William Lane Craig, professor of philosophy at Talbot School of Theology, "employs postmodern hermeneutics in reading the instructions on a

---

[15] John Frame reminds us that Lyotard's deconstructionism "had not done away with metanarratives, but has only substituted one for another" (*A History of Philosophy and Religion*, 2).

[16] *Naming the Elephant*, 40.

[17] *Trilogy*, 280.

medicine bottle."[18] Nihilists may mean well, but they cannot consistently live without meaning.

It is true that when Christians behave in a way that is inconsistent with their worldview, they often suffer the consequences. Though Christians are not exempt from the consequences of their hypocrisy, nihilists are *required* to be hypocritical if they want to function at all. If nihilists seek to live according to their worldview by refusing to submit to absolutes, then they will knowingly jeopardize their health in the process. In other words, Christians are frustrated when they fail to practice what they believe, while nihilists are frustrated when they practice what they believe. Because of this, nihilism can not be a worldview that is intellectually worth accepting.

Conclusion

The circular problem with the naturalistic worldview is that naturalism leads round to determinism and empiricism, and empiricism says truth is only obtained inductively by sense perception, and this leads around to determinism, which concludes by coming back around to relativism and nihilism, which says nothing makes sense. Naturalists start the conversation by saying that the laws of nature control everything, but conclude by denying that there are such things as universal laws of nature. Ultimately, the collective system of the naturalistic worldview, with all of its logical consequences, ends in meaninglessness. It is not that science is defective, but that, if there is no God, science only leads to despair and irrational absurdity. It is clear that the naturalistic worldview cannot support its own basic presuppositions; hence it deconstructs under the pressure of its own weight. Without presupposing God, madness is all that remains.

---

[18] William Lane Craig, *Reasonable Faith* (Wheaton, IL: Crossway, 2008), 229.

15

The Irrationality of Existentialism

The folly of existentialists is that they embrace relativism but continue to search for individual purpose and meaning. Who are the existentialists? They are those who build on the foundation of naturalism — man's self-sufficiency — but paradoxically refuse to accept the dreadful implications of naturalism — life is meaningless. Though they have rejected all set reference points, existentialists continue to write down their beliefs as if their particular philosophies could be trusted.

The Absurdity of Jaspers & Sartre

The German existentialist Karl Jaspers (1883-1969), for instance, was unwilling to lay down his pen and accept the fatalism that flows out of naturalism. If naturalism is right, man is not free. Man is merely a hydrated dust-ball. Man's thoughts and emotions are merely a cluster of chemical impulses that are controlled by the laws of physics. For this reason, according to Jaspers, modern science and empiricism cannot provide psychologically satisfactory answers to our most basic questions — such as the meaning of life. Scientific knowledge can only take us so far and leaves us to make a choice. We will either sink into despair or take a transcendental leap of faith, which Jaspers called *transcendence*. *Transcendence* refers to Jasper's method of intense self-contemplation. It was an internal search for existential, self-prescribed meaning. In his own words: "Only transcendence can make this questionable life good, the world beautiful, and existence itself a fulfillment."[1] Only afterwards are we comforted with our own limitless freedom and the experience of 'authentic existence.' This process, Jaspers said, is the purpose of philosophy:

> But philosophical thought begins at the limits of this rational knowledge. Rationality cannot help us in the essentials: it cannot help us to posit aims and ultimate ends, to know the highest good, to know God and human freedom; this inadequacy of the rational gives rise to a kind of thinking which, while working with the tools of understanding, is more than understanding. Philosophy presses to the limits of rational knowledge and there takes fire.[2]

John-Paul Sartre (1905-1980) believed that ultimate personal freedom only exists when there is no God. Man can only be unshackled and free when he is able to create his own meaning. Naturalism and empiricism have ruled out God as a possible answer to the ultimate question – why are we here in the first place? But this should not depress us, for it opens up the possibility for us to choose our own way. Sartre explained:

> Atheistic existentialism, which I represent, is more coherent. It states that if God does not exist, there is at least one being in whom existence precedes essence (meaning), a being who exists before he can be defined by any concept, and that this being is man, or, as Heidegger says, human reality. What is meant here by saying that existence precedes essence? It means that, first of all, man exists, turns up, appears on the scene, and, only afterwards, defines himself. If man, as the existentialist conceives him, is indefinable, it is because at first

---

[1] Karl Jaspers, *Way to Wisdom*, trans. Ralph Manheim (New Heaven: Yale University Press, 1954), 126.
[2] Ibid.

he is nothing. Only afterward will he be something, and he himself will have made what he will be. Thus, there is no human nature, since there is no God to conceive it. Not only is man what he conceives himself to be, he is only what he wills himself to be after this thrust toward existence.[3]

At the heart of existentialism is a bold attack against the rule of God. We will make our own way in this world. We are free to do what feels right in our own eyes. It does not matter that freedom from God leads to our own incarceration, for at least we are free to act like madmen within our cells.

To understand the absurdity of existentialism, think about the design of a carpenter's hammer. Whoever designed the hammer had a particular purpose in mind – pounding nails into things. For the hammer, its design and intended purpose preceded its existence. Yet, for the existentialist, the hammer, by chance, just so happens to exist for no particular reason or purpose at all. It just happened to evolve from nothing. There is no God, thus no designer. The hammer just so happens to exist, and we just so happen to find it lying on the ground. What is it? It does not matter, we get to decide its meaning for ourselves. For us free thinkers, 'existence precedes meaning.' We are free to use the hammer however we please. How about we use the hammer as a bowl? For since we have sold our inheritance for some of Esau's delicious soup, we need a container in which to store it. Who cares if the hammer is inadequate and our soup spills on the ground in the process, at least we will not have God telling us what to do.

Moreover, nature itself sufficiently teaches us that design precedes purpose and not vice versa. The sun, the moon, trees, rivers, snakes, snails, lungs, bones, teeth, and everything else in nature have a pre-established purpose. These artifacts of nature

---

[3] Jean-Paul Sartre, *Existentialism and Human Emotions* (New York: Citadel Press, 1987), 15. Parenthesis is mine.

are good at what they do because they were made to do what they do. We may arbitrarily say that teeth are not for chewing and lungs are not for breathing, but we will look silly in the process. We may say that men and women are not created for each other, but the very design of the human anatomy tells us that same sex couples do not properly fit together and are unable to procreate. Existentialism is irrational, but man has proven that he would rather do as he wishes than maintain his sanity.

The Absurdity of Friedrich Nietzsche

No one, however, was as radical and, dare I say, bold as the German existentialist Friedrich Nietzsche (1844-1900). Nietzsche was courageous enough to take the ethics of naturalism to their logical and haunting conclusions – turning good and evil upside down. In one of his more popular passages, he vividly and unashamedly proclaimed the death of God:

> Have you not heard of that madman who lit a lantern in the bright morning hours, ran to the market place, and cried incessantly: "I seek God! I seek God!" – As many of those who did not believe in God were standing around just then, he provoked much laughter. Has he got lost? asked one. Did he lose his way like a child? asked another. Or is he hiding? Is he afraid of us? Has he gone on a voyage? emigrated? – Thus they yelled and laughed.

> The madman jumped into their midst and pierced them with his eyes. "Whither is God?" he cried; "I will tell you. *We have killed him* – you and I. All of us are his murderers. But how did we do this? Whither are we moving? Away from all suns? Are we not plunging continually? Backward, sideward, forward, in all directions? Is there still any up or down? Are we not straying as through an infinite nothing? Do we not feel the breath of empty space? Has it not become colder? Is not night continually closing in on us? Do we not need to light lanterns in the morning? Do we hear nothing as yet of the noise of the

gravediggers who are burying God? Do we smell nothing as yet of the divine decomposition? Gods, too, decompose. God is dead. God remains dead. And we have killed him.

"How shall we comfort ourselves, the murderers of all murderers? What was holiest and mightiest of all that the world has yet owned has bled to death under our knives: who will wipe this blood off us? What water is there for us to clean ourselves? What festivals of atonement, what sacred games shall we have to invent? Is not the greatness of this deed too great for us? Must we ourselves not become gods simply to appear worthy of it?"[4]

"*God is dead*," claimed Nietzsche. According to Nietzsche, modern man has finally removed the need for any supernatural explanation for the universe. The superstitious idea of God, which primitive man needed to explain such things as lunar eclipses and natural disasters, can no longer be sustained by modern and liberated thinkers.

Nietzsche understood the high cost of eliminating God from our lives – our morals would have to come from some other source. Since God is dead, we must look to nature for the answers. "Once the sin against God was the greatest sin," Nietzsche claimed, "but God died, and these sinners died with him. To sin against the earth is now the most dreadful thing, and to esteem the entrails of the unknowable higher than the meaning of the earth."[5] What do we learn when we look at nature? We learn the importance of reproduction, natural selection, and the *survival of the fittest*.

Nature is often cruel, but the process of evolving is the ultimate goal. Herein, Nietzsche claimed, lay the meaning for man's existence and his ethical code for living. He argued that

---

[4] Friedrich Nietzsche, *The Gay Science*, trans. Walter Kaufmann (New York: Vintage Books, 1974), 181.

[5] Friedrich Nietzsche, *Thus Spoke Zarathustra*, trans. Walter Kaufmann (New York: Penguin Books, 1966), 13.

civilization has evolved from the animal world by the assertions of the strong over the weak. Civilization will only continue to make progress when the noble, wise, strong, and mighty decide to conquer and overpower the weak and the feeble. Thus, selfish and ambitious desires are not to be considered as evil but good. Concerning Nietzsche's philosophy, historian Will Durant (1885-1981) remarked:

> If life is a struggle for existence in which the fittest survive, then strength is the ultimate virtue, and weakness the only fault. *Good* is that which survives, which wins; *bad* is that which gives way and fails...The ultimate ethic is biological; we must judge things according to their value for life.[6]

To live well, according to Nietzsche, is to allow all your intellectual powers and ambitious passions to run free from, and unshackled by, any superstitious religious restraints. Remarking on this ethical framework, Durant stated: "The best thing in man is strength of will, power and permanence of passion; without passion one is mere milk, incapable of deeds. Greed, envy, even hatred, are indispensable items in the process of struggle, selection and survival." [7] Nietzsche declared, "I have often dreamed it must be still more blessed to steal than to receive."[8] In his book *Beyond Good and Evil*, Nietzsche was audacious enough to say:

> To abstain from mutual injury, violence, exploitation, to equate one's will with someone else's...reveals itself as will towards the denial of life, the principle of dissolution and decay...life itself essentially consists of dispossessing, injuring, overpowering the foreign and the more feeble, suppression, severity, imposing one's own forms, annexing and – at least at mildest – exploiting.

6 Will Durant, *The Story of Philosophy* (New York: Simon & Schuster, 1961), 301, 318.

7 Ibid, 317.

8 Ronald Hayman, *Nietzsche* (New York: Penguin Books, 1980), 266.

Even Charles Darwin realized the counterproductivity of hospitals and medical care:

> We civilised men do our utmost to check the process of elimination; we build asylums for the imbecile, the maimed, and sick....Thus the weak members of civilised societies propagate their kind. No one who has attended to the breeding of domestic animals will doubt that this must be highly injurious to the race of man. It is surprising how soon a want of care, or care wrongly directed, leads to the degeneration of a domestic race; but excepting in the case of man itself, hardly any one is so ignorant as to allow his worst animals to breed.[9]

Austrian neurologist Sigmund Freud (1856-1939), who prized Nietzsche as having "more penetrating knowledge of himself than any man who ever lived or was likely to live," bemoaned the reduction of the infant mortality rate brought about by technical progress of medicine because it "works against the beneficial effects of natural selection."[10]

For this reason, Christianity promoted "what Nietzsche called a 'slave morality' that legislates dulling norms of rectitude, thereby fostering herd like quiescence and stigmatizing the

---

[9] Cited in Jim Nelson Black, *The Death of Evolution* (Grand Rapids: Zondervan, 2010), 129-130.

Building off Darwinism, Ernst Haeckel (1834-1919), a German biologist, naturalist, and philosopher, assisted in laying the foundation in 1899 for *evolutionary racism* and *social Darwinism* in his book *The Riddle of the Universe*. Haeckel sought to provide a naturalistic worldview that explained all the mysteries of the universe, such as consciousness, by scientifically reducing everything to matter and energy. Among other things, Haeckel believed that the different races have evolved independently from one another, which propelled the idea that some races were more advanced than others. *The Riddle of the Universe* sold half a million copies alone in Germany, making Haeckel one of the most influential thinkers of his time, which created the intellectual climate for Nazi Germany to thrive a few decades later.

[10] Sigmund Freud, *Civilization and Its Discontents* (New York: W. W. Norton & Company, 1961), 40.

'highest human types.'"[11] Rather than Christian virtues, such as pity, compassion, and kindness being helpful, they are detrimental to the all-important evolutionary process. Christians believe in the dignity of man because man is made in the image of God. Man is not an animal, thus human life is sacred and in need of protection. This includes infants in the mother's womb and the elderly who need constant care. In Christianity, the strong should protect the weak. But, according to Nietzsche, these Christian virtues topple the mighty and rebel against nature's law.[12]

In this evolutionary program, social progress requires the strong to willfully, actively, and forcefully choose to obtain more power, and the only way to do so is to remove the weak and mentally impotent. In the same way a farmer seeks to weed out his feeble cattle by breeding the stronger cattle, society ought to weed out those individuals who are deformed and incompetent.[13] Nietzsche claimed that marriage was made for this purpose,

[11] Helen Zimmern, from the introduction to Friedrich Nietzsche, *Beyond Good and Evil* (Mineola: Dover Publications, 1997), vii.

[12] In the same way Nietzsche hated Christ he hated the New Testament: "One had better put on gloves before reading the New Testament. The presence of so much filth makes it very advisable...I have searched the New Testament in vain for a single sympathetic touch; nothing is there that is free, kindly, open-hearted or upright. In it humanity does not even make the first step upward - the instinct for cleanliness is lacking...Only evil instincts are there, and there is not even the courage of these evil instincts. It is all cowardice; it is all shutting of the eyes, a self-deception. Every other book becomes clean, once one has read the New Testament" (*The Anti-Christ*, sect. 46).

[13] Being influenced by his half-cousin Charles Darwin, Francis Galton (1822-1911) advocated for *eugenics* (a term he coined) in *Hereditary Genius* (1869). Eugenics is concerned with advancing the human race, through what Galton called, "judicious mating" and compulsory sterilization. He defined eugenics as "the science which deals with all influences that improve the inborn qualities of a race; also with those that develop them to the utmost advantage" ("Eugenics: Its Definition, Scope, and Aims," *The American Journal of Sociology*. Vol. 10; July, 1904; Number 1). Otmar Freiherr von Verschuer (1896-1969), Karin Magnussen (1908-1997), Josef Mengele (1911-1979), and Nazi Germany took social Darwinism and the eugenics of Galton to its radical conclusion by experimenting on and executing those whom they deemed to be inferior.

"Thou shalt not only propagate thyself, but propagate thyself upward!"[14] He also felt war was a useful means to this end. This might sound contradictory to the enhancement of society, yet Nietzsche claimed that war should be encouraged. "You say that a good cause justifies war? . . . I say unto you: it is a good war that justifies any cause."[15] Superiority is established the same way apes show their dominance by fighting their opponents. War is natural. War is good. In the twisted words of this twisted man:

> What is good? All that enhances the feeling of power, the will to power, and power itself in man. What is bad? – All that proceeds from weakness. What is happiness? – The feeling that power is *increasing*, that resistance has been overcome. Not, contentment, but more power: not peace, but war, not virtue, but efficiency. The weak and the botched shall perish; first principle of our humanity. And they ought even to be helped to perish.[16]

Of course, this line of thinking was agreeable to Adolf Hitler who said: "Those who want to live, let them fight, and those who do not want to fight in this world of eternal struggle do not deserve to live."[17]

We must fight. If society is ever going to obtain more "power," it must first "will" it. We must choose power over submission and pity. Nietzsche believed the desire for power was imbedded within all men by nature. Evolution has instilled this appetite in us all. All men are self-seeking; to deny this, is to deny reality. On the other hand, to restrain this natural craving is detrimental to the self and to the collective. Nietzsche asserted,

---

[14] Ibid., 319.

[15] *Nietzsche.*, 259.

[16] This is odd, seeing that Nietzsche was very sickly most of his life. He was a feeble man who had to be cared for by friends and family. In the last ten years of his life he became mentally insane and needed constant care from his Christian mother.

[17] Cited in William L. Shirer, *The Rise and Fall of the Third Reich* (New York: Simon and Schuster, 1960), 86.

"What is most unforgivable in you is having the power to rule and not wishing to." To "will to power" is only natural.[18]

By choosing (will to) power, individuals not only improve themselves, but they assist in the creation of a new superior race of beings – a race of "*Supermen*" (one reason why he is known as Hitler's philosopher).[19] This superior race would improve society (the arts, sciences, literature, etc.). Yes, this would eliminate the physically weak and mentally feeble, but these people do not contribute to society anyway. They slow down the natural evolutionary process.

Nietzsche coined the term *superman* (*Übermensch, or overman*) to explain the next phase of man's evolution. Man has evolved from apes and that which will evolve from man is yet to appear. "What is ape to man?" Nietzsche asked, "A laughing stock or a painful embarrassment. And man shall be just that for the overman (superman): a laughingstock or a painful embarrassment. You have made your way from worm to man, and much in you is still worm. Once you were apes, and even now, too, man is more ape than ape."[20] Nietzsche went on to say, "Man is a rope, tied between beast and overman . . . What is great in man is that he is a bridge and not the end."[21] The end of man is 'Superman;' a new race of beings superior in every way to what humans are today. Whatever means is necessary to reach this end must be carried out.

Yet, there is one glaring inconsistency with the existentialism of Nietzsche – the superhuman race will not occur without a cognitive and willful intent (the will to power) within men, but supposedly past evolution took place without any cognitive planning within the species. It takes intelligent breeders to match

[18] *Nietzsche*, 266.
[19] See John Blanchard, *Does God Believe in Atheists* (Darlington, UK: Evangelical Press, 2000), 75.
[20] *Thus Spoke Zarathustra*, 12.
[21] Ibid., 14-15.

the stronger cattle together and it will take intelligent man to create the superman. Where in nature was the willful intelligence that brought about the evolutionary process? It could not have been God, for God is dead. In addition, the blind forces of nature often eliminate the strongest among us because they do not distinguish between the strong and the weak. But this undermines Nietzsche's foundation. If, as he claimed, evolution does not take place without willful intent, then evolution could not have occurred in the past without some external, intelligent guidance.

The Absurdity of Existentialism

Atheistic existentialism is built on the unsustainable foundation of materialism. If materialism cannot substantiate its own presuppositions, how can existentialism avoid an irrational conclusion as well?

It is true that if there were no God, there would be no meaning to life. But it is not true that finite man is sufficient to create his own meaning without any absolutes. Seeking meaning without any absolutes is like a disoriented, blind man throwing a dart at a cosmic target a billion miles away. Even if he happens, by chance, to throw the dart in the right direction, he does not have the arm strength to reach the desired destination. In the end, existentialism is a leap into the darkness without any warrant for belief. At best, existentialism is wishful thinking built on a dreadfully, pessimistic foundation.

This is part of the reason that space-age movies like Star Wars and Star Trek attract such a grand fan-base; because they latch on to the part of ourselves that says, "there must be greater purpose." The theater welcomes us into a world greater than our own. When existentialists start to get down, movies like Star Wars revive their hope - a hope in intergalactic governance. Right now, we're merely ruling little ole Earth. But if keep pushing forth the advancement of technology and the agenda of needing more engineers, we'll get there someday.

Intergalactic governance becomes there hope – how they find meaning – and they don't even stop to realize the absurdity of it all. How ultimately, it still doesn't matter what we all accomplish within the universe, because according to the theory of the Big Bang, which they hold, the Universe is still going to eventually end and destroy all our hard work.

Such wishful thinking, without God in the picture, will always leave us psychologically and emotionally unfulfilled. As finite individuals, we are not autonomous. We are not self-sufficient. We are born needy. We are born in search for something beyond ourselves. Principally, we are born in search of meaning and happiness. We cannot help but look for these things. This is true. But the answer is not found in this world.

Freud agreed that we all seek after happiness; however, he despised any form of religious solution. In regards to belief in God, he denounced it: "The whole thing is so patently infantile, so foreign to reality, that to anyone with a friendly attitude to humanity it is painful to think that the great majority of mortals will never be able to rise above this view of life."[22]

Though Freud despised religious faith, he understood that atheism had its consequences: "One can hardly be wrong in concluding that the idea of life having a purpose stands and falls with the religious system."[23] Though Freud did not think any definitive answer could be given for the meaning of life, he concluded that people will not give up looking for happiness: "They strive after happiness; they want to become happy and remain so."[24] Yet, after listing the various unsuccessful ways people typically try to find happiness, Freud acknowledged: "The

---

[22] *Civilization and Its Discontents*, 22.
[23] Ibid., 24-15.
[24] Ibid., 25.

programme of becoming happy, which the pleasure principle imposes on us, cannot be fulfilled; yet we must not – indeed, we cannot – give up our efforts to bring it nearer to fulfillment by some means or other." [25] Though he compels us to keep searching, he could not tell us where to look. Though he didn't want us to give up, he knew it was futile to keep looking.

Freud was right about humanity's desire to be happy. It is self-evident that we do not inherently possess happiness, or otherwise we would not be looking for it. Freud was also right in concluding that without God, happiness is nowhere to be found. The well-meaning therapist may tell us that we do not need others to be happy. She may even encourage us to love ourselves more and look within ourselves for the answers that we are searching for. But this advice becomes foolish to the one who is banished to a deserted island. If we were left totally alone, we would cling to a volleyball and make him into an image of a friend and call him Wilson. We could love ourselves all we want, but we would still go mad. Insanity would overtake us because the despair of loneliness would be overwhelming. The very thought of living our lives alone is utterly depressing. This is because we were not made to be alone (Gen. 2:18). We were made in God's image so that we may have fellowship with God.

Even if we had all the power, fame, and fortune imaginable, we would still be lonely and miserable without any true friends. We may think that all we need is money to be happy, but even with unlimited buying power we would still be searching. "The eye is not satisfied with seeing, nor is the ear filled with hearing" (Ecc. 1:8). The bodily passions and the cravings of the five senses are never satisfied. We may love our exotic sports cars, but they will never love us back. There must be something more to life than just accumulating possessions. Likewise, fame and power do little to meet the deepest longings of the heart.

[25] Ibid., 34.

When I was younger, I traveled to Europe and toured the Swiss Alps alone. The sights were breathtaking, but the experience had an empty feeling to it. Who enjoys going to the movie theater or a nice restaurant alone? We naturally want to experience life with someone else. All of our best memories, the ones we could not stand to lose, have at least one other person included in them. We are made for relationships.

A few months ago, I had the privilege of holding my third son, Britain, just moments after his birth. There is no feeling like it in the world. My own son! For those fleeting moments, the beauty of new life removed the scales from my eyes and allowed a glimpse into the meaning of life. When we have found that which is worth dying for, then we have discovered that which is worth living for. Though little Britain did not know or love me, I could not help but find the greatest joy and happiness in clinging to him.

As much as I love and find happiness in my baby boy though, such happiness, as unnerving as it is, will not be permanent. There will be many years where I will sacrifice myself in service to him, while he in return gives me more defiled diapers. You see, in fatherhood and motherhood, there is a greater happiness still that lurks, and has yet to be found. It is the child in all of us crying out for a father who despite our inadequacies, loves us permanently and infinitely, even when we do not deserve it. Because when we are sacrificially serving and loving our children, we instinctively want and wish for a similar kind of love ourselves. A loving relationship we know we are all lacking, and if sought after in this world, truly, will never be found. There is only one who gives everlasting and unfailing love such as this, and it is God. As George Park Fisher summarizes, "There is in the human spirit a profound need for God. This is grown out of the fact that we are not only finite, but consciously finite, and not sufficient for ourselves."[26]

We were made in His image so that we may have a relationship with Him, but we will not recover our joy and purpose until that image and relationship is renewed in Christ. For this reason, I agree with Alister McGrath, professor of science and religion at the University of Oxford, who said: "We are created with an inbuilt yearning for God, famously expressed in the prayer of Augustine of Hippo (354-430): 'You have made us for yourself, and our heart is restless until it finds its rest in you.'"[27]

To treasure Christ and to know that He treasures us is the key to happiness; it is the true meaning of life. If we were made for Him, then we will never be fulfilled without Him. God's commandments to love Him with all of our hearts and to love our neighbors as ourselves aren't given merely to restrict us from having fun. They are keys to our own personal meaning and happiness.

Nietzsche may have thought that selfishness and lust for power were the keys to life, but in those last few years of his life he depended on the unselfishness of his mother. After all his friends forsook him and he went completely insane, he would have died all alone if it were not for his Christian mother showing him love and compassion.

Existentialists may not want to submit to God's design for them, but no matter what they choose to dedicate their lives to, they will remain miserable outside of a personal relationship with God through Jesus Christ. Frustration only comes when trying to use something for which it was not designed.

---

[26] *The Grounds of Theistic and Christian Belief*, 90.
[27] Alister McGrath, *Why God Won't Go Away* (Nashville: Nelson, 2010), 145.

Pragmatism may work in the short term, but eventually the shoe will fall apart if we keep using it as a hammer. In the same way, when I was much younger, I had the clever idea to clean my fish tank with toilet tissue. As you might suspect, rather than cleaning the tank, the tissue did what tissue is designed to do – dissolve in water in a fairly quick fashion. As I attempted to clean the algae off the sides of the tank, things went from bad to worse. The tissue broke up into a billion pieces, which clogged the filter and fogged up the water. Just how the tissue disintegrated and lost all purpose, so too do we lose our purpose when we do not dedicate our lives to what we were designed to do.

Conclusion

Ultimately, we were created to walk with God. If we evict Him from our lives, we drive ourselves into captivity. God does not need us in order to be happy. He, as God, is self-sufficient. The Father, Son, and Holy Spirit are eternally happy and glorified with the love that they have for each other from all eternity. We, on the other hand, will never find purpose, meaning, or happiness without Him. No amount of power or money will ever satisfy us. Not even ruling and having governance over the universe will leave us satisfied. We are not self-sufficient. We will never find the love we are looking for apart from Him. We were not designed to live life without a relationship with God. This is why we need divine revelation. Thus, we only hurt ourselves when we forsake God and close our ears to what He has said to us in His Word. No wonder so many people, who are separated from the joy of the Lord, are so miserable. And they will remain in this wretched state as long as they continue to intellectually and practically live their lives without Him.

16

The Irrationality
of Postmodernism

"How beautiful it all seemed at the time of the Enlightenment," the British journalist Malcolm Muggeridge observed, "that man triumphant would bring to pass that earthly paradise whose groves of academe would ensure the realization forever of peace, plenty, and beatitude in practice. But what a nightmare of wars, famines, and folly was to result therefrom."[1]

The Rise of Postmodernism

The cultural historian Jacques Barzun (1907-2012) linked the decline of culture with the decline of faith:

Nietzsche's observation of eighty years ago that "God is dead" was taken up again recently as a liberating idea, but all it records is that the citizens of the modern industrial world do not habitually reckon with Providence or appeal to a deity. They appeal and reckon with machinery, medicine, money, and the forces of the unconscious. These are not gods: the relation of humble intimacy, sacrifice, and mutual love, is lacking.

[1] Malcolm Muggeridge, *The End of Christendom* (Grand Rapids: Eerdmans, 1980), 8.

Thrown back wholly on themselves, men feel their insufficiency. They see more and more clearly that they are not in control of their individual lives or collective destiny, and that many of their practical goals elude their reach.[2]

Without a grand purpose to guide us, emptiness and futility is what remains. According to Barzun:

Despair, indifference, the obsession with cruelty and death, the Samson complex of wanting to bring down the whole edifice on one's head and the heads of its retarded upholders – those passions seize the souls of the young generations and turn them into violent agents of change, or disabused skeptics and cynics.[3]

In his bestselling book *The Culture of Narcissism*, the Neo-Marxist historian Christopher Lasch (1932-1994) gave a vivid and pessimistic description of the decadence of our times. "Plagued by anxiety, depression, vague discontents, a sense of inner emptiness, the 'psychological man' of the twentieth century seeks neither individual self-aggrandizement nor spiritual transcendence but peace of mind, under conditions that increasingly militate against it."[4]

Slavery to the vanity of our own selfishness is the high cost of being liberated from God. According to Muggeridge, Barzun, and Lasch, we now live in the age of despair, but it is the world of our own making. We have traded hope for despondency, life for death, meaning for emptiness, truth for nihilism, love for selfishness, and God for a bowl of Esau's soup. But the exchange cost us everything.

We wanted to be left alone, and now we have discovered the desolation of our own isolation. We were naïve to think we could travel alone and not feel lonely and miserable when we finally

---

[2] Jacques Barzun, "Toward the Twenty-First Century," in *The Culture We Deserve* (Middletown, CT: Wesleyan University Press, 1989), 172.

[3] Ibid., 163.

[4] Christopher Lasch, *The Culture of Narcissism* (New York: W. W. Norton & Company, 1991), 13.

arrived at our destination. But here we are – addicted to our psychotropic, antidepressant medications.

We did not become depressed overnight however. We traveled a long way through the many years of Modernity, through the Age of Enlightenment, and the great gains of the scientific revolution. According to the Canadian philosopher Charles Taylor's epic work *A Secular Age*, it has been a 500-year journey. During which we have gone from the impossibility of not believing in God in the 16th century to where unbelief is "not only easy, but inescapable." [5] We have become, as it were, "disenchanted" with the supernatural.[6]

This disenchantment is linked with, among other factors, the false but optimistic notion of our intellectual self-sufficiency. With an imminent God being pushed aside and our becoming overly fixated on our own autonomy and independence we have entered what Taylor calls "the age of self-authenticity."[7]

Rather than living within the box, we feel the need to blaze a new trail for ourselves. "With the demise of God and the meaningful cosmos," says Taylor, "we are the only authorizing agency left."[8] In this we have moved away from finding our identity in God, the church, the state, or even our nuclear family to seeking *meaning* and personal value in our own individual self-

[5] Charles Taylor, *A Secular Age* (Cambridge, MA: Harvard University Press, 2007), 25.

[6] This disenchantment, says Taylor, was not merely the result of the scientific revolution, for he says, "a crucial part of my argument for the 'deconstruction' of the death of God view, is that the arguments from natural science to Godlessness are not all that convincing" (Ibid., 557). Rather secularization and disenchantment has its roots, in part, in the rise and spread of deism in the 17th and 18th century.

[7] "The age of authenticity," according to Taylor, has been shaped by many factors, including consumerism, egoism, individualism, hedonism, and even expressivism – where fashion has become a vital part of personal self-expression and identity. The sexual revolution of the 1960's was also a part of the push to find personal meaning and freedom from any external norms.

[8] Ibid., 587-589.

expression.[9] Self is ultimate. Sadly, this was reinforced when Abraham Maslow (1908-1970) placed "esteem" and "self-actualization" at the top of man's hierarchy of needs. "Self-actualization" and the "ethic of authenticity" have replaced our dependency on any transcendental and objective standard.

Our dependence on God has been supplanted by the lust for self-identification. For we no longer need to deny ourselves and bring our lives into conformity to God's will to find fulfillment. We are now encouraged to find our purpose in *being ourselves* – whatever that may look like.[10]

Of course, this intellectual independence, selfishness, and even *narcissism* can be traced back to Adam and Eve when they questioned the wisdom of God and took hold of the forbidden fruit. Man has always placed his own wisdom above God's. As a cultural shift, the roots of humanism and intellectual autonomy can be traced through the rationalism of René Descartes. He believed that mankind was self-sufficient in obtaining knowledge of all things though their own intellectual capacities.[11] John Locke disagreed in part with Descartes, arguing that experience, not reason, must be relied upon. However, like Descartes, Locke contended for mankind's self-sufficiency.

Rather than truth descending from God, man could climb upwards on his own. If man is left to himself, then Immanuel Kant was right – God lies behind a transcendental wall.

---

[9] "Commodities [such as Nike shoes] become vehicles of individual expression, even the self-definition of identity" (Ibid., 483).

[10] "The pursuit of happiness," says Taylor, "has come to seem not only not to need a restrictive sexual ethic and the disciplines of deferred gratification, but actually to demand their transgression in the name of self-fulfillment. The people who feel this most strongly are, of course, precisely those for whom many of these disciplines have become second nature, not needing a strong ethical/spiritual backing to maintain themselves" (Ibid., 493).

[11] This may not be a fair charge against Descartes. See footnote 13 on page 94.

Kant may have thought he was rescuing faith from knowledge, but he actually ignited a fire that would burn until every particle of truth was consumed.

Though Kierkegaard sought to rescue religion from Kant's wall by turning faith into a passionate and existential leap, he too failed to stress that religious truth is foremost an objective certainty that has been historically revealed to us in an infallible book.

Man is sufficient; science is sufficient. The great philosophers of Modernity, such as Descartes and Locke, did not need any supernatural guidance. These men attempted to construct their respective theories of knowledge from a finite starting point – themselves. Their aim was to answer every possible question and obtain universal knowledge. By working upwards, they thought they could reach the heavens.

Their attempt to attain universal knowledge, however, would be like trying to construct the Tower of Babel on a frozen lake. No matter how solid the construction may be, if the foundation is insufficient to hold the weight, the structure is bound to fall. Modernity and her philosophers may have had high hopes to reach the pinnacle of knowledge, but the higher she climbed, the more she realized that ultimate truth could not be found from a finite starting point. Before making it to the top, the integrity of her presuppositions began to be in doubt as the foundation started breaking apart underneath her feet. If she cannot be certain of the end of truth, she can not be certain of its beginning.

The Arrival of Postmodernism

With the loss of hope of obtaining universal knowledge, according to the French philosopher Jean-François Lyotard (1924-1998), the construction of any grand metanarrative has fallen down.[12] Like a collapsed building, knowledge itself has collapsed into pieces and there is no foundation with which to rebuild it. We are lost. We are adrift, according Sartre, in a rudderless boat in an endless sea. We are eternally floating in the air – a dark hole – with no knowledge of which way is up or down. Everything is in flux. Everything is contingent and relative. Without God, there is no eternal reference point to keep us from losing our bearings in this dark world. All is fragmented. There are just bits and pieces that cannot be connected.

Who is right? No one knows. All that we know is that we had better not think we know because certainty has become the hallmark act of intolerance.

This is where Modernity has brought us – nowhere. Because of her embarrassment, she has run off into the darkness with her twin sister, Postmodernity, sweeping into the vacuum to take her place. The difference between them is that Modernity gave us hope and promised to lead us into all truth, while Postmodernity is honest when she promises us nothing but hopelessness and despair.

The absurdity of it all led the French Noble Prize winner Albert Camus (1913-1960) to begin his book, *The Myth of Sisyphus*, with these words: "There is but one truly serious philosophical problem, and that is suicide. Judging whether life is or is not worth living amounts to answering the fundamental question of philosophy."[13]

Camus concluded, as King Solomon did long ago (when contemplating the futility of life "under the sun"), that all of life is meaningless and all of its fruitless toil amounts to nothing. Everything is meaningless, even the great discoveries of science.

---

[12] See Jean-François Lyotard, *The Postmodern Condition: A Report of Knowledge*, trans. Geoff Bennington and Brian Massumi (Minneapolis: The University of Minnesota, 1983).

[13] Albert Camus, *The Myth of Sisyphus*, trans. Le mythe de Sisyphe (New York: Vintage Books, 1991), 3.

"Whether the earth or the sun revolves around the other is a matter of profound indifference. To tell the truth, it is a futile question."[14] And he is right, if there is no meaning to life, what does it really matter?

Camus compared life to the ancient myth of Sisyphus who was cursed to carry a heavy rock up a steep mountain that only became steeper as he climbed. The closer he came to reaching his goal, the more difficult the process became until, finally, it was entirely impossible. It was inevitable, at a certain point in his journey, that the stone would fall off his back and roll all the way back down to the base of the mountain. Turning around in despair, Sisyphus realizes as he marches down after his stone, that his lot in life was to continue to repeat this grinding process over and over without end.

Hard work is manageable when there is a reason or motive to work, but when the work becomes pointless, then despair is all that remains. Life and all of its meaningless labor amounts to nothing. We live and hope for tomorrow, but tomorrow only brings us closer to death.

Yet, we live as if we will never die – until the knowledge of death is unavoidable. Rationality and science are of no comfort. We are alone; we work but to no avail. When we wake up to the realization of our own death, we cannot help but contemplate the absurdity of life – a life without meaning or purpose.

Once despair and absurdity set in, we discover that if there is nothing worth dying for, then there is truly nothing worth living for either. "From the moment absurdity is recognized, it becomes a passion, the most harrowing of all."[15]

Man longs for meaning, but because it is fool's gold, the absurdity of it all must be embraced:

[14] Ibid., 3-4.
[15] Ibid., 22.

I don't know whether this world has a meaning that transcends it. But I know that I do not know that meaning and that it is impossible for me just not to know it. What can a meaning outside my condition mean to me? I can understand only in human terms. What I touch, what resists me – that is what I understand. And these two certainties – my appetite for the absolute and for unity and the impossibility of reducing this world to a rational and reasonable principle – I also know that I cannot reconcile them. What other truth can I admit without lying, without bringing in a hope I lack and which means nothing…?"[16]

Though "life is a bad joke," according to Camus, the only way to get through it was to rebel and embrace the absurdity of it all. Rather than looking to God, as Solomon once did, Camus suggested we accept our fate and acknowledge the meaninglessness of life and continue to march up the pointless mountain. He tells us to defy the truth by strapping that rock on our backs and climbing the mountain of absurdity because the only other option is suicide.

Though Camus embraced the absurdity of life, other atheists could not bear to succumb to such despair. According to many atheists, we must create our own way in the world. We must create meaning for ourselves. For example, the French biochemist Jacques Monod unashamedly put man in the place of God by dogmatically preaching that we, as autonomous creatures, are free to choose our own meaning:

The ancient covenant is in pieces; man at last knows that he is alone in the unfeeling immensity of the universe, out of which he emerged by chance. Neither his destiny, nor his duty have

[16] Ibid., 51.

been written down. The kingdom above or the darkness below; it is for him to choose.[17]

Social theorist Jeremy Rifkin was even more daring when he said:

> We no longer feel ourselves to be guests in someone else's home and therefore feel obliged to make our behavior conform with a set of pre-existing cosmic rules. It is our creation now. We make the rules. We establish the parameters of reality. We create the world and, because we do, we no longer feel beholden to outside forces. We no longer have to justify our behavior, for we are now the architects of the universe. We are responsible to nothing outside ourselves, for we are the kingdom, the power and the glory for ever and ever.[18]

With God pushed aside, external values and meaning are pushed aside as well. How to live and what to live for are not questions that have external answers. Mankind is left alone to discover or create these answers. "If God is dead," then, Muggeridge concluded, "somebody is going to have to take his place. It will be megalomania or erotomania, the drive for power or the drive for pleasure, the clenched fist or the phallus, Hitler or Hugh Hefner."[19]

Some existentialists have concluded that the meaning of life is 'power' and others have resorted to a life of 'hedonism.' But regardless of what answer is supplied, existentialism is finite man's attempt to create meaning in a meaningless world without a divine dictionary.

---

[17] Cited in Ravi Zacharias, *A Shattered Visage: The Real Face of Atheism* (Grand Rapids: Baker Books, 1990), 41-42.

[18] Cited in John Blanchard, *Does God Believe in Atheists* (Darlington, UK: Evangelical Press, 2000), 121.

[19] Cited in Ravi Zacharias, *A Shattered Visage: The Real Face of Atheism* (Grand Rapids: Baker Books, 1990), 25.

The Despair of Postmodernism

The implications of Postmodernity are dreadful. If God is exiled, it is man who will go into captivity. If we cast out the warmth of the light, cold and dreary darkness is bound to consume us. If we have sought to be enlightened without looking at the Light, it is no wonder that all we discover is dark. If we throw away God's law, let us not be surprised if we cannot find our way. If we do not want to gaze on heavenly things, let us not be shocked if hell is all we see.

Our captivity is of our own making. We have pushed God out of sight so that we can be free to create our own world without Him. We have made Him irrelevant to life in hopes that we find personal freedom. We have claimed that we can climb our mountains and unlock all the secrets of the universe for ourselves. We have forsaken God by exalting our experiences, our wisdom, and ourselves.

We are self-sufficient, so we think. But after all our searching, boasting, and self-exaltation, we have awoken to the depressing realization that we have lost our dignity, freedom, and meaning.

We went to sleep thinking that we were gods, but woke up to discover that we are less than dogs. Without God, we are mere beasts seeking to gratify our lower passions, barking and sniffing around in dumpsters and trash heaps for our next meal. We used to sit upright, but now we go about crawling on all fours.

Though we were made for greatness, we have settled for the trifles and vanities of this world. Without God, our dignity has been marred with dirty, hedonistic pleasures that enslave and destroy our souls. The very thing we have chosen to love is the very thing that is killing us. We were called to be the crown of creation. We were made in the likeness of God, and we were given the noblest of all tasks – to find happiness, purpose, and freedom in loving, worshiping, and obeying the King of Glory.

We were created to walk beside the living God, but we have pushed Him off the path and we have lost our own way in the process. Without God, misery, hopelessness, and despair is all that remains for us, and we only have ourselves to blame. By throwing God overboard, we did not realize that by being made in His image, we would be dragged into the cold, dark, watery grave as well. [20] If we have killed God, then we have killed ourselves along with Him.[21]

Conclusion

Everyone's presuppositions about God, knowledge, and ethics determines their worldview. As we have seen, *naturalists* begin with a precommitment to the belief that God is irrelevant. When the cosmos is all that remains, there is neither any epistemic warrant for knowledge nor any ethical foundation for the purpose of life. And when there is no warrant for knowledge and ethics, then there is no warrant to believe anything at all. In the end, *naturalism* is an atheistic and self-contradictory worldview that only ends in despair.

From the starting presupposition that the cosmos can explain itself without any supernatural revelation comes materialism, empiricism, determinism, relativism, nihilism, and existentialism. On the foundation of naturalism, Modernity began with the confidence that man was self-sufficient to discover an all-encompassing explanation of all things.

---

[20] George Park Fisher was right when he said: "Atheism is an insult to humanity" (*Grounds of Theistic and Christian Belief*, 62). Fisher explained that it is a "gross affront" to "reason and moral sense" to tell a man to "abstain from frivolity" and to "act from an intelligent purpose, for the accomplishment of rational ends; but the universe, he is told, is the offspring of gigantic frivolity" (Ibid.).

[21] As Francis Schaeffer put it, "If God is dead, then man is dead, too." Cited in William Lane Craig, *Reasonable Faith*, 77.

The original objective of Modernity was not to kill God as much as it was to explain all things, including God, without the assistance of God. Modernity was rooted in the *self-confidence* of man's *self-sufficiency*.

Yet, after many years of disappointment, when it became evident that a grand metanarrative could not be discovered from a finite reference point, Modernity has succumbed to Postmodernity. And Postmodernity has not declared the death of God but the death of truth. Because we are not *self-sufficient*, this is what we get when we refuse to look to God – meaninglessness and hopelessness.

17

The Irrationality of All Nontheistic Religions

Sin against a holy God is the problem, and our guilt is the evidence that we all know this to be true. Naturalism is an attempt to remove guilt by removing God, but because God cannot be killed, our guilt remains alive.

As we have seen, naturalism ends in absurdity because it cannot support its own presuppositions. Not only can naturalism not give an account for sin and guilt, it cannot give an account for its own foundation – logic, mathematics, and the laws of physics.

Since it is irrational to embrace naturalism, we will now need to examine the next options – impersonal-supernaturalism and personal-supernaturalism.

Do the various impersonal-supernatural worldviews, such as Hinduism, Jainism, Buddhism, and the like provide us with any coherent solutions? Can consistency be found in any of the non-Christian, personal-supernatural religions, such as Judaism and Islam? First we will examine the coherency of impersonal-supernaturalism in this chapter and then turn our attention to the non-biblical personal-supernaturalism in the following chapter.

The Absurdity of Impersonal-Supernaturalism

Eastern religious thought, as with all forms of mysticism, can be henotheistic, polytheistic, pantheistic, dualistic, monistic, animistic, agnostic, and even atheistic. Though this sounds complicated, no matter what the various mystical religions believe about the nature of the Ultimate Being (i.e., God), they all believe that the Ultimate Being is impersonal and utterly unknowable. No matter if this God (if it can even be called God) exists as a force entirely separate from nature, within nature, or one with nature, regardless, it is always a God that is not a personal and knowable being.

Since, even within polytheism, there is one Ultimate Being behind all the multiple deities, henotheism is not out of the question. Because this Ultimate Being may be one with nature, panentheism is also included. Because this force may manifest itself in different degrees and strengths within the universe, polytheism and animism are a part of some Eastern religions. Since this ultimate force transcends all that is knowable and is beyond the concepts of *being* and *existence*, agnosticism and even atheism have found their way into Eastern practices.

Eastern religions are not concerned about pinpointing and defining the nature of God, for this is impossible for an Ultimate Being that is ineffable (unknowable). What concerns these religions is how to escape the sufferings, or pollutions, or finiteness, or individuality of our physical life that is bound to the material and physical world. The objective is for our souls to be reunited with this impersonal and unknowable Ultimate Being.

Different Eastern religions may emphasize a slightly different path or manner of obtaining union with the Ultimate Being, from various forms of ethical behavior to mystical enlightenment, but they all would have us find a way to escape the evil and suffering of this world through some manner of enlightenment or nirvana with the Ultimate Being. The goal is annihilation – to cease to exist as a personal and conscience being by being united to the ultimate impersonal and unconscious being.

Hinduism

In Hinduism, the Ultimate Being is Brahman, which is something that cannot be defined, for it is undifferentiated and beyond existence or being itself. Brahman could be nothing as much as it could be something. To be reunited with Brahman, the soul must be liberated (Moksha) from the wheel of karma and Samsara (reincarnations) by reaching nirvana through either the Way of Works, or the Way of Knowledge, or the Way of Devotion. Only afterwards will the soul be free from the pain and suffering that comes with being chained to a physical and bodily existence.

Jainism

In Jainism the path (Dharma) for the soul to escape its physical bondage is through right belief, right knowledge, and an ascetic denial of the flesh as listed in the "Five Great Vows" of renunciation which are: (1) killing, (2) lying, (3) stealing, (4) sexual pleasure, and (5) worldly attachment.

Buddhism

Nirvana, the release of suffering and binding attachment, is reached in Buddhism not through extreme asceticism or hedonism, but through a Middle Path of knowledge and enlightenment. Enlightenment is obtained through the Eightfold Path: (1) Right knowledge – acceptance of the four Noble Truths, (a) believing in the existence of suffering, (b) suffering is caused by our bodily cravings, (c) we cannot be free without our bodily cravings being extinguished, and (d) bodily cravings are extinguished by following the Eightfold Path. (2) Right resolves – renouncing bodily pleasures and harboring ill towards any living creature. (3) Right speech – cease lying, gossiping, and idle talking. (4) Right behavior – do not kill, steal, or fornicate. (5) Right occupation – earning your living without exploiting or harming others. (6) Right effort – resolving to put the proper effort in eliminating our sinful qualities and increasing our good qualities until we are perfected. (7) Right contemplation – being observant, strenuous, and alert in striving to free ourselves from desire and suffering. (8) Right meditation – once we have abandoned all desires and are free from suffering, then nirvana can be reached through right meditation. Afterwards, we are one with the Ultimate Being (Brahman).

Other Eastern (Mystical) Religions

Along with Hinduism, Jainism, and Buddhism, many of the other mystical worldviews such as Taoism, Shintoism, Sikhism, and the New Age movement hold to an impersonal Ultimate Being. These different worldviews may give different answers regarding how we are to become enlightened or united with deity, but the one thing they hold in common is that the Divine (what ever its relationship is to the universe) is utterly unknowable. Ultimate Being does not have properties that are in any way similar to anything that we know. Ultimate Being is entirely transcendent; it is not a person or even a conscious being. It is not even a force because a force implies power, and power is something that can be experienced and talked about. Even the phrase *Ultimate Being* is merely an empty symbol that points to something that is beyond *being* altogether. It is beyond existence or being. What is it? The point is, we cannot know.

The Inconsistency of an Unknowable God

This leads to a major inconsistency. If we cannot know God, if God cannot even know Himself, and if God cannot communicate Himself to us, then we cannot know that God is unknowable in the first place. To say that God transcends all knowable concepts is at best wild speculation. Even if an unknowable God did exist, it would be impossible to know that He existed. Thus, what guru has the right to say that this Ultimate Being transcends all conceivable concepts? How does he know God is unknowable? Did God tell him? Did the guru see this unknowable God behind a rock? Did he have a magical encounter with this unknowable being?

Moreover, if a guru says that he has experienced this unknowable God, does he not deny the unknowablity of God? An experience with God is at least a connection with God. Any connection demands that there is at least a point of similarity between God and man. To connect with God there has to be some kind of analogous relationship with God – be it ever so slim. Wherever this point of similarity may lie, it means that God cannot be absolutely transcendent from man. If God is utterly unknowable, it is a contradiction to claim that there is a path to enlightenment. Is the guru not talking out of both sides of his mouth when he says, "God is unknowable, but here is how you can know/experience him"? I guess that these are the same gurus that enjoy listening to one-handed people applauding their teachings.

Without an authoritative revelation from a personal God, who is to say that mysticism, contemplative prayers, yoga, asceticism, self-flagellation, Upper Way, Middle Way, or Lower Way brings enlightenment and union with the unknowable God. Without a God who can communicate, finite and fallible man is left to grope around aimlessly in the darkness. Man may arbitrarily articulate various conjectures on how to live, but without any concrete authority, impersonal-supernaturalism (in any of its forms) is basically no different than the absurdity of naturalism, for knowledge is restricted to only that which is contained in the visible universe. Thus, because the mystical worldviews are existentialist in practice – believing they must find meaning on their own because their God has restricted access to them from finding it – it is no wonder that many succumb to agnosticism and atheism. For if God is unknowable, then what's the point in trying to know God. However, once agnosticism and atheism are admitted, all knowledge ends in relativism and nihilism, which causes impersonal-supernaturalism to be inconsistent with itself.

The Inconsistency of Confusing God with Nature

Somehow this ineffable God, who is beyond existence and being, is the ground of all existence and being. God is supposedly the ground of all that is conceivable but is one which cannot be conceived. In other words, an Ultimate Being that does not exist created all that does exist, and this leads to a host of internal contradictions.

A Blind Unintelligent Force

This Ultimate Being is not a conscious and intelligent being, but somehow is the ground of all intelligence. The laws of logic, the laws of physics, mathematics, and willful intent within the human race is all rooted in a blind, unconscious, unintelligent force. How does an unintelligent power create (or emanate) a universe that is full of intelligence? If an enlightened guru says that the intelligence that is evident throughout the universe is the intelligence of the unintelligent force, then where is this intelligence located?

Mother Nature and Father Time are anthropomorphic terms that impart human intelligence into nature itself. But does the universe have a soul? Does it have a brain? Does it think? Does it have a plan? Does it have a design? If the universe is a force, does it blow around blindly without any direction or intent? How can there be a supernatural element to the universe that is dumber than a dog or a cockroach? How can the supernatural be unintelligent?

If we seek to answer this dilemma by saying that there is no supernatural element behind or within the universe, then we abandon impersonal-supernaturalism and are forced to embrace the absurdity of naturalism.

Pantheism

Pantheism is the belief that God and nature are one and the same. Paul Harrison, the President of the World Pantheist Movement, gives a simple definition of pantheism: "All is God."[1] Benedict de Spinoza (1632-1677), the great prophet for pantheism, preached that, "besides God no substance can be, nor can be conceived...Hence it follows with the greatest clearness...that God is one, that is to say, in nature there is but one substance."[2]

> The key to Spinoza's philosophy is his monism: that is to say, the idea that there is only one substance, the infinite divine substance which is identical with Nature: *Deus sive Natura*, 'God or Nature'. The identification of God and Nature can be understood in two quite different ways. If one takes Spinoza's message to be that 'God' is just a picturesque way of referring to the ordered system of the natural universe, then he will appear to be an atheist. On the other hand, if one takes him to be saying that when scientists talk of 'Nature' they are really talking all the time about God, then he will appear to be, in Kierkegaard's words, a 'God-intoxicated man'.[3]

Though many pantheists want to hug trees as they worship the universe, at the heart of their mystical worship is atheism.

---

[1] Paul Harrison, *Elements of Pantheism* (Shaftesbury, UK: Element Books, 2013), 1.

[2] Benedict De Spinoza, *Ethics*, trans. W. H. White in Great Books of the Western World, ed. Robert Maynard Hutchins (Chicago: Encyclopedia Britannica, Inc. 1952.), Vol. 31, 360.

[3] Kenny Anthony, *The Oxford Illustrated History of Western Philosophy*, ed. Kenny Anthony (Oxford: Oxford University Press, 1997), 147.

Because pantheism is simply naturalism with the term *God* added to their love of Nature, pantheism partakes of the same inconsistency as naturalism. Why worship Nature, when Nature cannot give account for its own existence?

Panentheism

Panentheism is similar to pantheism, but rather than God and Nature being one, panentheism says that nature is *separate from* but *located in* God. Rather than being monistic, panentheism is dualistic. Nature is in God. As the body is the house of the human soul, the universe is the house of the World-Soul. But what are the properties of the World-Soul? If the World-Soul is impersonal, if it cannot think or have willful intent, what good is it? Does it even exist? If the World-Soul remains an impersonal and unknowable force that cannot communicate itself to us, then we still remain alone with no ultimate meaning and purpose in life.

Polytheism

Many of the polytheistic religions, such as Hinduism and Buddhism, are rooted in a mixture of henotheism and atheistic beliefs. Though this sounds strange, we must remember that there is one Ultimate Being (henotheism), Brahman, which is completely unknowable and is beyond the idea of *being* and *existence* (atheistic).

Even more perplexing is the idea that this non-existent and unknowable God created or emanated all that exists in the universe. Because the universe is the emanation of God, God is everywhere in the universe. The various powers of Nature are manifestations of Brahman. Because these powers are manifestations of Brahman, they deserve worship and are given proper names. Brahma is the creator of the universe, while Shiva is the god of destruction. Vishnu is the goddess of preservation. Ganesha, the elephant-god, is the god of wisdom and knowledge.

These are but a few of the 33 million gods of Hinduism. Yet, these polytheistic gods are not all together distinct deities as much as they are different manifestations of the unknowable and impersonal being, which supposedly goes beyond *existence* and *being*. Though some of these gods are stronger manifestations of Brahman, they all remain as expressions of the different attributes of Brahman. This means that even the weakest idols supposedly have some spark of deity within them. As there can be *many* distinctions that can be made in the universe, so there can be *many* gods who manifest the *one* Ultimate Being.

An elephant-man can be created out of stone and placed in a temple to be worshiped. The worshipers may believe that this idol contains within it the spirit of Ganesha, but they are worshiping a manifestation of a god that is merely a manifestation of Brahman, which is a god that does not even exist. Because Brahman is beyond the reach of worship, polytheists worship various emanations of Brahman. If, however, Brahman is utterly beyond the universe, then how are these polytheistic gods (Shiva, Vishnu, and Ganesha) emanations of Brahman? Does not an infinite gap between Brahman and Ganesha still remain? If we can connect with the various polytheistic gods, which somehow are connected with Brahman, would that not mean that there is a real connection between Brahman and us? And if there is a real connection between Brahman and us (via the gods), would this not make Brahman knowable? Is this not a fundamental contradiction?

Confounding Transcendence and Immanence

This points to the main inconsistency within pantheism, panentheism, and polytheism, which is the mixing together of the utter transcendence with the utter immanence of God. Because God and the universe are made out of the same ontological stuff, then epistemologically speaking, God is both entirely separate from the universe and entirely one within the universe at the same time. In either way, however, God is unknowable.

If one circle represents God, and if another circle represents the universe, then if God is totally transcendent, this means there is absolutely no overlap or connection between these two circles. If God is totally separate from the universe, with no analogous connection, then God forever remains unknowable. According to the pantheistic philosopher Benedict de Spinoza: "Things that have nothing in common with one another also cannot be understood through one another, or the concept of the one does not involve the concept of the other."[4]

On the other hand, if God is totally imminent, then these two circles perfectly overlap each other with no distention between them. If the universe and God are one and the same, then this too makes God unknowable and useless.

Therefore, it is not only a contradiction for God to be both transcendent and imminent, but without God making man in His own image, it would be impossible for man to know God.

---

[4] Benedict De Spinoza, *Ethics*. Trans Edwin Curley (New York: Penguin Books, 1996), 2.

For knowledge of God to be possible, the two circles that represent God and the universe cannot either be totally separate or be totally overlapping, but merely connecting with each other. In other words, to resolve the tension, God and man must neither be one and the same nor totally different, but rather analogous to each other.

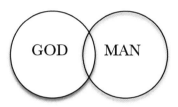

Various mystics may claim that we can climb our way to enlightenment and lose our individuality and bodily passions as we are merged into the Ultimate Reality, but whatever path they suggest we take, afterwards they are forced to deny the validity of that path when they say that God is beyond knowledge itself.

The Neoplatonic philosopher Plotinus (204-270) would have us escape individuality and be united with the One (Ultimate Being) by first meditating on universal concepts and afterwards having us turn off all cognitive thought as we take a leap into the darkness. Buddha would have us travel down the Eightfold Path before we lose consciousness and individuality as we are merged into Brahman as a drop of water is absorbed into the sea.

The ladder reaching up to God, however, falls apart at the last step. If God is utterly unknowable, there is no ladder long enough to reach Him. Plotinus may say that universal concepts (such as *unity* and *oneness*) are closer to the One than particular concepts (e.g., a blade of grass and an individual oak tree), and Hinduism may say that Vishnu is a greater manifestation of Brahman than Hanuman (an ape like god that assists Rama, who is the seventh avatar of Vishnu), but regardless of which god or concept is the closest to the Ultimate Reality, there remains an infinite gap between that last step and nirvana.

The gods are merely symbols, and the symbols become even less than symbols because there is no connection between the symbol and Ultimate Reality. No matter how close together the steps at the bottom of the ladder are, it will always remain impossible to climb our way to an unknowable God seeing there is an infinite gap between the last step and the ineffable being. Thus, mysticism, in all of its forms, undermines its own foundation.

In addition, if we blend God's transcendence with His imminence, then this impersonal God becomes the cause of evil. If God is all, or is in all, with no distinction, then this Ultimate Being is also one with all that is evil. As long as the physical universe is an emanation of God, then evil must also be an emanation of God as well. Ultimately, then, God is to blame for all the evil and suffering in the world.

It is not that mystical thinkers are not aware of these logical contradictions. In fact, many of them would argue that logical consistency is merely a Western concern. Though they may say such things, however, they don't really mean what they say. They value honesty as much as we do. If we travel to the East, we will notice that even there, $1 + 1 = 2$. In the same way that the laws of physics apply to us in the West, they apply to those living in Asia.

No matter where we travel, we will discover that the laws of logic are universally true. A contradiction is a contradiction no matter where it is located or who says it.

Conclusion

Like naturalism, *impersonal-supernaturalism* cannot give consistent answers to the three ultimate questions of life concerning God, knowledge, and ethics. Rather than saying God is irrelevant, *impersonal-supernaturalists* claim that God is unknowable. In both cases, their worldviews end in the same place – self-referentially absurd. For without a personal God who has revealed Himself to man, there are no grounds for knowledge and ethics; and without just grounds for knowledge and ethics, there are no grounds to justify their starting presupposition of a non-existent and impersonal God.

18

The Irrationality of Islam & Judaism

With both naturalism and impersonal-supernaturalism failing the test of coherency, all that remains is personal-supernaturalism. Within this category of thinking, there are three major possibilities – Judaism, Islam, and Christianity. What separates Christianity from Judaism and Islam is the teaching that salvation is by God's grace alone. Therefore, rather than going over the particular truth claims of each of the non-Christian, theistic worldviews, it is sufficient to show how Judaism and Islam fail to remain consistent with themselves by showing the logical impossibility of sinners meriting their salvation before a just and righteous God.

The Inconsistency of an Unjust God

Judaism and Islam (along with many cults within Christianity) teach salvation by good works. In fact, every world-religion, besides Protestant Christianity, demands that we merit our way to God. There is, however, a fatal flaw in this approach – it makes God unjust.

A just God cannot allow sin, any sin, to go unpunished. The law, by its very nature, demands satisfaction. The law demands perfection, but this is something we cannot fulfill. None of us are perfect. I would even argue that it is impossible for us to do one perfect deed, which would include having perfect motives. Every good act, if it is going to be a perfect act, must be done for the glory of God alone. Because we are selfish individuals, this is impossible.

Nevertheless, for the sake of the argument, let us suppose that it was possible for us to accumulate more good works than bad works. This still does not tip the scales in our favor. A murderer may be perfect in every area of his life from birth until death except for the fact that he committed murder. Yet in the eyes of the law, the murderer is still guilty and must pay for his crime. A lifetime of goodness does not cancel out one single transgression. The law requires that we live perfectly from start to finish. This includes loving God with all our hearts and loving others as ourselves in every thing we think, say, and do. Sin is anything that comes short of this standard. A just God cannot say, "Well, you're close enough." Justice requires perfection, and any sin requires a penalty. This is the nature of the law.

If God, as the Lawgiver and Judge, overlooks even the slightest transgression, then He becomes unjust. Any injustice in God makes Him a sinner. For instance, if your little girl was abducted and abused, with all the forensic evidence, including DNA and eye witnesses, pointing to Mr. Joe Blow as the perpetrator, it would be unjust for the Judge to dismiss the case because Mr. Joe Blow has been an outstanding citizen and a good father. It would make no difference even if Mr. Joe Blow were deeply and sincerely apologetic. If justice is going to be served, then Mr. Joe Blow must pay. Thus, is it just for the Judge to let Mr. Joe Blow walk away as if he had done nothing? If you loved your little girl, then it is only reasonable to assume that you would not be content with the Judge releasing her murderer as if he was innocent.

It is not that good works do not merit favor and blessing from a just God, but rather that the law requires perfection. Because none of us, besides Jesus Christ, is perfect, none of us can be saved by our good works. We need forgiveness, but Judaism and Islam do not have any legal way for a just God to forgive us. Thus, there is no salvation in such a flawed system.

If God is just, and we at the same time have to work our way into God's good favor, then we are in trouble. If God is not just, then we are also in trouble – for who knows what will happen. How a just God can forgive the unjust is safely and beautifully preserved in the Christian worldview, in which God has sent His only begotten Son to fulfill the requirements of the law and to endure the justice and wrath of the law on the cross for all those whom He legally represents.

> But now the righteousness of God has been manifested apart from the law, although the Law and the Prophets bear witness to it – the righteousness of God through faith in Jesus Christ for all who believe . . . It was to show his righteousness at the present time, so that he might be just and the justifier of the one who has faith in Jesus (Rom. 3:21-26).

God can be gracious and just at the same time, for justice and mercy kiss each other at the foot of the cross. For the sake of those who believe, God made Jesus "to be sin who knew no sin, so that in him [believers] might become the righteousness of God" (1 Cor. 5:21). We can do nothing to earn or gain God's legal approval, but by faith alone, in Christ alone, we may be forgiven of all our sins. In Christ alone we may be declared innocent and righteous before a just and holy God.

This is the gospel of free grace, which is the only answer to man's guilt. We can seek to do all the good we want, but the skeletons in our closest will always remain behind closed doors, for our shame and guilt cannot be washed away by religious acts of compensation.

Guilt is the problem, and good works are not the solution. We need the offended party to forgive us. We need a legal substitute to stand in our place, to pay for our crimes, and to merit the righteousness that we need to stand before a just God. We need God to forgive us, and only the God of the Bible is able to forgive us while remaining true to His own righteous character. The gospel of Jesus Christ makes forgiveness possible. For this reason, Christ is the only way to God. The Lord Jesus made this abundantly clear when He said, "I am the way, and the truth, and the life. No one comes to the Father except through me" (John 14:6).

The Inconsistency of a Monistic God

Moreover, the injustice in these non-biblical gods is only half of the problem. For God to be just, He must be righteous, loving, relational, and able to communicate His law to man. Yet, only the triune God of the Bible possesses such attributes.

The Problem of Righteousness

For instance, sin and guilt come from the failure to obey God's moral law. But where does the law come from? What makes the law good? In Plato's *Euthyphro*, Socrates asked if the law is good because the gods have declared it so, or if the gods have declared it good because it is good. This however is a false bifurcation. The first option diminishes the law as it makes the standard of goodness merely arbitrary in the thoughts of God. The second option overly exalts the law as it places God underneath its rule. What Socrates failed to understand is that there is a third option that is rooted in the trinitarian nature of God.

God's moral law is not an external or abstract code of conduct that exists outside of the character of God. God is not under law, but rather the law is a reflection of the moral character of God. God is love. God is righteous. Thus, it is God Himself who is the standard of morality. This also means that the law is not an arbitrary construction in the mind of God.

Because God is love, love is the essence of the law. The law demands love and prohibits selfishness. With this in mind, both law and love layout the terms for a right relationship with God and others. If there were no God and only a single person existed, sin and selfishness could not exist. A single individual in complete isolation could not steal, cheat, gossip, lie, covet, or kill. He also could not be unselfish or selfish. He could not be bad, but neither could he be good. It takes at least two persons for morality to exist. In this way, the law and love exist because of relationships.

Thus, the purpose of the moral law is to create and sustain happy and meaningful relationships with God and with one another. Because we were made for relationships, the key to our happiness is found in loving God with all of our hearts and loving our neighbors as ourselves.

The Problem of Love

In like manner, though there is only one God, there are three persons in the Godhead. God is one in nature but three in persons. This, I believe, not only makes God eternally complete and happy in Himself, but also provides God an avenue to eternally express His love – a love that is not inwardly focused. God the Father eternally loves and seeks the glory of the Son and the Holy Spirit.

Likewise, the Son and Holy Spirit eternally seek the glory of God the Father (John 16:14-15). Each of the three persons know and love each other perfectly. This love is not inwardly focused, for God, by His very nature, is the ultimate giver. As Michael Reeves points out: "If God were just one person, then love of the other would not be central to his being."[1]

---

[1] Michael Reeves, *Delighting in the Trinity* (Downers Grove, IL: IVP, 2012), 112.

Jonathan Edwards also recognized that God's goodness required for Him to be more than a monistic being:

> It appears that there must be more than a *unity* in infinite and eternal essence, otherwise the goodness of God can have no perfect exercise. To be perfectly good is to incline to and delight in making another happy in the same proportion as it is happy itself, that is, to delight as much in communicating happiness to another as in enjoying of it himself, and an inclination to communicate all his happiness; it appears that this is perfect goodness, because goodness is delight in communicating happiness.[2]

Augustine, in his book *The Trinity*, went a step further and said not only must God not be monistic, but he must be triune for Him to love.[3] Not just two, but three persons are needed for God to be love because, as Augustine explains, love requires three things: a subject, an object, and an expression. That is, love involves a person who loves, a person who is loved, and a channel of communicating love from the lover to the beloved, and that these three requirements, can truly only be eternally satisfied by the Father who loves the Son through the Holy Spirit, and visa versa.

How does the Father love the Son? He loves by giving Himself. But how does the Father give Himself to the Son? He gives Himself to the Son by the operation of the Spirit. The Spirit exhaustively knows the Father (by His co-indwelling in Him) and takes what belongs to the Father and communicates it to the Son. In other words, God loves by giving Himself to the Son by the *means* of the Holy Spirit.

---

[2] Jonathan Edwards, "Miscellany" 96, in *The Works of Jonathan Edwards*. Vol. 13, ed. Thomas A. Schafer (New Haven: Yale University Press, 1994), 263. The Word in italic is present author.

[3] Augustine, *The Trinity*, trans. Edmond Hill, ed. John E. Rotelle (New York: New City Press, 1992).

The Problem of Relationships

But even though this view is appealing, I remain unconvinced that *only* a triune could God have the propensity to love. So really, it is not so much as three "persons" (as we would recognize the term) are necessary, but two, for there must be at least two eternal and coequal persons subsisting within the Godhead, giving and receiving love with each other, for God to be love. According to C. S. Lewis:

> All sorts of people are fond of repeating the Christian statement that 'God is love'. But they seem not to notice that the words 'God is love' have no real meaning unless God contains at least two Persons. Love is something that one person has for another person. If God was a single person, then before the world was made, He was not love.[4]

In reference to this statement, Robert Letham, senior lecturer in systematic and historical theology at Wales Evangelical School of Theology, states, "If he were not love, he could not be personal, either."[5] Letham went on to say:

> Only a God who is triune can be personal. Only the Holy Trinity can be love. Human love cannot possibly reflect the nature of God as a Trinity of persons in union and communion. A solitary monad cannot love and, since it cannot love, neither can it be a person.[6]

Furthermore, God's glory is not a single attribute as much as it is the radiance of all God's attributes. Glory shines forth out of God. God's glory is the proper value that comes with knowing and appreciating God, therefore, God's glory requires an eyewitness. It requires appreciation. These requirements can only be eternally satisfied by a multiplicity of persons within a Godhead who perfectly appreciate each other.

---

[4] *Mere Christianity*, 152.
[5] Robert Letham, *The Holy Trinity* (Phillipsburg, PA: P&R, 2004), 444.
[6] *Ibid.*, 446.

So the eternal glory that is shared within the Godhead consists of each of the three persons giving Himself to the other persons, and the other persons properly admiring the beauty, majesty, and honor of the other. The glory of God is the infinite value that each of the three persons of the Trinity place on one another. Or to put it another way, it is this appreciation between the three persons of the Godhead that allows the Father, Son, and Holy Spirit to love and glorify each other perfectly.

This means that the intertrinitarian love is not selfish. The Father's love does not seek it's own, but rather the glory and honor of the Son, and likewise the desire of the Son and Spirit is to shine forth glory and honor upon the other persons of the blessed Trinity. In this we see the perfect relationship that is rooted in love and righteousness.

The Problem of Communication

Love, by its very nature, seeks to give and share. Yet, if God was a single person, the desire to share and communicate would not be essential to His nature. And if sharing was not essential to God's nature, why would He share and reveal Himself to us? For this reason, Michael Reeves asks:

> If God is a single person, and has always been alone, why should he speak? In the loneliness of eternity before creation, who would he have spoken to? And why would he start now? The habit of keeping to himself would run deep. Such a God would be far more likely to remain unknown.[7]

In other words, if God was not essentially a relational and personal being, there would be no inherent motive to share, love, and communicate Himself to us. But God is love because God is trinitarian. Thus, it is inherent within His nature to communicate and share Himself.

---

[7] *Delighting in the Trinity*, 80.

Because God is love, the Father loves by communicating and sharing the greatest object of His affection – His Son (Matt. 16:17). The Son, in turn, loves us by revealing the Father (John 14:6), and the Spirit loves us by sharing the Father and the Son (1 Cor. 1:30). Each person, it is seen, finds pleasure in revealing the glory of the other persons. Therefore, we can know God because God is triune and He naturally gives, shares, and communicates Himself to others – something that could not be said about a monistic deity.

Moreover, when God communicates love and joy to us, according to Jonathan Edwards, He is not simply conveying the concepts of love and joy, but rather He communicates in such a way that he bestows the affections of love and joyfulness. [8] Philosophers and theologians can seek to explain the theoretical meaning of these concepts, but they cannot actually give the experience of love and joy to their readers. God, on the other hand, because He is the source of all love and joy, can bestow these things by giving us Himself. God is love and in Him is unspeakable joy.

Therefore, to the degree we know and experience God will be the measure in which we will know and experience love and joy.

God delights in communicating happiness to others as much as He delights in enjoying happiness for Himself. For God enjoys sharing the enjoyment that He enjoys, and since God finds enjoyment in Himself, He thus loves communicating Himself to others.

So what is God's love? It is the three persons of the Trinity investing their happiness in the happiness of each other by seeking to share their happiness with each other so that they remain united together in a single happiness. As we like to share

---

[8] See chapter 1 of William M. Schweitzer, *God is a Communicative Being: Divine Communicativeness and Harmony in the Theology of Jonathan Edwards* (London: T&T Clark, 2012).

our favorite things with the people we love the most, each person of the Godhead loves to share their life, glory, love, and joy with each other. Because God loves the Son, He loves to share His Son with the Spirit. They each love to share themselves and each other. And this is how God loves us. God shares His life, glory, love, and joy with us so that we too can be satisfied in the life, glory, love, and joy that comes from a saving knowledge of Him (John 17:22).

In other words, the loving relationship that the Father, Son, and Holy Spirit share with each other from all eternity is the relationship that God has freely chosen to share with His people (John 17:26). The Father gives His Son to His people. The Son, as the eternal Word, reveals the Father. And the Spirit brings believers into communion with the Father and the Son. The greatest gift of all has been offered to mankind – an invitation to join in and experience the glorious joy and unending love found only between the Mosh High Father, Son, and Holy Spirit. Now, this is love!

Without the Trinity, morality and love would only be an abstract concept in the mind of God. Allah may be a god who can command obedience, but his commands would not be rooted in love. As single-person god, Allah is inherently selfish. In eternity past, Allah may have admired himself, but he could not have enjoyed or loved anyone else. Allah is left to his own self-consciousness.

Self-appreciation is warranted if you happen to be God, but self-appreciation alone does not warrant an eternal morality, for it lacks any meaningful relationship since there is no *essential* and *inherent* desire to personally communicate and share with others. So indeed, since Allah cannot account for his own eternal righteousness, he fails to be a god of love.

Conclusion

God's law, God's love, God's personhood, and God's communi-cativeness are essential and eternal because God is triune. Only the God of the Bible can explain why there is an universal moral standard and only the God of the Bible is able to justly forgive all those who come to Him in repentance and faith through the work of His Son dying on the cross. In short, no other worldview, philosophy, or religion has a coherent answer for man's guilt.

19

The Irrationality of
Non-Trinitarian Religions

Guilt remains the problem. A guilty conscience not only testifies that we know there is a just God, but it also testifies why we are unreceptive to such knowledge. Because we stand guilty before a holy God, we would prefer either that God be impersonal or that He not exist at all.

Because of our sins, we have a hostile relationship with God. The previous chapter explained why Christ is the only remedy for a guilty conscience. Only in Christ can sinners be forgiven and reconciled to God. But this reconciliation with God raises another dilemma for non-trinitarian religions. Namely, a *relationship* with God requires an analogous correlation between similar yet different things. That is, there must be both 'unity' and 'diversity' for relationships to exist in the first place. But where does the 'unity' and the 'diversity' come from?

The Problem of the 'One' and the 'Many'

The problem begins by asking which is ultimate or primary – 'unity' or 'diversity'? No matter which one we choose, we end up destroying the other in the process.

Though William of Ockham (1288-1347), an English Franciscan philosopher, claimed that only *particulars* existed, it appears that most people have chosen 'unity' as the ultimate reality. For example, Muslims view the 'oneness' of God (*Tawhid*) as ultimate reality. In Judaism, it is the indivisibility of Yahweh. Brahma is 'Ultimate Reality' in Hinduism and Buddhism. The oneness of God's essence is the unifying force behind pantheism. For Aristotle, it is the pure "impartible and indivisible" substance of the Unmoved Mover. [1] And the unifying concept in Neoplatonism is the 'One.'

Choosing 'unity' as ultimate means that everything (all forms of 'diversity') can be reduced to the 'one.' But this type of reductionism has its consequences.

Though we naturally want to classify things together, like the 37 different species of cats (e.g., lions, tigers, and house cats) into the cat family (*felis genus*), it is impossible to find a single unifying component or concept that unifies all cats together. We cannot reduce the cat family to fur, tails, or pointed ears because fur, tails, and pointed ears are not restricted to the cat family. Not only that, if we seek to identify them as a distinct *genus*, cats are more than just a ball of fur, or a wagging tail, or pointed ears. If we reduced things down to a single trait or a single idea, we end up destroying that which we were trying to explain. Once a cat is reduced to a ball of fur, then we no longer have a cat.

Thus, those religions that seek to make their monistic god the ultimate reality have a hard time explaining why there is 'diversity' in the world. And this is not to mention that this reductionism must be applied to God as well, and when God is reduced to a single attribute or a particular trait, he/it is nothing more than a mesh of unknowable substance.

[1] The Unmoved Mover of Aristotle is a non-trinitarian being: "How can they be right who say that the first principle is unity and this is substance, and generate number as the first product from unity and from matter, assert that number is substance? How are we to think of 'two', and each of the other numbers composed of units, as one?" (*Metaphysics*. Trans. W. D. Ross. Stilwell, KS: Digireads Publishing, 2006., 11.2).

On the other hand, if we seek to do away with any unity principles or classifications, making *diversity* the ultimate reality, then God disappears from existence. Not only that, we destroy knowledge altogether, seeing that knowledge of the world comes from classifying and contrasting different and similar things together. If there is only *diversity*, as postmodernism would suggest, then there is no similarity and analogous relationship between things. But, if there are no similar or analogous relationships between things, then it becomes impossible to know those things.

Though this may only seem like a philosophical knot, there is an answer found in the Bible. Ultimate reality is both 'unity' and 'diversity,' such as we discover in the doctrine of the Trinity. The 'one and the many' are *equally ultimate* as there is only one God who subsists in three distinct persons. We can have both unity and diversity as ultimate because we have a triune God who is ultimate.

The *equal ultimacy* of God is important, even vital, for a cohesive worldview. Though some argue that the Trinity is a contradiction, it is the doctrine of the Trinity which provides the coherency of the Christian worldview. Without the Trinity, everything deconstructs into meaninglessness.

For instance, Allah is one. In the Qur'an it reads: "He is Allah, the One" (Surat Az-Zumar 39:4). But this does not mean one in number, for that which has no second cannot exist in a numerical form. According to Vincent J. Cornell, a scholar of Islamic studies and director of the King Fahd Center of Middle East and Islamic Studies at the University of Arkansas: "'God is one' in the sense that there is no multiplicity or division conceivable in Him, neither outwardly, nor in the mind, nor in the imagination. God alone possesses such unity."[2]

Concerning Judaism, the renowned Rabbi and Torah scholar Moshe ben Maimon ("Maimonides," 1135-1204) stated:

> This God is one; He is neither two nor more than two; He is simply one. His unity is not like any other oneness that exists in the world. His is not the unity of a kind that encompasses many other single particulars; and it is not like the unity of a body that is divided into parts and extremities; rather it is a unity that is entirely unlike any other sort of oneness in the universe.[3]

Likewise, the theistic god of Aristotle, the Unmoved Mover, is an immaterial, infinite, eternal, immutable being who is pure actuality. Because He is immaterial, He is a simple being without body, parts, or composition. Because He is eternal, He exists in a timeless and motionless state. He is pure actuality (*actus purus*) that is without any movement whatsoever. He is not like man who is in flux and ever changing. God is perfectly immutable. God is not becoming − He is what He is and all that He is without any change or differentiation.

Man knows there is an infinite, eternal, and immutable God, but without special revelation, natural theology will never properly lead us to believe God is a Trinity. All these wonderful attributes (immateriality, infinity, eternality, and immutability), however great they are, without the balance of the Trinity, logically lead to the inconsistency of monistic pantheism.

---

[2] Vincent J. Cornell, "God in Islam," in the *Encyclopedia of Religion*, Ed. Lindsay Jones, Vol. 5, 2nd Edition (New York: Macmillan Reference of Thompson Gale, 2005), 3561-3562.

[3] *MT, Hilkhot Yesodei Ha Torah*, 1:7, Cited in Micah Goodman, *Maimonides and the Book that Changed Judaism* (Philadelphia: The Jewish Publication Society, 2015), 5.

The Problem of Differentiation

If God was not triune, then Aristotle is right – there are no grounds for any distinctions within God at all.[4] Without any inherent distinctions, God would not only be timeless (for that requires a separation in the mind of God between successive and distinct thoughts), but He would be one with His attributes, which is Biblical.

However, all of His attributes would also be one *with each other* without any differentiation at all, which is problematic.[5] It is problematic because without distinctions between His attributes there is no difference between God's omniscience and God's omnipotence. God's acts of power would be identical to His thoughts and decrees. As Aristotle argued, "If they are one in number, all things will be the same."[6] In fact, all of God's attributes, as in pantheism, would become one single attribute without any differentiation (which is an extreme and unbiblical view of divine simplicity).[7]

---

[4] According to Aristotle: "The infinite cannot be a separate, independent thing. For if it is neither a spatial magnitude nor a plurality, but infinity itself is its substance and not an accident of it, it will be indivisible; for the divisible is either magnitude or plurality" (*Metaphysics*, 11.10).

[5] The Dutch Reformed theologian Geerhardus Vos (1862-1949) explained why this was problematic: "May we also say that God's attributes are not distinguished from one another? This is extremely risky. We may be content to say that all God's attributes are related most closely to each other and penetrate each other in the most intimate unity. However, this is in no way to say that they are to be identified with each other. Also in God, for example, love and righteousness are not the same, although they function together perfectly in complete harmony. We may not let everything intermingle in a pantheistic way because that would be the end of our objective knowledge of God" (Theology Proper, vol. 1 of *Reformed Dogmatics*, trans. and ed. Richard B. Gaffin. Bellingham, WA: Lexham Press, 2012-2014., 5).

Scott Oliphint reminds us that "The doctrine of simplicity, in its best formulations, has never affirmed that God is some sort of Being in which no distinctions do or can reside" (*God with Us*, 64).

[6] *Metaphysics*, 11.2.

[7] Ironically, though Aristotle rejected polytheism for theism, the theism that he embraced leads right back to the pantheism that produces the polytheism that he rejected. It is no wonder that the further a society moves away from the

The Problem of Movement

For Aristotle, immutable means immobile. To be purely simple without parts or differentiation means that there can be no movement of self. And by the word *movement,* Aristotle is not only referring to a change of physical location but also to any temporal change occurring through the intentional exertion of power. Any intentional exertion of power requires a differentiation between the moment before and the moment after the act of power. This differentiation brought about by sequence, succession, or time is impossible for a simple, immutable God without parts.

Even if He wanted to, God cannot enter into space or time at all – a God of pure unity is completely locked out. Thus, immutability is not merely the idea that God's essence does not change, but that God cannot create change. God cannot create the universe or anything else, for this implies movement or succession within God.

The Problem of Thought & Emotions

Moreover, without any differentiation, there is no difference between God's mind, heart, and will, for they are all immutability one. This would indicate that it is impossible for God to emotionally interact with creation without there being a change in His eternal state of being. According to the preeminent medieval Jewish Rabbi, Maimonides, there cannot be a change in God's emotions without there being a change in God's nature: "It is written, I am God who does not change (Mal. 3:6). And if He were sometimes angry and sometimes happy, He would be changing."[8]

---

knowledge of theism, the more pantheistic and even animistic it becomes. Because of inward guilt, man naturally wants to worship a mediator (e.g., an emanation of God) that buffers them from the wrath the ultimate God.

[8] Cited in *Maimonides and the Book that Changed Judaism*, 8.

Not only is God without any emotional change, God's emotion must be singular. He cannot single out and focus on an individual event in history and have an emotional opinion or judgment about it. He knows nothing of time related events and therefore He has no new experiences.

Consequently, God cannot have what Jonathan Edwards identified as a *will of decree* and a *will of command*. Biblically speaking, these two wills are unified in that they both seek God's glory, but they seek God's glory from different perspectives. God's *will of decree* is God seeking His own glory in the grand scheme of things, which is God's eternal plan that cannot be violated. God's *will of command* is God seeking His own glory in every particular event in history, which is often violated.

Nevertheless, if God cannot differentiate between temporal events, He does not have a *will of command*. He is not inflamed by the unjust acts of men because these acts are undifferentiated from the rest of God's knowledge and emotions. He is completely apathetic to the affairs of men.

If God is angry with the wicked, then He must have been timelessly angry with them before the foundation of the world. Whatever God's emotional state is from eternity past, He must remain in that state without change. It is impossible for God to be appeased or provoked, for it is impossible for Him to have emotional opinions about any single event in time. God is timeless, thus He must be timelessly angry. In God's motionless state, He only perceives all things in one continuous gaze without any cognitive and emotional differentiation about any particular incident in history.

But then again, if there is no differentiation in God, there is no difference between God's anger and God's satisfaction. What does it mean for God to be angry if God's wrath is identical to God's love and pleasure?

The Problem of Consciousness

But this not only robs God of any emotional and personal interaction with creation, it robs God of all cognitive interaction. Once God's emotions are limited by God's heart being absorbed into the sea of God's simplicity, God's mind must be absorbed into this same ineffable sea as well.

If God cannot distinguish between His attributes, according to Pseudo-Dionysius, as pointed out in chapter 3, God cannot distinguish between Himself and that which is not Himself. Such contemplation implies a distinction between the self-awareness of the one who is thinking and that which is being thought upon.

For Aristotle, though God is pure thought, he cannot think in any true sense of the word because *thinking* consists of composite thoughts. Thinking is differentiating between things. And because "thought is moved by the object of thought," [9] contemplation cannot be contributed to the unmovable God. Consequently, God cannot know the *particulars* of the universe, for He can only know that which is indivisible. Because the only indivisible substance is God, God can only know Himself.[10]

Thus, the god of Aristotle, according to B. A. G. Fuller (1879-1956), a former president of the American Philosophical Association, "knows only himself with a knowledge in which there is distinction neither of self from not-self, nor of the activity of thought as such from it's content."[11] Fuller went on to explain: "All God's life and thought are locked up. He knows nothing but it, nothing but himself."[12] For this reason, Aristotle said that God is "thinking upon thinking."[13] That is to say, God's essence cannot be distinguished from God's thought. If God is what He

[9] Ibid., 11.7.
[10] Ibid., 12.9.
[11] B. A. G. Fuller, "The Theory of God in Book Λ of Aristotle's Metaphysics" in *The Philosophical Review*, Vol. 16, No. 2 (Mar., 1907), 170-183., 173.
[12] Ibid., 175.
[13] *Metaphysics*, 12.9.

is, then He is that which He contemplates. God is what He is without any differentiation, then whatever information is in the mind of God is the very essence of God. Pure simplicity, without any inherent diversity of any kind, leads to this conclusion – a God who cannot consciously think.

The Problem of Divine Revelation

We have already seen, in chapter 18, how a non-trinitarian God would have no intrinsic motive to communicate and reveal Himself, but even if He did try to reveal Himself, it would be impossible. Without any differentiation, God's knowledge of Himself is ineffable. A God who cannot separate one thought from another thought can only know Himself in one simple and indivisible pure act. But with all particulars removed from the mind of God, what is left? Something completely unknowable. For this reason, Fuller concluded: "It is like consciousness without anything but its mere name to be conscious of, and therefore meaningless."[14] And if God's knowledge of Himself is bound to a pure act of thought without distinctions, how can he speak to man in an intelligible way? At best, the inconsistency found in mysticism is all that remains when God's knowledge of Himself is indivisible and unknowable.

The Problem of Creation

Moreover, if there is no distinction between God's thoughts, there also can be no distinction between God's knowledge of Himself and God's acts. If there are no distinctions between the various attributes of God, then God's creative acts of power must be eternal in the same way God's knowledge is eternal. God's mind is ineffably united, without any distinctions, to God's will, to God's emotions, and to God's acts of power. God does not have passions because God does not have parts, but neither does

14 Ibid., 177.

He have a mind or a will. With no differentiation within the mind of God, there is no *intentionality* with God. This means that God did not choose to create, for He has always been and remains in a timeless state of creating. Because He is barred from time, as Aristotle argued, the universe must be eternal.[15]

Again, according to this view of God, there can be no movement or motion in God without there being a distinction within the essence of God. Consequently, this not only makes the universe eternal, it makes the universe necessary and essential to the essence of God. That is, if the act of creating cannot be separated from the undifferentiated attributes of God, then God's act of creating the universe becomes timelessly and eternally one with the essence of God. God and the universe are blended together where the one becomes the other. This would also mean that there was never a time *before the foundation of the world* where nothing existed but God alone. As in monistic pantheism, creation is an essential property of God. God and creation are eternally united and inseparable. This ceases to make creation a free act of God's will that is subject to time, but merely an eternal emanation that cannot be separated and distinguished from God's essence. For God to be who He is, creation has to be what it is – making both God and the universe necessary and essential to one another.

The Problem of Transcendence and Immanence

With God being completely unknowable in His unified essence He becomes wholly other. Yet, His transcendence is conflated oddly enough with His immanence because the universe is a timeless emanation of God's being. Of course this leads to a clear contradiction: God cannot be both entirely other and entirely the same with the universe.

---

[15] *Metaphysics*, 12.6. For a Christian thinker who defends the eternality of the universe see *Eternal God* by Paul Helm (New York: Oxford, 2012), 234-250.

Conclusion

Not only is the god of pantheism one with the universe, the god of pantheism ceases to be loving and personal. He is a simple being who apathetically and blissfully exists in a cemented state of pure and indivisible thought of Himself without any personal concern or contemplation of the ever changing affairs of the universe that is full of particulars.

One may argue that this god of Aristotle is not Allah or the god of Judaism, but this is where a pure unitarian/monistic god leads. For instance, the Arab-Islamic scholar Muhyiddin Ibn 'Arabi (1165-1240) reduced the 'oneness' of God (Tawhid) in Islam to its logical conclusion – pantheism. Ibn 'Arabi believed that the single and indivisible reality simultaneously transcends and is manifested in all things. Likewise, the Jewish philosopher Baruch Spinoza did the same with Judaism in his book *Ethics*.[16] And though many Muslims and Jews do not agree with Ibn 'Arabi or with Spinoza, this is where the ultimacy of God's 'oneness' logically ends.

If we start with pure unity without any intrinsic diversity, then Ultimate Reality becomes more of a blind, unknowable, and impersonal force than a personal and loving God who remains distinct from the universe. A single-person god, if he/it could even be defined as a person, cannot love, care, and express a diversity of emotions because there is no differentiation within his/its essence, thoughts, or acts. Such a god as Allah or the god of Judaism becomes the god behind pantheism. And, as we have already seen in chapter 17, pantheism is an incoherent worldview.

---

[16] See Benedict De Spinoza, "Of God" Part 1 in *Ethics*. Trans Edwin Curley (New York: Penguin Books, 1996).

20

The Irrationality of
Unitarian Monotheism

We have already seen the irrationality of pantheism in chapter 17, but thankfully we are not abandoned to merely the light of natural theology – the god of Aristotle. God has revealed Himself to us in His Word, where we learn that He is one God subsisting in three distinct persons that remain eternally united and separate from each other. God is personal, loving, and caring because there are three distinct loving and caring persons within the Godhead that internally (*ad intra*) and relationally interact with each other.

The Solution for Differentiations

It is true that God is a simple being that is not composed of non-divine parts. For instance, if the attribute of *power* was not essential to God's nature, then power would cease to be divine, which would cause God to be dependent on something outside of Himself for Him to be *omnipotent*. Because God cannot be dependent on anything other than Himself, He cannot be composed of any non-divine parts.

God's simplicity implies that His nature consists of His attributes, and His attributes do not exist independently or outside of God. This also implies that each attribute is inseparably necessary and essential to the other attributes of

God. That is, it is logically impossible to separate or remove any of the attributes of God without destroying God in the process. Each of God's attributes properly describe each of the other attributes of God in the same way that they each describe God. Because God is love, God's love is sovereign, eternal, and omniscient in the same way that God is sovereign, eternal, and omniscient. Finally, this implies that each and every attribute of God (in-and-of-itself) consists of the fullness of God. In this way, God is a *simple* being without *non-divine* parts. He is what He is.

God being *simple*, however, does not mean that He is without any *formal differentiations* within Himself. [1] Saying that God cannot be a collection of *non-divine* parts (i.e., parts that are not in-and-of-themselves fully God) is not the same as saying that God cannot subsist in different divine persons that are (in-and-of-themselves) fully God (i.e., *autotheos*). For instance, because each of the three persons of the Godhead are (in-and-of-themselves) fully God, *formal differentiations* and relations are inherent and necessary in God. According to Oliphint, "These personal distinctions and relations are all identical with him; they are not 'added' to him from the 'outside.'"[2] In other words, the differentiations within God are essential to who God is.

Formal differentiations within the Trinity imply that God is not only able to distinguish between things outside Himself, but that He is able to distinguish between different things inside Himself. For example, God the Father knows that He is neither the Son nor the Spirit, the Son knows that He is neither the Father nor the Spirit, and the Spirit knows that He is neither the Father nor the Son.

---

[1] By *formal differentiation* I mean something more than a *conceptual distinction* (*distinctione rationis*, a distinction in thinking) that exists only within our finite minds to help us make sense of an ineffable God that transcends human language.

[2] K. Scott Oliphint, "Simplicity, Trinity, and Incomprehensibility of God" in *One God in Three Persons*, Ed. Bruce Ware and John Starke (Wheaton, IL: Crossway, 2015), 230.

Moreover, the *formal differentiations* between the three persons of the Trinity are not merely conceptual distinctions within the mind of God; rather, they are an essential part of His ontology.[3] Jay Wesley Richards, a senior fellow at the Discovery Institute, reminds us that "the Father and the Son could not change places."[4] Richards went on to elucidate:

> There is some fact about the Father that makes him the Father and not the Son, and some fact about the Son that makes him the Son and not the Father, even if we can refer to these separate facts by means of single asymmetrical relation. Moreover, the relation of the Father to the Son is not the same as the relation of the Father to the Spirit. Therefore, if one wishes to retain the trinitarian distinction, one must deny that every essential divine property or relation is strongly equivalent.[5]

Consequently, there can be and there are essential and eternal distinctions within the very being of God.[6] This implies that God's simplicity must be understood in light of the diversity found in the Trinity.[7] Specifically, God's simplicity does not

---

[3] The Eunomians (i.e., neo-Arians) denied the orthodox doctrine of the Trinity by applying Aristotelian logic to the doctrine of divine simplicity. In gist, they argued that if there are no distinctions within God, then only the Father exists *a se* (dependent on nothing outside of Himself). Ultimate *oneness* is reducible to the Father – He alone possesses the simple essence of Divinity. The essence of the Son is generated from the Father and the essence of the Spirit proceeds from the Father and Son as they are ontologically and eternally subordinate to the Father, who alone is Almighty God. See Thomas H. McCall "Trinity Doctrine, Plain and Simple" in *Advancing Trinitarian Theology* (Grand Rapids: Zondervan, 2014), 46.

[4] Richards, Jay Wesley, *The Untamed God* (Downers Grove, IL: IVP, 2003), 230.

[5] Ibid.

[6] Scott Oliphint seeks to maintain balance when he reminds us: "An important aspect of this doctrine of God's simplicity is that these distinctions in God are not thought to exist as real 'things' in God. That is, they should not be thought as things at all, so that the Godhead is a composition of 'things upon thing'" (*God with Us*, 65).

[7] For an excellent article on the relationship between divine simplicity and the Trinity see Thomas H. McCall "Trinity Doctrine, Plain and Simple" in *Advancing Trinitarian Theology* (Grand Rapids: Zondervan, 2014).

cancel out His multiplicity. "To avoid the blank identity of pantheism," Van Til claimed, "we must insist on an identity that is exhaustively correlative to the differentiations within the Godhead."[8]

If there were no *formal differentiations* within God, as with Allah, the Aristotelian Unmoved Mover, and the god behind pantheism, then God would become pure unity without any diversity at all. In fact, as pointed out in the last chapter, unitarian monotheism, in all of its forms, is reducible to monistic pantheism.

The Solution for Divine Revelation

Furthermore, if there are no differentiations within God, then there cannot be any differentiations within the mind of God. Consequently, without God being able to distinguish between His various thoughts and attributes, then, as in monistic pantheism, God would be utterly unknowable even to Himself.

And if God cannot know Himself, what hope do *we* have of knowing God? If God cannot distinguish His knowledge from any of His acts of power, it would be impossible for Him to reveal Himself to man. For instance, what does it mean to say that God is love if God's love is identical to God's omniscience? What would God's omniscience mean if it was one and the same with God's hatred? Terms describing God would cease to mean anything if they can mean everything. Thus, if God's knowledge of Himself was restricted to a single attribute, then our knowledge of Him would be no knowledge at all.[9] Without

---

[8] Cornelius Van Til, *An Introduction to Systematic Theology*, 2nd ed., William Edgar (Philipsburg, NJ: P&R, 2007), 273.

[9] B. A. Bosserman explained: "Unitarian theologies...succumb to a stultifying sort of mystery where god is identical with, or subject to, an ineffable void, that renders him incapable of speaking altogether, or of speaking with authority. For, nothing can be accurately predicated of a strictly unitary deity, since the multiplicity involved in predication is at odds with his nature. If such a being were to enjoy negative definition as he exists in contrast to the created sphere, it

distinctions within God, says Calvin, "only the bare and empty name of God flits about in our brains, to the exclusion of the true God."[10]

Commenting on this, the Princeton theologian B. B. Warfield (1851-1921) remarked: "According to Calvin, then, it would seem, there can be no such thing as a monadistic God; the idea of multiformity enters into the very notion of God."[11] In this, Calvin understood that for God to reveal Himself to man, He must be tripersonal. Only a God whose diversity is *equally ultimate* with His simplicity is a God that can be known.

Jonathan Edwards also rooted divine revelation in the doctrine of the Trinity. According to Edwards, God is a *communicative* being. Expounding upon Edwards' view, William Schweitzer writes: "In asserting that God is a communicative being, Edwards is referring to a logically and temporally prior theology whereby God is inherently communicative *ad intra* (i.e., internally) among the persons of the Godhead." [12] That is, although the economic Trinity communicates to man and angles *ad extra* (i.e., externally), God's essential communicativeness is not dependent upon man or angels or anything else outside of Himself. This is because, ontologically speaking, the Father communicates to the Son, and the Son and the Father communicate to the Spirit. In this, communication is essential to the very nature of God.

Therefore, the economic Trinity is able to communicate *ad extra* (i.e., externally) to man, only because the ontological Trinity communicates *ad intra* (i.e.., internally) with Himself. The Father,

---

would only demonstrate his dependence on the temporal universe in order to enjoy the sort of differentiation, purpose, and relationship that he lacks in himself" (The *Trinity and the Vindication of Christian Paradox*, 101).

[10] Calvin, *Institutes*, 1.13.2.

[11] B. B. Warfield, "*Calvin's Doctrine of the Trinity*," Works of Benjamin B. Warfield (Grand Rapids: Baker Books, 2003), 5.191.

[12] William M. Schweitzer, *God is a Communicative Being: Divine Communicativeness and Harmony in the Theology of Jonathan Edwards* (London: T&T Clark, 2012), 17.

Son, and Holy Spirit love, enjoy, and glorify each other by revealing themselves to one another, communicating to one another, and sharing themselves with one another. And it is only because they are inherently able to communicate and share themselves with each other like this that they are intrinsically able to communicate and share themselves with us, who are made in the image of God.

In other words, divine communication is possible because God is triune. As all three persons of the Godhead are involved in the process of communication: The Father reveals the Son (Matt. 16:17), the Son reveals the Father (John 14:6), and the Spirit reveals the Father and the Son (1 Cor. 1:30). Each person finds pleasure in revealing the glory of the other persons. Hence, we can know God because God is triune – something that could not be said about a monistic deity.

The Solution for Thoughts & Emotions

Also, a multi-personal God is required for a God who can differentiate between His different attributes, thoughts, emotions, and acts. Only a multi-personal God can have a *will of decree* and *a will of command* that allows Him to be both impassibly at peace in regard to the grand scheme of things and emotionally grieved in regard to particular sinful acts as they transpire in history. Like a 1,000 piece jigsaw puzzle that can either be fully constructed into a single picture or broken apart into its individual pieces, God is able to see all of history at one glance and also examine each singular event separately. When He considers the complete historical picture, He is eternally happy. He is impassibly satisfied with the outworking of His *will of decree* because ultimately, all things are working together for His glory as planned. And while God is able to examine single pieces of the puzzle independently from the whole, and be grieved accordingly, He is also able to be angry with those who transgress His *will of command* because in those temporal moments He ceases to be glorified.

God's essence does not change, but this does not mean that He does not have particular opinions/judgments about things that do change. The English puritan Stephen Charnock (1628-1680) understood that a display of changing emotions is not only consistent with the immutability of God but is required:

> God is not changed, when of loving to any creatures he becomes angry with them, or of angry he becomes appeased...God always acts according to the immutable nature of his holiness, and can no more change in his affections to good and evil, than he can in his essence... Though the same angels were not always loved, yet the same reason that moved him to love them, moved him to hate them. It had argued a change in God if he had loved them always, in whatsoever posture they were towards him.[13]

Consequently, God can be grieved after the fall of man and be appeased by the atoning work of Christ on the cross because He, who controls time, can differentiate between time related events.

The Solution for Relationships

The differentiation within the Trinity is also what allows God to be personal and relational in His nature. God did not have to take on relational properties when He created man; rather, He is eternally and inherently relational. Hence, without any change taking place in His nature, He is capable of personally interacting with those whom He created in His own likeness.

The Solution for a Separate Universe

The ontological differentiation between the Father, Son, and Spirit is as vital as God's oneness. The ontological differentiation within God is vital in keeping the essence of God from becoming

[13] Stephen Charnock, *The Existence and Attributes of God* (reprint, Grand Rapids: Baker, 1996), 1:345.

conflated with the universe. This is because the *equal ultimacy* of God not only allows for diversity-in-unity, but it also explains why an immutable God was able to create a distinct universe out of nothing (*ex nihilo*) at a particular point in time.

Aristotle believed that motion (e.g., the pure motion of the stars) was eternal, for every act of motion within the universe must be caused by a previous act of motion, which must be indefinite. Though motion is infinite, there must be a prime mover to prevent the logical inconsistency of an eternal regression. The solution, according to Aristotle, is that motion is the eternal effect of the eternal Unmoved Mover – making the unmovable God and the forever moving universe coeternal and coessential.

Aristotle was right – motionlessness and motion must both be eternal. There is no way around this. For instance, if *motionlessness* (i.e., an Unmoved Mover) was not eternal, then we would be left with an eternal regression of causes with no explanation of what or Who set off the first cause. On the other hand, if *motion* was not eternal, then motion would not be essential to God's nature. And if motion was not essential to God's nature, then God would depend upon something outside of Himself to move and act. And if God was immobile and unable to exert acts of volitional power, then He could not have created a temporal universe out of nothing. So, motionlessness and motion must both be eternal.

But how can both realities be eternal without God and creation being coeternal and coessential? How can an unmovable God create something temporal if creating the universe requires an act of movement within God? How can God be unmovable, yet capable of moving Himself to create? How do we have a God who is above time and space, but is not locked out of time and space? How do we have a God that is immutable to time-bound events, but is also able to carryout time-bound events, such as creating and governing the universe?

The only solution is found in the triune God of the Bible. God is immutable without being restricted to a static and motionless state. This is because God is one in His essence and three in His persons. He is unchanging in His essence (which safeguards us from open theism).[14] However, in this immutable and eternal state of perfection, the Father, as a distinct person, is intrinsically and internally (*ad intra*) moved to love and glorify the Son, and likewise the Son and the Spirit are moved to love and glorify the Father. They each are incited to share, communicate, give, love, and glorify the other by the infinite worth that they consistently see in the other. They are in an eternal state of *interacting* and sharing their glory with each other. That is, within the Godhead there is an eternal state of movement (i.e., interaction) between

---

[14] The proponents for open theism, such as Richard Rice, Clark Pinnock, and John Sanders, may say that God is unchanging in His essence, but they undermine their claim by making the *diversity* of the tripersonal relationship of the Godhead ultimate over the *oneness* of His unchanging essence. That is, the *oneness* of God's essence ends up being at least partially absorbed into the *diversity* of God's tripersonal interaction within creation. By elevating the *diversity* of God over the *oneness* of God, God's sovereignty, omnipotence, and omniscience no longer remain immutable. God's knowledge, emotions, and power become limited to the multiplicity of things taking place outside His being. Rather than being immutably closed, God is open to change. Rather than the Almighty controlling all things, He is more of a powerful demigod. He is able to properly adjust His plans as needed, but remains restricted to the diverse whims and decisions of man. His knowledge is dependent on creation.

The trinitarian God, however, is able to interact with creation in a personal and imminent way because He is inherently able to differentiate between things within Himself and things outside of Himself. Because *diversity* is essential to His nature, God is able to distinguish between His thoughts, emotions, acts, and time related events. Yet, He remains transcendent and separate from creation because His *unity* is also equally essential to His nature. Because He is able to differentiate between His will of decree and His will of command, He is able to providently and emotionally interact with creation in a personal way. But, He also knows and sees all things at once. And, ultimately, nothing can cause God to suffer because He knows and controls all things without there being any change within Himself.

In sum, without the *diversity* of the three persons, God's simplicity would lead to pantheism. Conversely, without the *oneness* of God's essence, the relational properties inherent within the Trinity would lead to open theism. Though from different directions, both pantheism and open theism make God dependent on creation. The equal ultimacy of the oneness and diversity of the Trinity is the only safeguard to keep us from falling on either side of the ditch.

the three persons without any change taking place in the unity of God's immutable essence.

The word *automobile* originated from the compound of two French words *auto*, which means *self*, and *mobile*, which means *movable*. Thus, an *automobile* is something that moves itself. But truly this cannot be said of man-made vehicles that require a driver and fuel. Vehicles don't move themselves. Strictly speaking, the word *automobile* applies only to God. Only the triune God is autonomously self-moving. Unlike Aristotle's Unmoved Mover, the God of the Bible does not need the universe as a vehicle of movement. God is not dependent on anything outside of Himself. God is not cemented in an immovable state, for He can act, move, create, and do as He pleases.

To think, to love, to share, to communicate, and to act are all intrinsic abilities within a triune God. Because the triune God is not restricted from having acts of motion within Himself, creating and governing a universe that is separate and bound to time is not an impossibility. Creation does not have to be eternal. Although God is not bound by time and space, He is not locked out of time or space either. The God of the Bible is Lord of time and space as He is personally ever-present in all the particular affairs of this world.[15] In short, because the three persons of the Trinity interact internally (*ad intra*) with one another, the Godhead was able to create externally (*ad extra*) a temporal universe out of nothing at a particular moment in time.

---

[15] And according to Michael Reeves, love was "the motive behind creation" (*Delighting in the Trinity*, 47). For His own glory, God chose to share His love with His people. Or as Jonathan Edwards worded it: "God's end in the creation of the world consists in these two things, viz. to communicate himself and to glorify himself. God created the world to communicate himself, not to receive anything" (Jonathan Edwards, *Approaching the End of God's Grand Design*, 1743-1758, ed. Wilson H. Kimnach. vol. 25 of *The Works of Jonathan Edwards*. New Haven: Yale University Press, 2006., 116).

The Solution for God and Time

This brings us to one of the most difficult questions of theology: What is God's relationship to time? If time is *the measurement of movement*, then God's relationship with time is unlike our relationship with time.

We are restricted by time because *movement* exists independent of our own existence. We can't slow down the rotation of the earth or speed it up. Time ticks at the same rate regardless of how we feel about it. Moreover, *movement* changes us. We grow from young to old, with our bodies changing along the way. The older we become, the more we realize that our lives are slipping away from us. And there is nothing we can do about it. In short, we are bound to time because our existence is bound to *causation* or *movement* outside of our control.

God, on the other hand, is not moved or changed by any external causation or movement. This is because there is no causation or movement outside of God's control. The causation within a solar system or the falling sand within a hourglass do not move (or even exist) independently from God's will and power. Because God's ontological existence stands independent of any external movement, His nature cannot be changed by movement or time. With this in mind, God's nature is timelessly changeless.

The timeless and immutable nature of God, however, does not mean that God is restricted from moving Himself. Even though God cannot be moved or changed by external causes, He can internally move Himself in accordance with His immutable nature. This is because *motion* – all motion – occurs directly or indirectly by the power of God who does all things according to His predetermined counsel. As we have seen, God is capable of temporal acts of power (i.e., creating and governing the universe) because *movement* is inherent within His multi-personal existence.

So then, God's relationship with time must be understood in light of His triune nature. While God is changeless in the *singularity* of His immutable nature, the interaction between the *plurality* of the divine persons is not static. In other words, God can be *both* timelessly changeless within His unified essence *and* capable of moving Himself due to the inherent interaction between the three divine persons.

Thus, time, as with movement, is neither something that exists independently of God nor is it something that restricts God. Rather, both time and movement are ultimately controlled by the interaction between the *diversity* of divine persons as they think and act in accordance with the *oneness* of their immutable nature.

The Solution for God's Transcendence and Immanence

A monistic deity, on the other hand, would be completely locked out of time. An atemporal god, such as Allah, has its consequences. The consequence in this case would be that, since a monistic deity cannot display intentional and temporal acts of power, the universe would have to be eternal. That is, seeing that there is a universe, there could not have been a time when there was nothing but God if God was atemporal.

If God is bound by timelessness, where did the universe come from? The only possible answer that retains God as Creator is the notion that the universe has always existed as an eternal emanation flowing from the undifferentiated essence of this Unmoved Mover. As light flows from the sun, the universe has to be timelessly flowing out of God. Ultimately, without the Trinity, God and the universe would be one and the same, as light is made of the same stuff as the sun. Consequently, even though an atemporal god would be wholly other in His unknowable transcendence, He would be one with the universe in His ontological immanence. While this is a blatant contradiction, it is the result of a god who is barred from any temporal movement.

This obvious inconstancy, however, is safely resolved with the God of the Bible. With the Trinity there is a clear Creator/creature distinction, since God created the universe out of nothing at a particular point in time. God alone existed before the foundation of the world. There was nothing else but God until God (at a particular point in time) freely and intentionally spoke the universe into existence out of nothing.And because the universe and God *do not* consist of the same ontological substance, God remains transcendent. But He is also immanent because He is not barred from time as He personally interacts with those whom He has made after His own likeness. This *unity* and *diversity* between God and creation is possibly only because there is unity-in-diversity within the Godhead.

Conclusion

Only the trinitarian God of the Bible can be both ultimate and personal. For this reason, the Trinity is the only solution to the ultimate questions of life relating to (1.) *metaphysics*, (2.) *epistemology*, and (3.) *ethics*. *First*, as already pointed out, *metaphysics* is concerned about what is real or ultimate; and only the *equal ultimacy* of unity and diversity within the Trinity can properly explain the eternality of God and the existence of the temporal universe. *Second*, the *epistemological problem* of how we know what we know is exclusively resolved with the triune God of the Bible who is able to reveal Himself to man. As we have seen, all knowledge is rooted in the revelation of God, and only a trinitarian God can reveal Himself to man. *Third*, and finally, *ethics* can only exist if God is inherently personal and relational, which cannot be said of any monistic deity. And because the multi-personal God of the Bible is inherently relational, in Him we have an absolute standard to follow.

Non-trinitarian religions, such as Judaism and Islam, cannot give an account for the 'one and the many,' the distinction between the thoughts and acts of God, a temporal universe, and standards for moral righteousness that are vital for loving relationships. In short, non-trinitarian worldviews cannot coherently tell us (1.) what is real, (2.) how we know that it's real, or (3.) how we should live.[16]

If we don't have a trinitarian God who remains ontologically distinct from creation and who is able to reveal truth to man, then we must conclude that truth, all truth, is impossible to discover. The gist of the argument is that, without anchoring our beliefs in the God of the Bible, *absurdity* is all that remains. Christianity, as it has proven itself to be, not merely supplies the least contradictory worldview available, but truly, it gives the only worldview that is not contradictory. Because the Christian worldview is the only worldview that maintains coherency, it then is logically deducible that it is the one and only appropriate way to perceive Ultimate Reality. Believing in the Bible does not take a blind leap of faith, but rather the opposite – it is the only rational thing to do.

---

[16] Though all non-trinitarian worldviews can be classified into three categories: (1.) naturalism, (2.) impersonal-supernaturalism, and (3) personal-supernaturalism, they are reducible to *absurdity* because they end in the same place – monistic pantheism. Peter Jones, director of truthXchange, rightly states that there are only two overarching worldviews: "One-ism" and "Two-ism." "One-ism," according to Jones, is the belief that all things share the same essence, while "Two-ism" is the belief that God and creation possesses two different essences. As we have seen, even non-trinitarian personal-supernaturalism (i.e., Islam & Judaism) is reducible to monistic pantheism (See Peter Jones, *One or Two*. Escondido, CA: Main Entry Editions, 2010., 17).

PART 5

The Grounds For Belief

Come now, let us reason together, says the LORD:
though your sins are like scarlet, they shall be as white as snow;
though they are red like crimson, they shall become like wool.
Isaiah 1:18

21

Supported by Presuppositionalism

There are three primary and interconnected presuppositions to every worldview, which, as we have already noted, are the answers we give to the God, knowledge, and ethics questions. These are foundational and necessary questions that must be answered. We have also seen how every possible combination of answers to these three ultimate questions are reducible to one of the three overarching worldviews – *naturalism*, *impersonal-supernaturalism*, and *personal-supernaturalism*.

But the problem with *naturalists* and *impersonal-supernaturalists* is that the answer they give to the God question inadvertently undermines any possible answer they can give to the other two questions about knowledge and ethics. Without a personal God who has spoken to man, there is no solid foundation for knowledge or ethics. And if *naturalists* and *impersonal-supernaturalists* have no foundation for their knowledge and ethics, it would be absurd to trust a *naturalist* or *impersonal-supernaturalist's* beliefs about a God they don't know or don't think exists. Such "knowledge" is truly mere subjective though and opinion. Indeed, it is absurd to think they are right about the God question when they have no right to think they are right about anything.

This leaves us with *personal-supernaturalism*, but within this system of thought, only the trinitarian God of the Bible is able to supply us with mutually cohesive answers to life's ultimate questions. This is because a non-trinitarian deity (as we find in Islam and Judaism) logically leads back to an impersonal god that cannot communicate or have any inherently ethical values.

Thus, only when we have the trinitarian God of the Bible do we have grounds for knowledge (how we know what we know) and ethics (how we should live). Only the Christian worldview stands up against the test of logical cohesiveness.

The Transcendental Argument

So it is clear, in order to maintain a cohesive worldview, we must presuppose the God of the Bible, and this brings us to the main thrust of this book – the transcendental argument (a.k.a., *presuppositionalism*), which asks, *what are the necessary preconditions for the existence of knowledge?*

As we have noted throughout the book, logical and ethical absolutes must be presupposed in order to construct a trustworthy worldview. This is why all non-biblical worldviews are inherently flawed – they begin with faulty presuppositions (Part 4). And as we have also showed, logical and ethical absolutes can only be cohesively maintained within the biblical worldview, which shows (1.) divine communication (2.) from a personal/trinitarian God (3.) that is directed to those who are ontologically distinct from God (4.) but also are made in His likeness.

Divine Communication

We need a God who is capable of communicating to us, for without divine communication, there is no grounds for logical and ethical absolutes, and without absolutes, the absurdity of nihilism and relativism is all that remains.

Because *naturalism* begins by ruling out any form of divine intervention, supernatural communication is not even a consideration. *Impersonal-supernaturalism* is also unable to supply the necessary preconditions for knowledge and ethics because *impersonal-supernaturalism* says God and the universe consist of the same ontological stuff – God becomes one with nature and ceases to be personal. Without a personal God who can communicate, as with naturalism, *impersonal-supernaturalism* leaves finite man completely to himself (in a closed universe) to vainly search for objective meaning that is nowhere to be found.

A Trinitarian God

As indicated above, for divine communication to be possible, we need a personal God, but, as chapters 18-20 show, the only way for an Ultimate Being to be both *ultimate* and *personal* is for Him to be multi-personal.

The Ultimate Being must be both one and many for Him to be a communicable being. For instance, without *unity*, there would cease to be any one thing that was Ultimate. Without *diversity*, there would cease to be any formal differentiation within God, which would hinder God from distinguishing between things and communicating accordingly. Thus, only the trinitarian God of the Bible, who is both *one* and *many*, meets the necessary preconditions for divine communication.

A Creator/Creature Distinction

Another necessary precondition for divine communication is the Creator/creature distinction. This is because when *unity* is ultimate, as with Islam and Judaism, everything is reducible to pantheism. Because pantheism destroys the possibility of divine communication, as we have seen in chapter 19, Islam and Judaism cannot *consistently* give an account for divine communication.

The God of the Bible, on the other hand, is capable of speaking not only because He is trinitarian, but also because He is ontologically different from man. God is an eternal and self-existing spirit, while man was made from the dust of the ground, and the dust of the ground was ultimately created out of nothing (*ex nihilo*). This distinction is vital to prevent God and the universe from merging together into one substance. And this ontological distinction must be maintained for God to be both personal and capable of speaking.

An Analogy of Being

There must be a Creator/creature distinction, but there also must be a real point of connection between God and man if communication is to take place.

A link between God and man is possible because *ontology* (i.e., the nature of *being*) cannot be separated from *epistemology* and *ethics* within God's essence. This is because God *is*, in His essential being, epistemologically omniscient and ethically righteous. In other words, God is what He is. As God's ontological existence is the foundation behind everything else that exists, His knowledge is the foundation for epistemology, and His righteousness is the foundation for ethics. God is the standard and measure of all things. Therefore, because God *is* all-knowing and perfectly righteous, it is impossible to disjoin His being/essence (ontology) from His knowledge (epistemology) and from His righteousness (ethics).

This is important to note, because even though man is not made from the same ontological stuff as God, man is made in His epistemological and ethical likeness. What God formed from the dust of the ground, He also made a living soul by breathing the breath of life into him (Gen. 2:7). By this, I believe, man's original righteousness and knowledge of God (i.e., *sensus divinitatis*) was facilitated by the very breath and life of God. God not only created man ethically upright, He implanted within man the epistemological knowledge of Himself. Unlike the animals, man shares the communicable attributes of God. Because of this, there is an *analogy of being* between God and man.

This similarity between them establishes a real link. Being made in the image of God (*Imago Dei*) not only allows for man to know God, but more importantly, it allows for man to have fellowship with God.

It is true that the fall has separated man from the life of God, and that sin has defaced the *Imago Dei* within man, but nonetheless, the knowledge of God and the knowledge of *right-and-wrong* remain stamped on his conscience. Consequently, even with the unregenerate, there remains an analogous relationship – a real point of connection – between God and man.

Fallen man will never love God without being reconciled to God through Christ. As chapters 26 and 27 will show, only the *spiritual illumination* of the Holy Spirit can communicate to fallen man in such a way that they will lovingly embrace the truth of God's existence. This is because spiritual illumination restores the *Imago Dei* within them. By the Holy Spirit spiritually indwelling those whom He illuminates, He effectually imparts the love of God, the righteousness of God, and the (experiential) knowledge of God within them. In this way, the renewed man can personally know God because he has entered into spiritual fellowship with God.

Nevertheless, if there were no *analogy of being*, then God would be ineffable; and if God was ineffable, as explained in chapter 1, communication between God and man would be impossible. For this reason, a real point of connection between God and man is a necessary precondition for divine communication, and this necessary condition is only discovered within the biblical worldview.

Conclusion

Therefore, without logical and ethical absolutes, knowledge – all knowledge – deconstructs. The necessary conditions for logical and ethical absolutes are only met by the trinitarian God of the Bible who communicates to those whom He has made in His likeness. The biblical worldview is the only coherent worldview because of the impossibility of the contrary. It is the only coherent worldview because it alone meets the necessary preconditions for logical and moral absolutes.

22

Supported by Cohesiveness

How can an all-benevolent and all-powerful God create a world filled with so much evil? If God is good, why did He not create an eternal and perfect world where evil is impossible? If God wanted, He could have made man eternally good. He could have prevented the fall. He could have prevented all the sorrow, disease, crime, exploitation, slavery, sex trafficking, murders, and war that have plagued the world for all these years. But He didn't. How can this be? How can an all-knowing and all-powerful God still be considered holy if He knowingly created a world such as the one we have – a world full of evil?

The contemplation of this question has caused many to abandon belief in God. The atheism of C. S. Lewis was based on this dilemma: "My argument against God was that the universe seemed so cruel and unjust."[1] This lead John Stuart Mill's father to reject the God of the Bible. As we have already seen in the testimony of Mill:

My father's rejection of all that is called religious belief was not, as many might suppose, primarily a matter of logic and evidence: the grounds of it were moral, still more than intellectual. He found it impossible to believe that a world so

[1] *Mere Christianity*, 45.

full of evil was the work of an Author combining infinite power with perfect goodness and righteousness.[2]

It is true that Lewis abandoned atheism after further contemplation of this dilemma. Lewis realized he had no grounds to judge God as being evil because atheism cannot give account for moral distinctions in the first place.[3] But even so, the dilemma still remains within the Christian worldview – how can a good God create a world full of evil? This is supposedly where the Christian worldview falls apart.

Those who use this argument as a means to undermine Christianity do not realize that the theological solution to the problem is the very thing that saves the Christian worldview from incoherency. The theological answer to this problem is what makes the Bible coherent and perfectly compatible with science.

The naturalistic worldview only makes room for nature and science, and thus it does not remain consistent with its own presuppositions. Not only is there is no room for moral distinctions and right and wrong in this system, there is no room for any immaterial absolutes. Without immaterial absolutes, there is no room for mathematics and the laws of physics that undergird science. Moreover, the various impersonal-supernaturalist worldviews (such as pantheism, panentheism, monism, and dualism) also confuse the relationship between God and the universe, and thus fail to be cohesive and trustworthy. They, too, cannot properly explain moral injustice and evil without an absolute standard or without blaming God in the process. The power of God and the laws of physics become one and the same. In the end, those holding to naturalism or impersonal-supernaturalism have no grounds to complain about suffering and evil.

[2] Cited in Bertrand Russell, *Why I Am Not a Christian*, 118.
[3] Ibid., 45.

In other words, in non-trinitarian worldviews, there is ultimately no such thing as good or evil. The Christian worldview, on the other hand, makes room for both God and nature, for the supernatural and the natural, for metaphysics and physics, for religion and science, for God and man, and for primary and secondary causes.

The two realms are not confused nor mixed together, for in their relationship with each other, God and the universe remain united but distinct. For this reason, God's supernatural power is perfectly compatible with the laws of nature, and this is the beauty of the Christian worldview. This is what allows it to be consistent with itself. Because of this, God remains perfectly good and all-powerful, while man is fully responsible for his own transgressions. There is an all-powerful and all-benevolent God who will hold man accountable for all the injustice, sorrow, and crimes that have turned the world upside down.

God is Good

God is good in His nature (Jer. 12:1), His law (Ps. 19:7-11), His works (Ps. 145:17), His judgments (Ps. 119:137), and in His mercies (Rom. 3:21-26). God is good because He seeks His own glory in all things (Col. 1:16-18). Each person of the triune Godhead loves the other persons of the Godhead perfectly. They each place the glory of the others above everything else (John 17:5-32). Because nothing is greater than God's glory, for God to be good He must seek His own glory above all things. To not glorify the most glorious being is to come short of the glory of God. Each of the three persons of the Godhead seeks to glorify the others. God loves humanity, but not above His own glory – this is why God is good.

Motives matter, even in God. Everything that God does is good because everything He does is done for His own glory. The chief motive behind every action of the Father, Son, and Holy

Spirit is to glorify one another. God created the universe for His own glory, "All things were created through Him and for Him" (Col. 1:16). He saves sinners for His own glory (Isa. 43:7; Eph. 2:6-7). And He answers our prayers for His own glory (John 14:13). Even sin is permitted because it will indirectly bring glory to God (Ps. 76:10). So, when we think about God's goodness, we must remember that His goodness is not principally derived from His love for man (though He does love man), but from His love for Himself, or otherwise God would cease to be good.

God is All-Powerful

In addition to being good, God is omnipotent. He is absolutely sovereign. He controls everything – from the number of hairs on each of our heads (Matt. 10:30) to the timing of each little sparrow that falls from the sky (Matt. 10:29). He controls the rise and fall of the nations of the world and the rise and fall of the birds of the air (Dan. 2:21). God appoints when and where each of us is born into this world (Acts 17:26); and He determines when each of us will depart from this world (Heb. 9:27). He tells the sea where it can go and where it can go no further (Job 38:11). He clothes the lilies of the field, and He feeds the mouths of the lions in the wilderness (Luke 12:27; Ps. 104:21). He controls the hearts of all men, for even the king's heart is in the hands of the Lord, and He turns it where ever He wishes (Pr. 21:1). He hardens whom He wants to harden and shows mercy on whom He wants to pardon (Rom. 9:18). Not one blade of grass is blown about in the wind without being obedient to God's eternal and predetermined counsel.

God determines everything that takes place in history, for His counsel shall stand. No one can say to Him, "What are you doing?" (Dan. 4:35). For does not the potter have the right to do what He wants with His own clay (Rom. 9:21)? Does a hammer have the right to say to Him who wields it, "don't swing me here or there" (Isa. 10:15)? Of course not. He is God and He does all things according to His own pleasure (Ps. 115:3; Eph.1:11). God would cease to be God if He ceased to be in control of all things.

God's sovereignty ensures that everything works together for His own glory. Though not all acts in-and-of-themselves, such as sin, bring glory to God, they do work together to accomplish a greater purpose. Everything, including Adolf Hitler and the terrible crimes of Lenin, Stalin, and Pol Pot, will bring praise to God, or otherwise God would not have orchestrated such calamities. Man's wicked plans will all be thwarted and turned around before it is all said and done, so that the name of the all-wise, all-good, and all-powerful God will be exalted. Anything less than an all-powerful God could not bring all things, including evil, to a glorious conclusion.

Compatibility

But, this brings us back to our alleged dilemma — if God is good and sovereign, how is He not responsible for all the evil in the world? We must also remember that within the Christian worldview, God is both transcendent and immanent. Unlike pantheism, God is not one with the universe. If that was the case, then evil could be directly assigned to the actions of God. Conversely, unlike deism, God has not abandoned or left the universe to itself — where evil has no greater purpose. This would make God negligently irresponsible.

Only the biblical worldview has the answer to why there is evil in the world. Because God is in control of all things, evil works together with all the other events in history for the glory of God and the good of those who love Him (Rom. 8:28).

According to the Scriptures, God does not control all things directly. He controls the universe, but He is not one with the universe. He has delegated and invested a measure of His power into nature itself. The physical universe is established with the laws of nature; and humans have been endowed with the power and volition to choose between right and wrong. In other words, God controls the laws of nature and the free actions of men, but He is not one with these things. God has created the universe to operate in an orderly and precise fashion, and He has created man to operate in accordance with his human nature. As gravity does what gravity does, and dogs do what dogs do, so men will act the way men act. Nature will function according to its established laws, and creatures – including humans – will function according to their established natures.

So, according to the Scriptures, God governs all things according to His own counsel and purpose but does so in a way that does not violate the laws of nature and the volition of man. As the American-Dutch theologian Louis Berkhof (1873-1957) explains, "In the physical world He has established the laws of nature, and it is by means of these laws that He administers the government of the physical universe."[4] Thus, the direct power of God and the indirect powers of nature cooperate and work together without mixture and confusion. God and the laws of nature (religion and science) are not one and the same, but they are perfectly compatible with each other. Theologically, this is known as *concurrence*, which Berkhof defines as follows: "Concurrence may be defined as the cooperation of the divine power with all subordinate powers, according to the pre-established laws of their operation, causing them to act and to act precisely as they do."[5]

Though God has overruled the laws of nature on a few special occasions, as when He caused an axe head to float on water (2 Kings 6:6), He typically and almost always utilizes the laws of nature to carryout His purposes. This frees God from being morally responsible for evil, but it also prevents evil from undermining and thwarting His eternal purposes. Moreover, this

---

[4] Louis Berkhof, *Systematic Theology* (Grand Rapids: Eerdmans, 1994), 175.
[5] Ibid., 171.

means that man is not a machine; the impersonal laws of physics do not determine his will. "The divine activity," according to Berkhof, "accompanies the action of man at every point, but without robbing man in any way of his freedom."[6] This means that God is sovereign and man is responsible.

Man was originally created innocent, but due to his own will, he fell from his original state (Ecc. 7:29). For this reason, God is not the author of sin, for evil is derived from the heart of man (Jam. 1:13-14). Man is responsible for departing from God. Though God permitted it, in no way did God push, tempt, or incite man to leave his original position of innocence.

Once man chose to leave his original upright state, his original nature was defaced. He was made in the image of God, but this image was marred when he no longer loved God with all of his heart. He no longer could love God because He no longer wanted to love God – love of self was now the dominant factor in man's heart.

Man remained *free* to do what he wanted to do, but this also means that he was *bound* to do only what he wanted to do. Because man had become enslaved to his own sinful nature, it was impossible for him to please God (Rom. 8:5). As a polluted spring cannot produce fresh water or a bad tree bear good fruit, a depraved man will not love God above himself. As the leopard cannot change his spots, a selfish man will never surrender all to God (Jer. 13:23).

On his own, man has forsaken God, and now man can never come to God on his own. Fallen man always moves away from God's glory. Because even man's best acts are *not* done for the glory of God, God considers these acts as sinful (Rom. 3:23). Just as methamphetamine pulls the addict deeper into the addiction, self-love draws depraved souls deeper into selfish and sinful

6 Ibid., 173.

behavior. Down, down, down man spirals out of control. As gravity pulls objects downward, man's heart pulls him away from God.

Though selfishness pulls man away from God, God remains in control over the selfishness of men. Man's nature pulls him downward, but only to the level or degree God allows. As padlocks and law enforcers prohibit many crimes from taking place, God has sovereignly placed many external restraints upon the human race to prevent society from nose-diving completely out of control. Man's conscience, the structure of the family, governments, social acceptability, police officers, and many other such things keep depravity in check. God controls the restraints, and thus indirectly controls the degree to which man is able to fall into sin.

Only in judgment does God remove His restraining hand and give people over to themselves. His righteousness is revealed from heaven each time He hands people over to their own lawlessness (Rom. 1:18). As Paul explained, the consequence of sin is God removing His outward restraints and giving man over to his own sinful desires. Isaiah understood this as well. In his prayer to God, Isaiah cried out: "There is no one who calls upon your name, who rouses himself to take hold of you; for you have hidden your face from us, and have made us melt in the hand of our iniquities" (Isa. 64:7).

Thus, sin is the just punishment for sin. If we don't want to live for God, then God justly takes a step back from us and leaves us to our own devices. Because of sin, God gives us what we want – more sin. God does not push us into sin; He simply turns us over to our desires and down we go on our own accord. We sin freely and willingly. The further we travel down the path of unrighteousness, the more God gives us over to ourselves (Rom. 1:24, 26, 28). There is no end to where sin will take us. And, left alone, we will never seek after God but will only move further and further away from Him (John 6:44).

Because sin comes from within our own hearts, we are fully responsible; because God controls the restraints and nothing occurs without His permissive will – including sin. Moreover, because He is good, He only allows that which will bring Him glory (Ps. 76:10). Thankfully, there is not one random sin that will not be utilized for good. Thus, God remains sovereign over sin, while we remain fully responsible.

God's sovereignty and man's responsibly can be seen in every act of evil, but they are most clearly revealed in the greatest evil that has ever taken place in the history of mankind – the death of Jesus. The Apostle Peter had the boldness afterwards to look at the Jews and say, "this Jesus, delivered up according to the definite plan and foreknowledge of God, you crucified and killed by the hands of lawless men" (Acts 2:23).

This is an amazing accusation, for Peter acknowledged that Christ was the Lamb slain before the foundation of the world when he said that Christ was "delivered up according the definite plan and foreknowledge of God." With this acknowledgment, why didn't Peter blame God for the death of Christ? How can Peter claim that God ordained the death of Christ, and then turn around and blame the Jews for murdering Him when he said, "you crucified and killed by the hands of lawless men"? In other words, how can God be good and allow such evil – the most evil act of all – to occur?

Does this not make God evil and the Christian worldview incoherent? No, not at all. For the answer is found in the different motives and reasons behind God's actions and man's actions. On God's part, He ordained the death of His only Son out of love for His people and for the sake of upholding His own righteousness. God was executing His justice for sin when He poured out His wrath on Christ on the cross. Therefore, God cannot be charged with murder or with guilt, for God's purpose was to condemn sin and uphold His own moral law. God was making sure His goodness and justice were upheld while providing salvation for guilty sinners. This is glorious. The eternal purpose of God in sending His Son to die for sinners is what brings glory and praise to Himself. The Jews, on the other hand, did not have such pure motives when they handed Christ over to be executed by the Romans. They murdered Him. They did not seek either justice or God's glory, for they were acting out of envy and hatred (Mark 15:10).

So in this one single act in history we can observe the sovereign hand of God and the free actions of men taking place without mixture and confusion. The Jews committed sin while God punished sin. As when Joseph's brother sold him into slavery in order to carry out God's purpose of saving many people from starvation, what the Jews meant for evil, God meant for good (Gen. 50:20). In this way, we see God sovereignly governing all things – even the evil acts of men – for His own glory and for the good of those who love him (Rom. 8:28). When God removes His restraints, He does so out of justice, but when man falls into sin, they are fully culpable.

To be upset with God for all the evil, suffering, and death in the world does not make sense when we are the one's responsible. It does not make sense to be upset with God when it was He, the offended party, who willingly took on human flesh and personally endured evil, suffering, and death. If anyone did not deserve to suffer and die, it was Christ. It does not make sense to be upset with the God who bore such evil and suffering so that He could recreate a new universe that is free from all evil, suffering, and death. It does not make sense to be upset with God for allowing such evil, suffering, and death to exist all the while not being willing to forsake the very sins that causes such evil, suffering, and death. In sum, it does not make sense for the unjust to accuse the only one who is just with injustice.

Conclusion

Consequently, if there is anything good or praiseworthy in the universe, then the glory belongs to God alone. We only have ourselves to blame for the corruptions and cruelty that have permeated the human race throughout the history of the world. Thus, both God's sovereignty and man's volitional freedom prevent the world from being meaningless. Only within the biblical worldview are the supernatural and natural powers perfectly compatible with each other. Only the biblical worldview saves the world from meaninglessness.

23

Supported by
Reason & Evidence

Because the Christian worldview makes room for the power of God and the laws of nature, it is supported by both natural and special revelation. Because God created the universe, reason and scientific knowledge point back to the God of the Bible, and the God of the Bible perfectly coincides with the laws of logic and the legitimate findings of science.

As we shall see in the following chapter, because of our inherent knowledge of God and the self-verifying nature of Holy Scripture, we do not need rational arguments or empirical evidence in order to believe the gospel of Jesus Christ; but, because the gospel is true, it is verifiable by logical argumentation and historical and empirical evidences.

Supported by Reason

The cosmological, teleological, and ontological arguments are all valid arguments within the Christian worldview.

The cosmological argument says that every cause has an effect, and because nothing in the universe is without motion, the universe must have an outside cause.

The teleological argument says that everything that has a design, such as pocket watches, pocketknives, and pockets themselves, must have a designer. This logically implies that the universe must also have a designer, since it shows signs of design.

The ontological argument is based on the logical principle that something which is greater cannot be produced by something which is lesser.[1] In this context, we would say that something greater than our capacities to conceive could not have initially been conceived by us. For example, we may well be able to imagine the perfect island, which means that our powers of imagination and thinking must be greater than this perfect island. In this case, the perfect island does not have to exist. However, the idea of God, an infinite and supremely perfect being, is too great a thought for a finite and imperfect mind to conceive by its own powers. In other words, if God did not exist, it would be impossible for our finite minds to have created such an infinite and perfect idea in the same way it would be impossible for the Neuschwanstein Castle to have been built out of a single brick.

Within the biblical worldview, in which the knowledge of God, logic, and morality are basic presuppositions, these rational arguments make sense. In fact, as we have sought to demonstrate, the Christian worldview is the only coherent worldview, and it alone passes the test of reason. It is true because of the impossibility of the contrary.

---

[1] This is true concerning René Descartes' version of the ontological argument. Anselm (1033-1109), Archbishop of Canterbury, however, framed the argument this way: "Even the Fool, then, is forced to agree that something-than-which-nothing-greater-can-be-thought exists in the mind, since he understands this when he hears it, and whatever is understood is in the mind. And surely that-than-which-a-greater-cannot-be-thought cannot exist in the mind alone. For if it exists solely in the mind, it can be thought to exist in reality also, which is greater. If then that-than-which-a-greater-cannot-be-thought exists in the mind alone, this same that-than-which-a-greater-cannot-be-thought is that-than-which-a-greater-*can*-be-thought. But this is obviously impossible. Therefore, there is absolutely no doubt that something-than-which-a-greater-cannot-be-thought exists both in the mind and in reality" ("Proslogion" in *Anselm of Canterbury: The Major Works*, Ed. Brian Davis and G. R. Evans. New York: Oxford, 2008., 87-88).

Supported by Scientific Evidence

Because polytheists in ancient Greece confused supernatural power(s) with the laws of nature, they were prone to think that their gods were *directly* behind solar eclipses and other unusual occurrences. Christianity is not polytheistic, however. Christians believe in secondary causes. When atheists critique such thinking (which seems to be their main argument), they are critiquing polytheism not Christianity. In Christianity, God and creation are distinct entities.

Long before the scientific revolution and the discoveries of Copernicus, Galileo, and Newton, Christians understood the teaching of Scripture that the universe operated according to the laws of nature. Augustine of Hippo (354-430), for example, believed that the moon influenced the tides and he accredited solar eclipses to the "fixed laws of the sun's course" rather than to any direct supernatural power. [2] Augustine distinguished Christianity from Greek pantheism in *The City of God* when he upheld the importance of secondary causes.

> We worship that God who has appointed to the natures created by Him both the beginnings and the end of their existing and moving: who holds, knows, and disposes the causes of things; who hath created the virtue of seeds . . . who hath created and governs the most vehement and most violent fire of this world, in due relation and proportion to the other elements of immense nature; who is the governor of all the waters; who hath made the sun brightest of all material lights, and hath given him suitable power and motion . . . Therefore He governs all things in such a manner as to allow them to perform and exercise their own proper movements.[3]

---

[2] Augustine, *The City of God*. Trans. George Wilson and J. J. Smith (Peabody, MA: Hendrickson, 2013), 79.

[3] Ibid., 212.

The God of Augustine was not a god of the gaps – a god that is only needed to explain the unexplainable. God is not needed to fill in the remaining holes of scientific knowledge, which would make Him a god that will be slowly squeezed out of existence as scientific knowledge increases. The God of the gaps is not the God of the Bible. Rather, the God of the Bible is needed to explain why the laws of nature are there in the first place. God explains why there is geometrical structure that governs the laws of nature, and no other explanation can give account for such order.

Christians understand that there is an orderly universe because there is an orderly Creator who upholds the universe in accordance with the laws of nature. As Lennox claimed: "At the heart of all science lies the conviction that the universe is orderly. Without this deep conviction science would not be possible."[4] Lennox went on to cite Nobel Prize-winner in biochemistry Melvin Calvin in his explanation of where this conviction comes from:

> As I try to discern the origin of that conviction, I seem to find it in a basic notion discovered 2,000 or 3,000 years ago, and enunciated first in the Western world by the ancient Hebrews: namely that the universe is governed by a single God, and is not the product of the whims of many gods, each governing his own province according to his own laws. This monotheistic view seems to be the historical foundation for modern science.[5]

In fact, a miracle would cease to be a miracle if Christians did not believe in the laws of science. Since Christians start by presupposing the God of the Bible, they have no problems with belief in supernatural events, such as the miracles and the resurrection of Christ, and they don't have any problem with

[4] *God's Undertaker*, 20.
[5] Ibid.

science either. There is nothing wrong with scientific knowledge. Christians are not at war with science. They are not at war with the laws of nature. Many of the great scientists of the past were devout Christians – Sir Isaac Newton being the chief among them. Christians can thank God for an orderly universe that allows us to learn from our past experiences and helps us to plan for the future. A transcendent and imminent God, whose sovereign rule is perfectly compatible with the laws of physics, provides us with a perfect foundation for all of our empirical and rational knowledge.

Seeing that all truth comes through general and special revelation, scientific and biblical truths are not at odds with each other. That is, as Francis Bacon maintained years ago, the book of God's word is not in conflict with the book of God's works. As Charles Hodge said: "All that the Scriptures teach concerning the external world accords with the facts of experience."[6]

Christianity is not at war with science, nor is science at war with Christianity, according to Richard Swinburne. Swinburne believes the scientific evidence of an orderly universe can *only* be understood when God is presupposed. It is not beyond the realm of science to postulate the existence of something that is unverifiable by sense perception (such as gravity) in order to make sense of the evidence at hand.[7]

For instance, Newton did not discover gravity by observing its immaterial properties. This is because gravity is an invisible force that cannot (in-and-of-itself) be observed. Though Newton could not give any direct empirical evidence for its existence, he concluded that an invisible force, such as gravity, must be presupposed if we are going to make any rational sense of the motions of the planets and objects falling to the earth.

---

[6] Charles Hodge, *Systematic Theology*, Vol. 3, (Grand Rapids: Eerdmans, 1981), 82.

[7] See Richard Swinburne, *Is There a God* (New York: Oxford, 1996), 67.

According to Newton, gravity is the best explanation for the movements of the heavenly bodies. Moreover, once the force of gravity was presupposed, it was possible to locate Neptune prior to its discovery in 1846. By observing the movement of Uranus, astronomers noticed a perturbation at a certain point in its orbit. It appeared that, in addition to the Sun, another large mass was pulling on it. The only hypothesis that could give an account to the irregularity in Uranus' orbit was the gravitational force of an unknown planet. By this means, without any direct sensory confirmation, the existence, basic size, and location of Neptune were predicted.

In the same way gravity is needed to make sense of the motion of the planets, God is needed to make sense of an orderly universe. Newton understood that for science to work there needed to be a God: "Gravity explains the motions of the planets, but it cannot explain who sets the planets in motion."[8]

According to Swinburne, though there is no direct sensory evidence for the existence of an invisible and incorporeal God, the physical evidence of an orderly universe presupposes Him. "The theist's starting-point," according to Swinburne, "is not that we perceive order rather than disorder, but that order rather than disorder is there."[9] What hypothesis can make sense of such order? It is only when we presuppose God that we have an explanation that makes senses. Theism "leads us to expect to find the things which we do find − when we would not otherwise expect to find them."[10] If there is an Intelligent Designer, then the order and design of the universe is what we would expect to find. Again he says: "The hypothesis of theism is a simple hypothesis which leads us to expect these observable phenomena,

[8] "This most beautiful system of the sun, planets and comets," claimed Newton, "could only proceed from the counsel and dominion of an intelligent and powerful Being" (*The Principia*. reprint. Thousand Oaks, CA: Snowball Publishing, 2010., 440).

[9] *Is There a God*, 67.

[10] Ibid., 43.

when no other hypothesis will do."[11] For this reason, Swinburne concluded that God exists: "Because theism satisfies the criteria well, the existence and regular behaviour of material objects provide good evidence for the existence of God."[12]

Likewise, Stephen Meyer explains that *intelligence* is the only scientific explanation for the specified information within living cells.[13] Given the criteria used by historical scientists to explain past events, Meyer asks: "What causes now in operation produce digital code or specified information?"[14] The obvious answer, according to Meyer, is *intelligence*: "Because we have independent evidence – 'uniform experience' – that intelligent agents are capable of producing specified information. Intelligent activity is known to produce the effect in question. The 'creation of new information is habitually associated with conscious activity.'"[15] Yet, according to Meyer, an intelligent mind is not merely an explanation; it's the *only* scientific explanation.

First, there is "no other causally adequate explanation" for the semantic language coded in DNA.[16] "Undirected chemical processes do not produce large amounts of specified information starting from purely physical or chemical antecedents."[17]

Second, the experimental evidence confirms the causal adequacy of an Intelligent Mind."[18]

In biology, where differential survival depends upon maintaining function, selection cannot occur until new functional structures or sequences actually arise. Natural selection cannot select a nonfunctional sequence or structure based upon the 'knowledge' that it may prove useful in the

---

[11] Ibid., 55.
[12] Ibid.
[13] Stephen C. Meyer, *Signature in the Cell* (New York: HarperOne, 2009), 156.
[14] Ibid., 171.
[15] Ibid.
[16] Ibid., 330.
[17] Ibid., 332.
[18] Ibid., 333.

future pending additional alterations...The causal powers that natural selection lacks – foresight and creativity – are attributes of consciousness and rationality, of purposive intelligence.[19]

Third, "intelligent mind is the only known cause of specified information."[20] "Undirected materialistic causes," says Meyer, "have not demonstrated the capacity to generate significant amounts of specified information. At the same time, conscious intelligence has repeatedly shown itself capable of producing such information."[21] With this, Meyer concludes by saying, "Since intelligence is the only known cause of specified information (at least starting from a nonbiological source), the presence of specified information-rich sequences in even the simplest living systems points definitely to the past existence and activity of a designing intelligence."[22]

Conclusion

Alvin Plantinga is right when he says that there is no conflict between science and theism. Natural law and a supernatural Christianity are perfectly congruent. The real conflict, according to Plantinga, is between science and naturalism.[23] We do not need God in order to explain how secondary causes work together within the universe, we need God to explain why there is such a thing as secondary causes in the first place. Why is there an orderly universe which makes science even possible? The evidence points us to the only plausible answer – God.

[19] Ibid., 336, 137.
[20] Ibid., 341.
[21] Ibid.
[22] Ibid., 343.
[23] Alvin Plantinga, "There is superficial conflict but deep concord between science and theistic religion, but superficial concord and deep conflict between science and naturalism" (*Where the Conflict Really Lies*. New York: Oxford, 2012., ix).

24

Supported by Historical Record

Not only is the biblical worldview supported by reason and scientific evidence, it is verified by historical evidence. Christianity is not merely theoretical dogma or a philosophical system of thought, but belief in real life, historical events that took place in time and space. The birth, life, miracles, death, resurrection, and ascension of Christ, which are essential to the gospel, were not secret events done in the darkness. Rather, they were performed in the open. Christ as a historical figure is well documented. The Apostle John gives his own personal testimony of His existence:

> That which was from the beginning, which we have heard, which we have seen with our eyes, which we looked upon and have touched with our hands, concerning the word of life – the life was made manifest, and we have seen it, and testify to it and proclaim to you the eternal life, which was with the Father and was made manifest to us (1 John 1:1-2).

The miracles of Christ, which testified of the divine power and veracity of Christ, were done for all to see. Over 500 people saw Him after He rose from the dead (1 Cor. 15:6). The empty tomb proved He was who He said He was – the Son of God. Not only did Christ Jesus raise Himself from the dead, He taught others about this reality. So if He did not come back to life, then He is truly the biggest fraud who has ever lived. But His closest followers were convinced of His resurrection. His followers were so convinced of His resurrection that they were willing to die for Him – in fact, many of them did lay down their lives for Him. Why would Peter, Paul, and John be willing to die for something they knew was a lie? Christ gained over 8,000 plus followers in just a few months after His resurrection. This seems impossible if the evidence did not substantiate the claims of Christ. Even Saul of Tarsus, who did not want to believe, not only stopped persecuting the followers of Christ, but he became the chief advocate for Christ after seeing the risen Lord.

In *The Resurrection of the Son of God*, N. T. Wright, the former Bishop of Durham, has provided the definitive apologetic on the historicity of Christ's bodily resurrection. All critics of the Easter Story who want to be taken seriously will be forced to interact with this massive and formidable work. After a thorough and almost painstaking review of the ancient literature dealing with the resurrection, from Homer's Hades to the Dead Sea Scrolls, Wright concluded that the Easter Story is not what we would expect if it were merely a fabrication or a later pollution of the original text. At least four unusual details are recorded in the gospel stories that do not make sense if they didn't take place.

"The first surprise," Wright says, "when we read the resurrection stories in the canonical gospels ought to be that they are told with virtually no embroidery from the biblical tradition."[1]

"The second feature of the resurrection narratives which should cause us considerable surprise has also to do with something they lack."[2] Wright explained, "that at no stage do

---

[1] N. T. Wright, *The Resurrection of the Son of God* (Minneapolis: Fortress Press, 2003), 599.
[2] Ibid., 602.

they mention the future hope of the Christian."[3] Almost every time Paul or the other Apostles speak of Christ's resurrection, they link it with the hope of believers overcoming the power of the grave. If the gospels were somehow reworked at a later date (as some have suggested), it is strange that they don't resemble the resurrection stories provided by Paul and Peter.

The third unusual detail is that the gospel stories of the resurrection of Christ are not influenced by any of the important Old Testament resurrection texts. First century Jews believed that those whom God would raise from the dead would come forth from the grave shining brightly as heavenly stars (Dan. 12:2-3). Resurrected bodies were thought to be glittery or shiny. Though this was ancient Jewish belief, the gospels do not depict Christ's resurrection in such a fashion. This is not "the sort of thing one would expect if the evangelists or their sources had wanted to say that Jesus had been exalted to a position of either divinity or heavenly glory."[4]

The fourth detail, which would not have been admitted if the resurrection of Christ were merely made up, is the presence of women at the empty tomb. This is because the testimony of women in that day was not considered valid in a court of law. "It is, frankly, impossible to imagine that they were inserted into the tradition after Paul's day."[5] Wright went on to explain:

> Even if we suppose that Mark made up most of his material, and did so some time in the late 60s at the earliest, it will not do to have him, or anyone else at that stage, making up a would-be apologetic legend about an empty tomb and having women be the ones who find it. The point has been repeated over and over in scholarship, but its full impact has not always been felt: women were simply not acceptable as legal witnesses. We may regret it, but this is how the Jewish world

3 Ibid.
4 Ibid., 605.
5 Ibid., 607.

(and most others) worked. The debate between Origen and Celsus shows that critics of Christianity could seize on the story of the women in order to scoff at the whole tale; were the legend-writers really so ignorant of the likely reaction? If they could have invented stories of fine, upstanding, reliable male witnesses being first at the tomb, they would have done it.[6]

Wright concluded by saying, "If you try to imagine three such people doing it independently and coming up with three different stories which nevertheless all share this remarkable feature, in addition to the others we have noted, I think you will find it incredible. I certainly do."[7] The only apparent reason for the gospels to record these unusual details is the fact that they did indeed occur in history.

Not only are the unlikely details recorded in the gospels, of which the earliest manuscripts date back to the second century,[8] but the life of Christ is testified to by many non-canonical texts, such as the Jewish historian Flavius Josephus (AD 37-120). In the year 93, Josephus published a history of the Jewish people in which he testified of the life of Christ:

> About this time there lived Jesus, a wise man, if indeed one ought to call him a man. For he was one who performed surprising deeds and was a teacher of such people as accept the truth gladly. He won over many Jews and many of the Greeks. He was the Messiah. And when, upon the accusation of the principal men among us, Pilate had condemned him to a cross, those who had first come to love him did not cease. He appeared to them spending a third day restored to life, for the prophets of God had foretold these things and a thousand other marvels about him. And the tribe of the Christians, so

---

6 Ibid., 607-608.

7 Ibid., 610.

8 See Philip Comfort, *Encountering the Manuscripts* (Nashville: Broadman & Holman, 2005), 126-139.

called after him, has still to this day not disappeared.[9]

The Roman historian Cornelius Tacitus (AD 55-120) gave not only an early second century testimony of the life of Christ but a vivid account of the persecution experienced by the followers of Christ when he explained how the Emperor Nero falsely accused Christians of the burning of Rome in AD 64:

> Nero fastened the guilt and inflicted the most exquisite tortures on a class hated for their abominations, called Christians by the populace. Christus, from whom the name had its origin, suffered the extreme penalty during the reign of Tiberius at the hands of one of our procurators, Pontius Pilate, and a deadly superstition, thus checked for the moment, again broke out not only in Judea, the source of this evil, but also in Rome, where all things hideous and shameful from every part of the world meet and become popular. Accordingly, an arrest was first made of all who confessed; then, upon their information, an immense multitude was convicted, not so much of the crime of arson, as of hatred of the human race. Mockery of every sort was added to their deaths. Covered with the skins of beasts, they were torn by

---

[9] *Jewish Antiquities*, 18.3.3 §63 (Based on the translation of Louis H. Feldman, The Loeb Classical Library.) Though this text has been considered as a later Christian interpolation, one of the leading authorities on Josephus, Paul Maier, the Russell H. Selibert professor of ancient history, Western Michigan University, argues for its textual faithfulness: "Josephus must have mentioned Jesus in authentic core material at 18:63 since this passage is present in all Greek manuscripts of Josephus, and the Agapian version accords well with his grammar and vocabulary elsewhere. Moreover, Jesus is portrayed as a 'wise man' [*sophos aner*], a phrase not used by Christians but employed by Josephus for such personalities as David and Solomon in the Hebrew Bible.

Furthermore, his claim that Jesus won over 'many of the Greeks' is not substantiated in the New Testament, and thus hardly a Christian interpolation but rather something that Josephus would have noted in his own day. Finally, the fact that the second reference to Jesus at *Antiquities* 20:200, which follows, merely calls him the *Christos* [Messiah] without further explanation suggests that a previous, fuller identification had already taken place. Had Jesus appeared for the first time at the later point in Josephus's record, he would most probably have introduced a phrase like '...brother of *a certain* Jesus, who was called the Christ'" (Paul L. Maier, "Josephus on Jesus," in *Josephus: The Essential Works.* trans. and ed. Paul L. Maier. Grand Rapids: Kregel, 1994., 284).

dogs and perished, or were nailed to crosses, or were doomed to the flames. These served to illuminate the night when daylight failed. Nero had thrown open his gardens for the spectacle, and was exhibiting a show in the circus, while he mingled with the people in the dress of a charioteer or drove about in a chariot.[10]

According to professor of New Testament studies at Acadia Divinity College, Lee Martin McDonald, even though the historical critical approach (due to its starting presuppositions)[11] cannot verify the divinity of Christ, it does without a doubt substantiate the life of Christ as an historical figure:

> Of course, historians as historians will never be able to affirm the christological affirmations or interpretations about Jesus in the church's earliest documents, but it is important that Christians know their faith in Jesus is not contrary to the available evidence from antiquity.[12]

In addition to the historical record, the overwhelming archaeological evidence, also, supports the reliability of the Scriptures. The ancient history of Northern America as recorded in the Book of Mormon has yet to be substantiated by any archaeological findings. Joseph Smith (1805-1844) apparently included a lot of fiction in his story. Yet, the Bible has not only been proven trustworthy by archaeology, it has proven to be a valuable resource for pointing archaeologists in the right

---

[10] *Annals* (ca. 116-117), 15.44.2-8, trans. J. Stevenson as cited in McDonald, *The Story of Jesus in History and Faith*, 137.

[11] The historical critical approach does not view the original sources as authoritative, for since the post-enlightenment period, historians, like scientists, operate from a naturalistic worldview that denies the possibilities of miracles. Jürgen Moltmann, for instance, says we are to reject miracles even before we investigate the evidence: "In face of the positivistic and mechanistic definition of the nature of history as a self-contained system of cause and effect, the assertion of a raising of Jesus by God appears as a myth concerning a supernatural incursion which is contradicted by all our experience of the world" (Cited in *The Story of Jesus in History and Faith*, 19).

[12] Lee Martin McDonald, *The Story of Jesus in History and Faith* (Grand Rapids: Baker Academic, 2013), 45.

direction. And even when the reliability of the biblical history has been challenged, these challenges have been answered by later archaeological findings. For instance, it was once thought that the Hittites were a biblical legend until their capital and many of their records were unearthed in Bogazkoy, Turkey. The Assyrian king Sargon, who is mentioned in Isaiah 20:1, was also considered fictional until Sargon's palace was discovered in Khorsabad, Iraq. Moreover, the capture of Ashdod, which is mentioned in Isaiah 20, was recorded on the palace walls. These are but a few of the thousands of archaeological evidences that validate the biblical record.

Not only have many of the ancient cities and civilizations of the Old Testament been unearthed, which provide empirical and historical evidence of the reliability of biblical history, the accuracy of the New Testament has also been firmly established by archaeology. James Charlesworth of Princeton Theological Seminary concluded:

> It would be foolish to continue to foster the illusion that the Gospels are merely fictional stories like the legends of Hercules and Asclepius. The theologies in the New Testament are grounded on interpretations of real historical events, especially the crucifixion of Jesus, at a particular time and place.[13]

History is no enemy to the gospel. Historical documents and archaeological evidences confirm, as external witnesses, that Scripture is trustworthy in its historical testimony. Moreover, the historical record verifies that the Scriptures have been faithfully transmitted. Of course there is Bart Ehrman who not only claims that the Greek New Testament text has been corrupted, but that all the extant manuscripts are polluted to the point that it is impossible to reconstruct a trustworthy critical Greek text of the

---

[13] James H. Charlesworth, "The Historical Jesus and Biblical Archaeology: Reflections on New Methodologies and Perspectives" in *Jesus and Archaeology*, ed. James H. Charlesworth (Grand Rapids: Eerdmans, 2006), 694.

New Testament. Ehrman is quick to point out the 400,000 variants within the extant New Testament Greek manuscripts, and how there are no two manuscripts in perfectly agreement with each other.[14]

Yet, Ehrman stands in opposition to the consensus of the community of textual scholars and the overwhelming textual evidence. In fact, no ancient piece of literature can boast of a more faithful transmission than the Scriptures. First, no other ancient book has more extant manuscripts than the New Testament – close to 6,000. Second, no other ancient work has extant manuscripts that are so close to the original *autographs* – P[52] dates between 100-115 AD, and we have a host of *papyri* manuscripts that date back to the 3rd and 4th centuries. Third, of the 400,000 variants, 75 percent are spelling errors, which do not do any damage to the faithfulness of the Greek text. Fourth, another 24 percent of the variants are concerned with word order, but this too does not create much of a problem seeing that the subject of each sentence in the Greek is determined by word endings rather than by word placement. Fifth, that leaves only 1 percent (around 400) of variants that are any importance, yet of those 400 variants, the majority are concerned with minor issues such as gospel *harmonization*. Sixth, only around 15 percent of the 1 percent of variants (about 50) is considered of any major significance, yet there is no doctrinal compromise in any of the variant readings. With such evidence, it is safe to say that the Scriptures have been faithfully persevered throughout history.[15]

Conclusion

The biblical worldview is not supported by the evidence, but as we shall see in the next chapter, it also is the only worldview that can be faithfully implemented in everyday life.

---

[14] See Burt Ehrman, *Misquoting Jesus* (New York: HarperCollins, 2005).
[15] For an introduction to New Testament textual criticism, see my book *Behind the Bible: A Primer on Textural Criticism* (Birmingham: SGCB, 2012).

25

Supported
by Experience

As with the scientific and historical evidence, our present and every day life experiences correspond to the truth claims of the Bible. All we have to do to verify the truth of Scripture is look at the world around us. The Bible says that people are depraved and selfish by nature. This is evident not only when we read our history books and local newspapers, but also when we go Christmas shopping. The spirit of giving has turned into the spirit of receiving. Commercialism, materialism, and greed deck the halls. Selfishness and greed is what we see in others and what we see hidden away in our own hearts.

The Bible is not painting an unrealistic story about humanity. Not only does it explain the origins of sin, but also why people behave the way they behave. And who but Nietzsche is against the golden rule? Who in their right mind is opposed to others loving each other as they love themselves? The Bible reinforces our inherent knowledge of right and wrong, it explains why we come short of this standard, and where our guilt comes from. The way the Bible explains our human nature and the world around us seems to be the way things actually are – a total mess.

Moreover, the Bible tells us that those who are supernaturally born again, though they are not perfected in this life, do have a true love for God and for one another. The love Christians have for each other is evidence that Christ has come to save sinners (John 17:21, 35). Christ followers, those who truly believe, have an observable testimony of a changed life. Believers have been inwardly transformed; this is evident by some who have been converted from various selfish addictions to unselfishly seeking to give all that they have to the service of God (1 Thess. 1:4-10). I don't know if you know any true believers in Christ (not merely professing believers), but if you do, then you cannot help but notice something is different about them.

Likewise, the Lord promised that His followers would be persecuted for their faith (John 15:20). And this is evident not only by the historical accounts, but also by the overall disdain Christians receive when they publicly express their faith before the unbelieving world.

The Practicality of the Christian Worldview

But, most importantly, the Christian worldview is the only worldview that we can implement in our daily lives without intellectually contradicting ourselves in the process. As in the words of Francis Schaeffer:

> The truth of Christianity is that it is true to what is there. You can go to the end of the world and you never need be afraid, like the ancients, that you will fall off the end and the dragons will eat you up. You can carry out your intellectual discussion to the end of the discussion because Christianity is not only true to the dogmas, but it is also true to what is there, and you will never fall off the end of the world![1]

Other worldviews fail at this point. Do postmodern thinkers, who intellectually boast in relativism, walk through walls? Do postmodern thinkers deny the principles of mathematics when balancing their checkbooks? Do they hope their spouses remain

[1] *Trilogy*, 289.

faithful to their wedding vows? Do they look both ways before crossing the street? Do they live as if there is no up or down? Do deconstructionists, those who think language is meaningless, stop speaking? Do they expect the teenager running the register at McDonald's to understand them when placing an order for a Big Mac? Do they buy into the excuse of their sons when they say, "I did not know what you meant when you said, 'You better be home by 12:00 pm.'" Do those in the Far East, who think the law of non-contradiction is only a Western way of thinking, not live by the law of non-contradiction in their everyday life? Do those who practice Zen really expect to hear a sound when they see a one handed man clapping? It is easy to create an intellectual philosophy, but the true test of any system of thought is seeing if it can be implemented and lived out in the real world.

Impossibility of a Total Rejection of the Christian Worldview

Opposing non-Christian worldviews cannot completely separate themselves from the Christian worldview. The knowledge of God, logic, and morality is inherent in all people. These are the core presuppositions behind the Christian worldview. In fact, knowledge of God, logic, and morality exclusively belong to the Christian worldview because only the Christian worldview can give a consistent account for their existence. But there they are. Non-Christians can twist, distort, and intellectually deny these realities, but because they are made in the likeness of God, they cannot completely separate themselves from them. Their very life is a light that they cannot extinguish. They can say they do not believe in any absolutes, but their lives prove their hypocrisy.

Some say that atheists, naturalists, and postmodern thinkers are forced to borrow capital from the Christian worldview to live their lives in the real world, but I think that they are born with these inherent principles within their consciences, and that they must suppress, distort, deny, and misuse these indestructible principles to justify their ungodly lives (Rom. 1:18). In short, man was made for a relationship with a holy God, but man, because of his innate selfishness, no longer desires a relationship with God. Irrational thinking and dysfunctional living are the consequences.

God exists because of the impossibility of the contrary. To make sense of the world around us, we must presuppose God – the personal, transcendent, and imminent trinitarian God of the Bible. God is a necessary condition for knowledge – all knowledge. He is the foundation for everything. As Lewis says: "I believe in Christianity as I believe that the Sun has risen, not only because I see it, but because by it I see everything else."[2] Without the light of God, we remain in the darkness. Knowledge, all knowledge, must begin with God, or otherwise nihilism and absurdity take over everything.

Yet, God has not left man in total darkness, for the knowledge of God has been implanted in all men. God has supplied us with the capacity to know the universe and ourselves because He made us in His image and endowed us with the innate knowledge of Himself. By the light of God, we can see light (Ps. 36:9).

When the knowledge of God is suppressed, however, incoherency is bound to supplant sound thinking. When we seek to cover up the light with the darkness, we are bound to stumble and fall. Some suppress the light of God with hedonistic pleasures and others with complex philosophical or religious beliefs. Regardless, all non-Christian worldviews, such as naturalism and impersonal-supernaturalism, end in absurdity. Only faith in Christ can rescue us from the darkness of our own making.

---

[2] C. S. Lewis, "Is Theology Poetry?" in *The Weight of Glory* (New York: HaperCollins, 2001), 140.

Conclusion

As light testifies of itself, the Bible, by its own internal witness, proves itself to be the Word of God. And it's not just that it says is the Word of God, but that without it, nothing makes sense; knowledge of any kind is ultimately impossible without the God of the Bible. Moreover, the rational, historical, and empirical evidence collaborates the testimony of Scripture. The Christian worldview is simply the only trustworthy worldview because of the impossibility of the contrary. "So the choice is this:" according to John Frame, "either accept the God of the Bible or deny objective morality, objective truth, the rationality of man, and the rational knowability of the universe."[3]

The absurdity of it all is that sinners will continue to choose absurdity over sanity. This is because sanity only comes by submitting one's thinking and life to the lordship of Christ, and this, my dear readers, is the heart of the problem.

[3] *Apologetics to the Glory of God*, 102.

26

Supported
by Revelation

Arguments, evidences, and proofs are not essential for us to either accept or reject the gospel of Jesus Christ.[1] The power and efficacy of the gospel does not consist in superior intellectual reasoning, but in the simple proclamation of the truth (Rom. 1:16). As presented in this book, it is not that the Christian worldview lacks intellectual integrity, but that belief in the gospel is not dependent on any external demonstration of its superiority over opposing worldviews.

Apologetic arguments have their place (for they are helpful in many ways), but they are not necessary in revealing the truthfulness of the gospel. Because the unshakable knowledge of a personal and just God exists within all people, as evidenced by their inward guilt, people are convicted by the truth of the gospel when they initially hear it.

Being made in God's likeness, men, even unregenerate men, have the intellectual capacity to recognize truth when they come into contact with it. The fact that we are all made in God's image

---

[1] John Calvin argued that those "who strive to build up firm faith in the Scripture through disputation are doing things backwards....For as God alone is a fit witness of himself in his Word, so also the Word will not find acceptance in men's hearts before it is sealed by the inward testimony of the Spirit" (*Institutes*, 1.7.4).

is what makes the knowledge of God, self, and the external world possible. This analogous relationship with God gives us the innate knowledge of the laws of thought (logic) and morality (God's law).

Therefore, though the fact that $2 + 2 = 4$ and the "golden rule" are not innate propositional concepts in our brains, they are propositional concepts that ring true once we, as rational beings, become aware of them. We cannot help but believe these concepts because these concepts agree and correspond with what we already innately know to be true – that we are personal beings in ethical relationships with God and with our neighbors. That is, because we all have an innate knowledge of God (which includes the laws of logic and the laws of morality), once $2 + 2 = 4$ and the golden rule are presented to our minds, we cannot help but believe them because they agree with what we already know to be true. The innate knowledge of God is kind of like a tuning fork, for when truth is presented to our minds, it resonates within our consciousness.

And, for those who deny these propositional truths, such as $2 + 2 = 4$, they must do so by denying common sense and suppressing that which is innate and self-evident within their own consciences. In the same way, the gospel is convicting because it corresponds with what we already know to be true. The light of the gospel, therefore, only brings additional responsibility and condemnation to those who hear it. Like light, truth is powerful.

But, when we hear the gospel, we all reject it. Even the best arguments cannot change a rebellious heart. Our problem is that the tuning fork of our heart is bent, since the *Imago Dei* no longer functions properly. It still works well enough for the gospel to bring a measure of certainty and conviction, but it is distorted enough that the gospel does not sound pleasant to our ears. Because of the self-love of our depraved hearts, our ears are out of tune and our eyes our out of focus. The gospel, however, is piercing and sharper than any two-edged sword. It is able to discern the intentions, motives, and thoughts of our hearts (Heb. 4:12). The Word of God speaks to us as if it knows us – as if it can see into our consciences. Even so, we cannot stand the sounds we hear because of the sins that it exposes within us (John 3:20). We know the gospel is true because it is testified by our guilt, but this same guilt causes us to deeply despise it. We hate self-condemnation and conviction. Moreover, our hearts have been distorted by sin to the point where we love ourselves above everything else. Thus, our minds and hearts are no longer in sync with the truth of God's Word.

Submission to the truth demands loving God above ourselves. Yet, if our primary reason for rejecting Christ is our embedded love for ourselves, how can we ever come to a saving knowledge of God? If truth alone is not enough to convince us to lay down our lives and turn to Christ, how will we ever be saved? We must believe to be saved, but how will we ever willingly embrace that which we deplore?

As long as we despise the God of the Bible, we will never freely and willingly surrender all to Him. We all need help. As God haters, we cannot convert ourselves. We need more than a slick pitchman to coach us into superficially repeating the sinner's prayer. The Bible makes it clear that faith and a personal knowledge of Christ come only by God's grace.

The only way we will ever embrace a holy and just God is for God to supernaturally reveal Himself to us as He really is – altogether worthy of all our love and acceptance. God must reveal Himself to our minds in such a way that our hearts perceive Him as altogether glorious. It is not that God must enhance His appearance so that we will like Him better, but He must change our hearts so that we can perceive Him as He truly is. Moreover, we must have help to see ourselves as we truly are – altogether undone and unworthy of the least favor of God. It is only when we see ourselves as deplorable and Christ as lovely that we will come to our senses, repent of our sins, and eagerly embrace what we know to be true. In other words, we who sit in darkness need to be enlightened in both our minds and our hearts. The image of God that has been defaced by sin must be renewed.

Divine Works

This divine revelation of God begins with the universe itself. Natural revelation is from God because God created the universe. This revelation is universal and self-authenticating. Because we are made in God's image, we cannot help but see the stamp of God everywhere we look. "There is no spot in the universe," according to John Calvin, "wherein [we] cannot discern at least some sparks of his glory."[2] For this reason, the English puritan John Owen rightly stated:

> There is no need of traditions, no need of miracles, no need of the authority of any churches, to convince a rational creature that the works of God are his, and his only; and that he is eternal and infinite in power that made them. They carry about with them their own authority. By being *what* they are, they declare *whose* they are.[3]

With this divine source of revelation, we all know (1) that there is a God (Rom. 1:19-20), (2) that He created the universe (Ps. 19:1), (3) that He is absolute (Acts 17:25), (4) that He is infinite (Acts 17:24), (5) that He is sovereign (Acts 17:26), (6) that He is all-powerful (Rom. 1:20), (7) that He is omnipresent (Acts 17:25), (8) that He is imminent (Acts 17:27), (9) that He is righteous (Ps. 97:6), and (10) that He is angry with sinners (Rom. 1:18). Because we are made in the image of God, we inherently

---

[2] *Institutes*, I.V.1

[3] *The Works of Owen* (Edinburgh: Banner of Truth Trust, 1995), Vol. 16, 310-311.

and immediately understand (11) that there is a universal law, (12) that we have broken this law (Rom. 2:15), and (13) that we will be held accountable to a just and angry God (Rom. 1:32). In essence, natural revelation reveals our guilt, leaving us to feel hopeless, as we wait for the coming day of judgment. For this testimony is constant (Ps. 19:2), universal (Ps. 19:3), and undeniable (Rom. 2:15), leaving us without any excuses (Rom. 1:20).

Natural revelation is vital, but it alone is not sufficient to bring us to love the God of the universe. Natural revelation leaves us condemned and guilty before a just God with no hope of salvation. The universe reveals a just and powerful God, but it does not reveal His merciful disposition and willingness to forgive.

Thus, left to ourselves, we will create all manner of religious means to appease God's wrath, or we will craft various philosophies that push the knowledge of God away by the exaltation of ourselves. Because of the false notions of our self-righteousness and autonomy, we will continually think too highly of ourselves and of our own abilities to seek after God. Natural revelation is vital, but it is not sufficient in bringing one to repentance and faith.

Divine Words

Because of our pride, we need special revelation. Broadly speaking, all of God's acts within history are considered a part of God's special revelation. But more narrowly speaking, special revelation is restricted to those historical acts of God, divine prophecies, and truths that have been recorded for us in the pages of Scripture. The Scriptures reveal the merciful disposition of God towards us in the gospel message that He sent His only Son to die for our sins – the just for the unjust. This is the goodness of God that leads sinners to repentance.

Just as natural revelation does not need any external proofs to verify its message, the Holy Scripture, because it is inspired by God's Spirit, needs no external argument, proof, or evidence to verify its infallible and authoritative nature. The Bible is self-sufficient and self-authenticating.

The veracity of Scripture does not stand on the approval of men, ecumenical councils, or churches, but on its own divine testimony. It does not even need apologists.

Not only does the Bible claim to be God's Word (1 Cor. 2:12-13, 2 Tim. 3:16, 2 Pet. 1:20), but it also handles itself as if it is God's Word. It speaks to us as if it is authoritative and infallible. As God's Word, the Scriptures demand belief and obedience in the same way God demands belief and obedience. "The authority of God shining in them," Owen claimed, "afford unto us all the divine evidence"[4] that is needed. In other words, the Bible proves itself to be the Word of God by its own internal evidence.

If the Scriptures prove themselves to be God's Word, why is it that so many reject the gospel? Why would any of us want to reject such good news? It is not as if the gospel is too complicated for us to understand. According to Owen, one "only possessed of reason and the ability to use it according to the measure of [one's] talents, can (without the aid of the Holy Spirit) discover the sense of the biblical propositions and grasp their signification."[5]

In fact, I would go as far as to say that the written Word of God brings a measure of conviction to all who hear it. It opens us up and exposes us for who we are. It shows us our sins and reinforces our guilt.

---

[4] *The Works of Owen* (Edinburgh: Banner of Truth Trust, 1995), Vol. 16, 307.
[5] *Biblical Theology*, 606.

Even those who are spiritually dead and incapable of loving the truth, cannot help, because they are made in God's image, but feel convicted by the truth when they hear it. For this reason, God will hold those of us who have heard the gospel to a greater accountability. None of us will be able to say to the Lord on the Day of Judgment, "I just did not realize that it was You speaking to me." Morcover, as we have already seen, the truth claims of the Bible are not rejected because the gospel is rationally incoherent or unsupported by historical evidence. Rather, the truth is rejected because the unchanged heart remains in love with the false notion of its own moral self-righteousness and/or intellectual autonomy.

The problem is that the wrong things are loved and hated because sin blinds. As Alvin Plantinga claimed: "Sin is a malfunction of the will, a skewing of affections; it is loving and hating the wrong things. Still, it also involves blindness, and inability to see the glory and beauty of the Lord."[6] This world and self are loved too much to be given up. It is for this reason that one remains spiritually dead and unwilling to embrace the gospel. It may be known that Christ is Who He says He is, but you may not be convinced that you like Who He says He is.

Though death is approaching, Esau's soup tastes too good for unbelievers to be overly concerned about eternity. The gospel is for those who know themselves to be sinners and see their need to be saved from their sins (1 Tim. 1:15). It seems the majority simply have no desire to be rescued from that which is slavishly loved – themselves.

Conclusion

Subsequently, all the apologetic arguments can be laid out with absolute certainty, and, as the Lord says, a man could even be raised from the dead, but because of our disdain for the gospel

---

[6] Alvin Plantinga, *Warranted Christian Belief* (New York: Oxford, 2000), 303.

that calls us to forsake all, we will stubbornly refuse this wonderful offer. For this reason, Jonathan Edwards says, "no signs that can be given will actually satisfy persons in such a case; let the signs that are given be never so good and infallible, and clearly laid down, they will not serve them."[7] Logical consistency, various proofs, and evidence are simply not enough to break a hard heart – something more is needed.

---

[7] Jonathan Edwards, *The Religious Affections* (Edinburgh: Banner of Truth Trust, 1994), 122.

27

Supported
by Illumination

Because of our spiritually dead state, we will continue to reject Christ until the Holy Spirit quickens our hearts and minds. We will not run towards Christ until the darkness is removed and we can see clearly. This is why spiritual illumination is needed.

Divine Light

Spiritual illumination is the influencing power of the Holy Spirit working by, in, and through the Scriptures to give light and spiritual understanding to the minds and hearts of God's people, which enables them to willingly believe, embrace, and obey the truth of God's Word. Thus, the testimony of the Holy Spirit is not a new revelation (independent of Scripture), but the Holy Spirit speaking in the words of Scripture.[1]

Spiritual illumination never goes beyond the truth presented in the text. It is the *written* Word that the Spirit uses to open the hearts of our understanding. When this occurs, believers know

---

[1] Edward Young claimed that Illumination "is not the communication to us of information beyond what is contained in the Bible. It is not the impartation of new knowledge. It is not a new revelation from God to man. It is rather that aspect of the supernatural work of the new birth in which the eyes of our understanding have been opened so that we, who once were in darkness and bondage of sin, now see that to which formerly we had been blind" (*Thy Word is Truth*. Edinburgh: Banner of Truth Trust, 1963., 34).

for certain that they are hearing God personally speak to them in the pages of Scripture (Luke 24:45, 1 Thess. 2:13-14).[2] Because of the testimony of the Spirit speaking to us in the truth claims of Scripture, the Scriptures are self-authenticating. As Calvin explained:

> Those whom the Holy Spirit has inwardly taught truly rest upon Scripture, and the Scripture indeed is self-authenticated; hence, it is not right to subject it to proof and reasoning...For even if it wins reverence for itself by its own majesty, it seriously affects us only when it is sealed upon our hearts through the Spirit...We seek no proofs, no marks of genuineness upon which our judgment may lean; but we subject our judgment and wit to it as to a thing far beyond any guesswork![3]

But let us not be confused, spiritual illumination is not the Spirit empowering the Scriptures (as if they are mere dead words), but the Spirit enlightening the minds and hearts of believers *by* the words of Scripture. The problem lies not in any deficiency in the *written Word*, but in the darkness and rebellion of our hearts (Eph. 4:18). In this sense, illumination is the Spirit of God speaking in, by, and through the *Scriptures* to bring light to blind minds and dead hearts so that they can properly receive and interpret the *Scriptures*.

This is why Edwards understood that the illumination of the heart does not occur without the illumination of the mind: "Holy affections are not heat without light; but evermore arise from the

---

[2] John Owen wrote that, "Once the mind of God had been reduced to writing, each mortal and individual man, to whom the Scriptures may come, *has God speaking to them no less directly than if he were hearing God speaking with His own voice to them*...Even the spoken voice cannot reach the ears of men but through a communication medium, that is, the air in which it is formed; so it cannot be denied that it is the voice of God speaking to men, though it is handed on through the communication medium of writing. It is in no way diminished by being reduced to writing" (*Biblical Theology*. 374-75).

[3] *Institutes*, trans. Henry Beveridge (Grand Rapids: Eerdmans, 1989), 1.7.5.

information of the understanding, some spiritual instruction that the mind receives, some light or actual knowledge."[4]

For this reason, embracing the truth claims of the Bible is not based on external evidence, rational arguments, or even on the coherent presentation of the Christian worldview, but in the Holy Spirit illuminating the truth of God's Word to us (Gal. 3:2, 5). As clarified by Calvin:

> Let it therefore be held as fixed, that those who are inwardly taught by the Holy Spirit acquiesce implicitly in Scripture; that Scripture, carrying its own evidence along with it, designs not to submit to proofs and arguments, but owes the full conviction with which we ought to receive it to the testimony of the Spirit. Enlightened by him, we no longer believe, either on our own Judgment or that of others, that the Scriptures are from God; but, in a way superior to human Judgment, feel perfectly assured – as much so as if we beheld the divine image visibly impressed on it – that it came to us, by the instrumentality of men, from the very mouth of God. We ask not for proofs or probabilities on which to rest our Judgment, but we subject our intellect and Judgment to it as too transcendent for us to estimate.[5]

Divine Faith

Spiritual illumination brings forth the new birth and faith. Once the eyes of our hearts can see clearly, we are born again. And, once we have new life in Christ, we cannot help but believe. The new birth does not force us to believe against our wills, but transforms our nature as it renews the *Imago Dei* with the infusion of the love of God so that we will be found willing.

Saving faith is not mere intellectual assent to the truth claims of the Bible. Demons acknowledge that Christ is the Son of God,

[4] Ibid.,192.
[5] Ibid.

yet they lack a personal relationship with Him. Many professing Christians also have only an intellectual understanding of the gospel. Though they do not deny the truth, they do not love the truth. They may profess to believe, but would not die for the truth.

In the same way that people believe in triangles and squares, nominal Christians believe in the Bible. But this speculative knowledge, which may even cause them to attend church and perform a few good deeds, is not saving faith any more than fear and trembling is evidence of saving faith within the demons (Jam. 2:19). Demons know God, but they do not love God. I am afraid that many, if not most, of professing Christians only possess this superficial form of faith – a faith that works without love.

Saving faith, however, establishes a personal and experiential relationship with Christ because it is motivated and derived out of a sincere love for Christ. Faith alone saves us, but faith works by love (Gal. 5:6). This love is the fruit of the new birth, where the old sinful and selfish nature is recreated in the likeness of Christ. The image of God that was defaced by the fall has been restored in Christ (Col. 3:10). We have been given the mind of Christ that gives us a proper discernment and love for the truth (1 Cor. 2:16). The tuning fork that was bent by sin has been renewed by love.

With a new heart, the gospel now resonates within our new natures and is altogether glorious. We willingly bow our knees to our Savior because, by God's saving grace, we now love the Lord Jesus above all things. Though His holiness and lordship was once a repellent, we now see these attributes as altogether glorious and worthy of all our adoration and worship.

Plantinga was right when he said: "The gift of faith and consequently regeneration isn't just a matter of restoring the intellect to a pristine condition in which we can once again perceive God and his glories and beauties; it also, and essentially, requires curing that madness of the will."[6]

After spiritual illumination and the new birth, our affections and will, because of our new nature, have been turned away from selfishness to a sincere love for God. As Plantinga went on to explain: "Regeneration consists in curing the will, so that we at last begin to love and hate the right things; it also includes cognitive renewal, so that we come to perceive the beauty, holiness, and delightfulness of the Lord and of the scheme of salvation he has devised."[7] Sin is now hated, and God is now glorious. But it is not as if reality has changed, it is simply that the darkness that once covered our eyes has been lifted.

Divine Love

In this sense, the saving knowledge of Christ comes not by apologetic argument but through spiritual illumination and regeneration. It comes by our minds being enlightened to the truth of God so that our hearts will be enflamed with a love for God. We must love the truth before we will embrace the truth (2 Thess. 2:10). Plantinga continued by saying:

> When the sources of affection function properly, we will love what is loveable, take delight in what is delightful, and desire what is desirable. We will love God above all and our neighbor as ourselves; we will delight in his beauty and glory, and in created reflections of that beauty and glory; we will desire what is in fact good for us.[8]

Calvin also realized that we will never commit ourselves to God until we see Him as altogether worthy of our devotion and service:

---

[6] *Warranted Christian Belief*, 303.

[7] Ibid., 304.

[8] Ibid., 309.

For until men recognize that they owe everything to God, that they are nourished by his fatherly care, that he is the Author of their every good, that they should seek nothing beyond him – they will never yield him willing service. Nay, unless they establish their complete happiness in him, they will never give themselves truly and sincerely to him.[9]

Divine Knowledge

It is this love, which comes from the new birth, which provides us with an experiential and personal knowledge of God. Paul summarizes all this in Ephesians 3:14-19:

> For this reason I bow my knees before the Father, from whom every family in heaven and on earth is named, that according to the riches of his glory he may grant you to be strengthened with power through his Spirit in your inner being, so that Christ may dwell in your hearts through faith – that you, being rooted and grounded in love, may have strength to comprehend with all the saints what is the breadth and length and height and depth, and to know the love of Christ that surpasses knowledge, that you may be filled with all the fullness of God.

First, we notice that *experiential* knowledge of God is supernaturally and sovereignly bestowed on us by God, "For this reason I bow my knees before the Father, from whom every family in heaven and on earth is named, that according to the riches of his glory *he may grant* you to be strengthened with power through his Spirit in your inner being" (vss. 14-16).

Paul is asking God to give or grant us this spiritual knowledge by strengthening our inner man. For Paul knew that, in our own natural capacities, we are insufficiently equipped and incapable of handling such weighty and glorious truths. To hold such weight, we need to be strengthened (κραταιωθῆναι, *krataiōthēnai*)

---

9 *Institutes*, 1.2.1

with God's power (δυνάμει, *duvámei*) through the work of the Holy Spirit. As it is written:

> "What no eye has seen, nor ear heard, nor the heart of man imagined, what God has prepared for those who love him" – these things God has revealed to us through the Spirit. For the Spirit searches everything, even the depths of God. For who knows a person's thoughts except the spirit of that person, which is in him? So also no one comprehends the thoughts of God except the Spirit of God. Now we have received not the spirit of the world, but the Spirit who is from God, that we might understand the things freely given us by God (1 Cor. 2:9-12).

This illumination and strengthening of the inner man is what brings forth faith, and this faith saves us because it legally and experientially unites us to the life of Christ. For by this faith, Christ dwells (κατοικῆσαι, *katoikēsai* – to house permanently) in our hearts (Eph. 3:17a). With Christ united to our hearts by faith, we are provided not merely an intellectual knowledge of Him, but a living and personal relationship with Him.

Christ is love. Consequently, the reason we need Christ to dwell in our hearts is so that we may be *"rooted and grounded in love"* (vs. 17b). Being rooted and grounded in love is the strengthening of our inner man that enables us to grasp a true knowledge of God. In other words, the power of God that was needed to strengthen us is the love of God that is written on our hearts.

The power that God uses to break our rebellious hearts is His love being poured out into our hearts. It is what brings about the new nature. As a result, the love of God within us not only gives us a love for God, but it also enables us to personally know God. The love of God disposes our old selfish natures that enslaved us to our own selfish passions of the flesh, and gives us a heart to know and willingly embrace God.

Why do we need to be strengthened with the love of God? According to Paul, we need to be rooted and grounded in love so that we "may have [the] strength to comprehend with all the saints what is the breadth and length and height and depth, and to know the love of Christ that surpasses knowledge" (vss. 18-19a). To know the love of God we need to be filled with the love of God. This is because God is love, and the fullness of His love in all of its depth, breadth, length, and height, is too great for us to comprehend without our first having the love of God living within us in the person of Christ. His love is inexpressible and beyond conclusive comprehension. We need strengthening in the inner man. We need to be rooted and grounded in love before we can comprehend the love of God.

This explains more fully how the love of God establishes a personal and experiential knowledge of God. Since God is love, when we experience the love of God, we experience God. Though we cannot visibly see Him, it does not mean we cannot emotionally and experientially know Him. As the Apostle John says, if "we love Him, God abides in us" (1 John 4:12). And this love that abides in us is the ingredient that we need in order to love and know Him in return, for "God is love, and he who abides in love abides in God, and God in him" (1 John 4:16). "Beloved, let us love one another, for love is of God; and everyone who loves is born of God and knows God" (1 John 4:7). As eyesight connects us with the world around us, faith, which works by love, connects us with God.

This love, in addition, is not merely a subjective and raw emotional experience, but rather it is an emotional experience that is firmly rooted in the objective knowledge of God that has been supernaturally revealed to us in God's written Word. With love being poured into our hearts by the divine illumination of God's objective Word, we are renewed in the likeness of God to love God.

For this reason, Paul concluded his prayer for us by adding, "that you may be filled with all the fullness of God (vs. 19b). Thus, being strengthened and rooted in the love of God not only gives us an experiential knowledge of the love of Christ, it enables (ἐξισχύσητε, *exischúsēte*, vs. 18a) us to be filled with all the fullness of God Himself.

Conclusion

But this, the necessity of love, brings us back to man's basic problem – man is separated from the love of God. Man's separation and rejection of God is rooted in the hardness of his heart (Eph. 4:18). Man may know right from wrong and the difference between love and selfishness, but he does not have the love (motive and power) to appreciate and fulfill this moral standard. Most importantly, man does not have the inward disposition to love God. Unregenerate man's inherent knowledge of God is not enough to provide a personal knowledge of God. You must love Christ to truly know Christ, and this takes spiritual illumination.

Consequently, intellectual and practical atheists do not lack warrant for belief in God, but they do lack the love that is necessary to submit to God. It does not matter if you are a nominal Christian or an outright atheist, what controls your beliefs and behavior is your deep-seated love for yourself. You are rooted in a love for self. Because you love yourself the most, you will not submit to the knowledge of God. You may make an empty profession of faith or contrive some complex philosophical system that denies the existence of God, but either way you seek to smooth over a guilty conscience without confessing your sins and bowing your knee to the lordship of Christ.

PART 6

The Call to Believe

whoever believes in him
will not be put to shame.
Romans 9:33

28

The Gracious
Call to Surrender

Dear reader, we cannot live a fulfilled and consistent life without God. Our guilt is the evidence of this. Our guilt is evidence of our unhappiness and foolishness. Though we each have tried in vain to cleanse our guilty conscience, it continues to speak out against us. But, even worse, it is our own voice that we each hear inside of our heads. We don't want to hear it, but we are constantly condemning ourselves. "Why did I do this?" "I shouldn't have done that." "I hope no one saw me do that." We love ourselves, so we hate this guilty feeling. We hate it when we know that we are wrong. Self-condemnation is the worst. If others condemn us, the possibility remains that they have misjudged us, but when our own heart speaks out against us, it is hard to deny culpability. We try to shut ourselves up, but as our conscience grows ever so dim as it becomes more and more hardened, we can never completely rid ourselves of the fact that we know we are sinful and deserving of God's judgment.

Guilt: A Universal Problem

What are we to do with our guilty consciences? Medication? Therapy? A pilgrimage to the Holy Land? Self-flagellation? Though guilt is ever present, we have each become an expert at silencing our conscience. Our first defense is crafting wonderfully worded excuses. We are good at finding supposed loopholes in the circumstances that happen to exempt us from what universally applies to others. We play dumb, as if we didn't know any better. Or, we see ourselves as having been unjustly placed in some kind of catch-22 circumstance. "We couldn't help it." We turn from being guilty to being a victim.

This, of course, leads to a second layer of defense – blaming others for our actions. "Lord, this woman, which you gave me, caused me to take hold of the forbidden fruit." "It is her fault, or maybe it's even your fault, God, for giving her to me."

If blaming others does not remove our shame, we seek to compensate by doing some good deeds. "Look at how good I am; I am not all that bad." "I go to church, and every now and then I plant a tree and give a few bucks to the homeless."

If the guilt lingers, we move into the distraction mode. We watch a lot of TV and keep ourselves entertained. Hopefully, if enough time and water passes under the bridge, we can begin to feel better about ourselves.

Yet, what we each find most helpful in softening our conscience is gathering a multitude of friends who will be ever so kind to reassure us that we are okay. We are looking for those friends that buy into our excuses, or help us create new excuses. We feel much better when they say, "I would have done the same thing." These are helpful friends. And if it is not these types of friends we are looking for, we find those whose moral actions and behavior are slightly worse than ours is. "I may occasionally slip up here and there, but at least I am not like Robert who is completely addicted to this stuff." "If I do a little, Robert does a lot." "Overall, in comparison, I am a pretty good person."

After years of suppressing our consciences, we find it much easier to continue in our sins without feeling as guilty. One of my homosexual friends admitted that he felt dirty the first few times he gave into his desires. His partner reassured him that this feeling was normal, and the key to working through it was not to think about it. In time, it will get easier and easier. But this is the case for all those who enter into sinful practices. Hardened criminals are not made overnight; it takes time to build calluses on a tender conscience.

Underneath all the calluses, no matter how many movies we have watched to distract ourselves and no matter how many friends have reassured us, down deep we know that we have sinned and come short of the glory of God. Because of our uncanny ability to forget and smooth things over, however, we have no idea how wicked and shameful we have been. We do not know the depths of our depravity. We each know that we are a sinner, but none of us can begin to comprehend how big a sinner we actually are in the sight of God. With mud-caked glasses it is hard to see how dirty we actually are. We see ourselves through sinful eyes. What must we look like to the one who is too pure to even look on sin?

Which of God's commandments have we not broken? We have stolen, lied, and cheated. We have been unfaithful, unforgiving, unkind, and unloving. We have given our lives to fulfilling the various passions of the flesh and have been more worried about being rich, popular, and powerful than being a thoughtful friend to those in need. We have given more time and energy living for ourselves than living for God.

Not only have we transgressed God's law, we have failed to do all the things that we should have done. We should have called grandma a few years back when she became ill. We should have stopped and helped that person on the side of the road. We should have done this or done that, but we were too lazy and self-focused. We have neglected to be thankful to God in all things. We have neglected the worship that is due to His name. We have not lived up to the standard.

This is not to mention the sins of our heart, such as anger, malice, bitterness, jealousy, covetousness, lustful thoughts, vain imaginations, and all manner of evil desires.

But what is more fearful than our hearts condemning us is knowing that God has personally chronicled everything that we have ever done. Every thought, word, and deed has been recorded. God is not fooled by our silly excuses. He has clearly manifested to us that those who practice such things are worthy of death (Rom. 1:32).

These sinful acts are treasonous. We have not only rebelled against our Maker and King, we have defected over to the kingdom of darkness. We have seditiously picked up our swords in opposition and have shaken our fists at Him in defiance. Our sins are a direct and bold attack against God. He has blessed us with life. He has showered us with good things, such as the rain and the sunshine. He has graciously been kind, long-suffering, and patient with us. He has sent us the gospel. He has given us plenty of opportunities to repent. He has seen fit to keep the blood pumping in our veins and uphold the beating of our hearts. But how have we responded to such kindness? We have defiled His name by the things we have watched and the jokes that we have entertained. We continue to bite the hand that is feeding us every time we utilize the gifts, money, resources, and health, which God has given us, for selfish, sinful, and disgraceful activities. The life that God has given us to serve Him, we have used to defy and curse Him.

Justice: A Universal Certainty

God's wrath is terrifying because it has been provoked by our rejection of His love. God finds infinite joy, happiness, and glory in His Son; His love for His Son is incomprehensible. God loves His Son, and He has also loved wretched sinners enough to give that which He loves the most – His only begotten Son (John

3:16). He did not hold back His greatest treasure, but freely offered Him – who holds life, meaning, and happiness in His hand. God gave the best He had to give. God has offered everything – something truly priceless. Yet, we have not only provoked God to wrath by our transgressions, but even worse we have spurned the love of a jealous God by rejecting His gift of love. The thing God valued the most is that which we have despised, as if His Son were not good enough. We, who are worthless, have rejected the One who is of infinite worth. We, who are unlovable, have turned away from God's immeasurable love. Thus, what anger must reside within God for the disgrace that we heap on Him when we turn our backs on His beloved Son?

Our rejection of God's love is open rebellion. Every moment we refuse to bow our knee and surrender all to His Majesty, we continue to provoke Him and to store up wrath for ourselves.

We are but a second away from running out of time. He will not hold back His wrath forever. The Day of Judgment is coming (Col. 1:6). Our guilt testifies of the certainty of this.

Death is coming, but we live as if it is not. As with our guilt, we have pushed this knowledge away from us. We have blinded ourselves to the severity of our condition and the gravity of the wrath of God. We have blinded ourselves with a false sense of security because of our self-righteousness. We have blinded ourselves with the pleasures and concerns of the world. We are more concerned about a pay-raise than saving our souls from hell. We are too busy fishing, hunting, playing golf, and keeping in shape than with getting right with God. We are too busy eating Esau's soup and playing a game of freeze-tag with our friends than seeking to meet with God. Because we still hear the birds singing and feel the warmth of the sun, we are under the false delusion that everything is okay.

We should be alarmed, but we are walking around in a haze. We are following the crowd, caught up in the madness, blown about by the latest fads and new releases. Like dogs roaming about looking for their next meal, we are carried about by the tide of hedonism. We are adrift, lost at sea, but completely unconcerned. As a mouse runs around and around in a wheel, we chase one pleasure after the next. The tide is rocking us asleep as it is taking us deeper out into the sea. We are unknowingly enslaved to our routines. Our daily lives, filled with pleasures in business and recreation, blind us to the approaching danger. As a herd of cows willingly follow each other to the slaughterhouse, we follow the course of this world unaware that it is reserved for fire.

It is only a matter of time before all this carelessness and false sense of security will be blown away. Death overtakes us all. In time, you will be standing before a holy God. No excuses. No self-righteousness. No atheistic worldview. Just you and your guilt, fully exposed before the Almighty God. But for now, your carelessness remains.

Forgiveness: A Universal Offer

The tragedy of it all is that, on your way to hell, you must purposefully walk over the dead and resurrected body of Jesus Christ; you must push Christ and His free offer of grace aside. If you face the wrath of God, it will be because you have refused the love of God. Having heard the gospel, you have been given a promise - a way of escape has been provided. Christ died for you. To remain in unbelief is to knowingly reject this gracious offer and say, "I don't want to think about that right now."

Moreover, if you push Christ out of your way, be fully aware of Whom you are rejecting. The gospel that offers you salvation cost Christ everything. For God to give you the universe, He would only have to speak the word. For God to save your souls from sin, He had to sacrifice His only Son. This free promise was not free for the One Who made it.

Christ laid aside His glory and became a man. He did not come dressed as a King but as a servant. He came into this world knowing that, as a man, He would face every temptation imaginable. After John baptized Him, Christ was led into a deserted area for forty days. During this time, all hell was unleashed on Him. The Devil and all his demonic forces threw everything that they had at Him. In utter hatred, the Devil sought to crush Him.

Christ was famished, tired, and beaten down in every possible way, and yet, He remained true to His Father. He resisted every temptation. He did not once shame or dishonor the One who sent Him into the world. He loved God and His neighbor with all of His heart, mind, and soul perfectly, entirely, and at all times. His life and earthly ministry was full of love, mercy, and compassion for others. He sought not fame, nor fortune, nor power. He was lowly of heart, gentle, and humble. He gave everything He had to the service of God and to assist others. He was sinless, righteous, perfect, and altogether glorious.

And this is not all – in this state of humility, sinlessness, and goodness, He willingly took sinners' place on the cross – the just for the unjust. He took our shame and guilt on Himself. The mocking we deserved, He willingly embraced. He was beaten, spit upon, and utterly humiliated as the chief of criminals. His own disciples and closest friends forsook Him in this dark hour. He was rejected because He was holy. But, worst of all, the anger and wrath of God, which we deserved, was poured out upon Him in full. He endured the judgment of God so that believers could be declared innocent.

What kind of king dies for His enemies? This is such a King, who offers those who repent a free pardon.

Christ rose from the dead, which proved His innocence. By His resurrection, Christ won the victory over sin, death, and the devil. We can be forgiven because the King of glory took care of justice for those who believe. What a Savior!

If you continue in unbelief, then this is the Savior you are rejecting. This is the gospel you continue to shun.

If God required a million dollars to wipe away our sins, many would pay the price willingly. If God required that we give up our firstborn to inherit eternal life, this too would be a price that some would be willing to pay. But, no! It is the offended party – God – who has laid down His firstborn for those who have sinned and rebelled against Him. Christ paid the ultimate price so you may be freely forgiven. Not only the just for the unjust, but the wounded party taking the place of the guilty party. Salvation is free, but this is what you refuse when you turn away in unbelief.

What kindness, what graciousness, and what goodness must you turn your back on when you reject the gospel? If you go to hell, it is because you refuse this offer; you turn your back on the goodness and mercy of God; you reject a Savior who died so sinners may live. And you reject Him why? Because you want to play freeze-tag with your buddies? Because you're too insubordinate to accept that their reigns a King over your soul? Because the pleasure of a twinkie sounds more desirable than the pleasure of being in a relationship with God?

Deciding not to follow Christ proves you don't want to be saved from your sins. Rather, your pride, ego, and self-centeredness keep you from accepting a Love to reside in your heart that is greater than all loves. It is *absurdity* to reject such a humble Savior, the King of Kings, the Lord of Lords. You reject life, meaning, purpose, and happiness so that you can hang onto sin, death, meaninglessness, and despair. You exchange the truth for a lie and heaven for hell. *This is the absurdity of unbelief.*

For those of you who are still carefree and unconcerned about the condition of your soul, there is not much more I can say. But, for those of you who have a broken and weary heart, for those who can see their sins and rebellion against their God, for those who truly hate their sins, for those who are ready to humbly ask God for forgiveness and surrender to the lordship of Christ, I have wonderful news. Look unto Jesus and you shall be saved. This is a promise that is certain to be fulfilled for all who believe. It is not by works but simply by believing this promise that we are made right before God.

He came to die for sinners (1 Tim. 1:15). He freely offers Himself to all who truly desire to be delivered from their sins and their guilt. Those who hide and cover their sins will remain in their sins, but those who repent – taking ownership and confessing their sins before God – and believe in their hearts that Jesus is who He says that He is shall be saved. Dear reader, there is forgiveness. Your guilt and sin may be removed as far as the East is from the West, and the perfect righteousness of Christ could be credited to your account. All your guilt may be washed away, and the blood of Jesus is able to cleanse you from all of your sins. "Come unto me," Christ says, "and I will give you rest." God made this promise. He cannot lie. He is able to save the worst of sinners. Salvation is free; you only have to believe.

And believing, my dear friends, is the *only* reasonable thing to do.

Bibliography

Ackley, Alfred H. *I Serve a Risen Savior*. Spring Hill, PA, 1887; d. Whittier, CA, 1960., both text and tune were published in the Rodeheaver hymnal *Triumphant Service Songs*, 1933.

Anselm of Canterbury. "Proslogion" in *Anselm of Canterbury: The Major Works*. Edited by Brian Davis and G. R. Evans. New York: Oxford, 2008.

Armbruster, Carl. *The Vision of Paul Tillich*. New York: Sheed And Ward, 1967.

Aristotle, *Metaphysics*. Translated by W. D. Ross. Stilwell, KS: Digireads Publishing, 2006.

Atkins, Peter. *Creation Revisited*. Oxford: W. H. Freeman & Company, 1992.

Augustine. *The City of God*. Translated by George Wilson and J. J. Smith. Peabody, MA: Hendrickson, 2013.

———, *The Trinity*. Edited by John E. Rotelle. Translated by Edmond Hill. New York: New City Press, 1992.

Ayer. A. J. *Language, Truth, and Logic*. New York: Dover Books, 1952.

Bahnsen, Greg L. *Pushing the Antithesis*. Powder Springs, GA: American Vision, 2007.

———, *Van Til's Apologetic*. Phillipsburg, NJ: P&R Publishing, 1998.

Barth, Karl. *Church Dogmatics*. Edited by G. W. Bromiley and T.F. Torrance. Edinburgh: T. & T. Clark, 1936-1969.

Barzun, Jacques. *The Culture We Deserve*. Middletown, CN: Wesleyan University Press, 1989.

Bavinck, Herman. *In the Beginning*. Edinburgh: Banner of Truth Trust, Reprint 1979.

_____, *Reformed Dogmatics*. 3 Vols. Translated by John Vriend. Grand Rapids: Baker, 2004.

Behe, M. J. *Darwin's Black Box*. New York: The Free Press, 1996.

Beyssade, Jean-Marie. "The Idea of God and Proofs of His Existence" in *The Cambridge Companion to Descartes*. Edited by John Cottingham. Cambridge: Cambridge University Press, 1995.

Berkhof, Louis. *Systematic Theology*. Grand Rapids: Eerdmans, 1994.

Berlinski, David. *The Devil's Delusion: Atheism and Its Scientific Pretensions*. New York: Basic Books, 2009.

Black, Jim Nelson. *The Death of Evolution*. Grand Rapids: Zondervan, 2010.

Blanchard, John. *Does God Believe in Atheists?*. Darlington: Evangelical Press, 2001.

_____, *Is Anybody There*. Darlington: Evangelical Press, 2006.

Boa, Kenneth D. and Robert M. Bowman Jr. *Faith Has Its Reasons: An Integrative Approach to Defending Christianity*. Waynesboro, GA: Paternoster, 2006.

Bonaventure, "The Journey of the Mind to God." *Late Medieval Mysticism*. Edited by Ray C. Petry. Philadelphia: The Westminster Press, 1962.

Bosserman, B. A., *The Trinity and the Vindication of Christian Paradox: An Interpretation and Refinement of the Theological Apologetic of Cornelius Van Til*. Eugene, OR: Pickwick Publications, 2014.

Bultmann, Rudolf. *New Testament and Mythology*. New York: Harper & Row, 1966.

Byl, John. *The Divine Challenge*. Edinburgh: Banner of Truth Trust, 2004.

Calvin, John. *Calvin's Commentaries*, Vol. 1. Translated by John King. Reprint, Grand Rapids: Baker, 2003.

_____, *Institutes of the Christian Religion*. 2 Vols. Edited by John T. McNeill. Translated by Ford Lewis Battles. Philadelphia: The Westminster Press, 1977.

_____, *Institutes of the Christian Religion*. Translated by Henry Beveridge. Grand Rapids: Eerdmans, 1989.

Camus, Albert. *The Myth of Sisyphus*. Translated by Le mythe de Sisyphe. New York: Vintage Books, 1991.

Charlesworth, James H. "The Historical Jesus and Biblical Archaeology: Reflections on New Methodologies and Perspectives" in *Jesus and Archaeology*. Edited by James H. Charlesworth. Grand Rapids: Eerdmans, 2006.

Charnock, Stephen. *The Existence and Attributes of God*. Grand Rapids: Baker, 1996.

Clark, Gordon. *Thales To Dewey*. Jefferson, MD: The Trinity Foundation, 2nd Ed., 1989.

Clifford, W. K. "The Ethics of Belief," in *Philosophy of Religion*. Edited by Charles Taliaferro and Paul J. Griffiths. Oxford: Blackwell, 2003.

Collett, Don. "Van Til and Transcendental Argument" in *Revelation and Reason*. Edited by K. Scott Oliphint and Lane G. Tipton. Phillipsburg, NJ: P&R, 2007.

Comfort, Philip. *Encountering the Manuscripts: An Introduction to New Testament Paleography and Textual Criticism*. Nashville: Broadman & Holman, 2005.

Cornell, Vincent J. "God in Islam," in the *Encyclopedia of Religion*, Ed. Lindsay Jones, Vol. 5, 2nd Edition. New York: Macmillan Reference of Thompson Gale, 2005., 3560-3567.

Craig, William Lane. *Reasonable Faith: Christian Truth and Apologetics*. Wheaton, IL: Crossway, 2008.

Crick, Francis. *The Astonishing Hypothesis: The Scientific Search for the Soul*. New York: Touchstone, 1994.

Davies, Paul. *Cosmic Jackpot: Why Our Universe Is Just Right for Life*. Boston: Houghton Mifflin Company, 2007.

Dawkins, Richard. *The Blind Watchmaker*. New York: Norton, 1996.

_____, *River Out of Eden*. New York: Basic Books, 1995.

_____, *The God Delusion*. Boston: Mariner Books, 2006.

_____, *The Selfish Gene*. New York: Oxford, 2006.

Dennett, Daniel C. *Darwin's Dangerous Idea*. New York: Touchstone, 1995.

Descartes, René. *Discourse on Method and Meditations on First Philosophy*. Indianapolis: Hackett Publishing Company, 3rd Ed., 1993.

Dionysius. "The Divine Names." *Dionysius the Areopgagite on the Divine Names and The Mystical Theology*. Translated by C. E. Rolt. Berwick, MI: Ibis Press, 2004.

Durant, Will. *The Story of Philosophy*. New York: Simon & Schuster, 1961.

Eckhart, Meister. "Another Sermon on the Eternal Birth," in *Late Medieval Mysticism*. Edited by Ray C. Petry. Philadelphia: The Westminster Press, 1957.

Edwards, Jonathan. *Approaching the End of God's Grand Design, 1743-1758*. Edited by Wilson H. Kimnach. Vol. 25 of *The Works of Jonathan Edwards*. New Haven: Yale University Press, 2006.

_____, *The Freedom of the Will*. Morgan, PA: Soli Deo Gloria, 1996.

_____, "Miscellany" 96, in *The Works of Jonathan Edwards*. Vol. 13. Edited by Thomas A. Schafer. New Haven: Yale University Press, 1994.

_____, *The Religious Affections*. Edinburgh: Banner of Truth Trust, 1994.

Ehrman, Burt. *Misquoting Jesus: The Story of Who Changed the Bible and Why*. New York: HarperCollins, 2005.

Evans, Stephen. *Passionate Reason: Making Sense of Kierkegaard's Philosophical Fragments*. Bloomington: Indiana University Press, 1992.

Fisher, George Park. *The Grounds of Theistic and Christian Belief*. New York: Charles Scribner's Sons, 1915.

Fletcher, James. *Situation Ethics*. Philadelphia: Westminster Press, 1966.

Flew, Antony. *There Is a God*. New York: HaperOne, 2008.

Frame, John. *A History of Western Philosophy and Theology*. Phillipsburg, NJ: P&R Publishing, 2015.

_____, *Apologetics to the Glory of God*. Phillipsburg, NJ: P&R Publishing, 1994.

_____, *The Doctrine of the Knowledge of God*. Phillipsburg, NJ: P&R Publishing, 1987.

Freud, Sigmund. *Civilization and Its Discontents*. New York: W. W. Norton & Company, 1961.

Fuller, B. A. G. "The Theory of God in Book Λ of Aristotle's Metaphysics" in *The Philosophical Review*, Vol. 16, No. 2 (Mar., 1907), 170-183.

Galton, Francis. "Eugenics: Its Definition, Scope, and Aims." *The American Journal of Sociology*, Vol. 10; July, 1904; Number 1.

Gerrish, B. A. *A Prince of the Church: Schleiermacher and the Beginnings of Modern Theology*, Philadelphia: Fortress Press, 1984.

Goodman, Micah. *Maimonides and the Book that Changed Judaism*. Philadelphia: The Jewish Publication Society, 2015.

Green, Ronald. *Kierkegaard and Kant: The Hidden Debt*. Albany: State University of New York Press, 1992.

Harrison, Paul. *Elements of Pantheism*. Shaftesbury, UK: Element Books, 2013.

Hawking, Stephen and Leonard Mlodinow. *The Grand Design*. New York: Bantam Books, 2010.

Hayman, Ronald. *Nietzsche*. New York: Penguin Books, 1980.

Helm, Paul. *Eternal God: A Study of God without Time*. New York: Oxford, 2012.

Henry, Carl. *God, Revelation and Authority*. Vol. 3. Waco: Word Books, 1979.

Hick, John. *Faith and Knowledge*. Ithaca, NY: Carnell University Press, 1966.

Hitchens, Christopher. *God is Not Great*. New York: Twelve, 2007.

Hodge, Charles. *Systemic Theology*, 3 Vols. Grand Rapids: Eerdmans, 1981.

Hume, David. *Dialogues Concerning Natural Religion*. Indianapolis: The Bobbs – Merrill Company, 1947.

Isaacson, Walter. *Einstein: His Life and Universe*. New York: Simon & Schuster, 2007.

James, William. "Pragmatism" in *Pragmatism in Other Writings*. New York: Penguin Books, 2000.

Jaspers, Karl. *Way to Wisdom*. Translated by Ralph Manheim. New Heaven, CN: Yale University Press, 1954.

Johnson, George. "Creation, in the Beholder." *The New York Times*, 20 May 2014, D3.

Johnson, Jeffrey D. *Behind the Bible: A Primer on Textural Criticism*. Birmingham: SGCB, 2012.

Johnson, Phillip E. *Darwin on Trail*. Downers Grove, IL: IVP, 2 ed. 1993.

Jones, Peter. *One or Two: Seeing a World of Difference*. Escondido, CA: Main Entry Editions, 2010.

Josephus, Flavius. *Jewish Antiquities*. Translated by Louis H. Feldman, The Loeb Classical Library. Cambridge, MA: Harvard University Press, 1970.

Kant, Immanuel. *Critique of Pure Reason*. Translated by J. M. D. Meiklejohn. Amherst, NY: Prometheus Books, 1990.

Kenny, Anthony. *The Oxford Illustrated History of Western Philosophy*. Oxford: Oxford University Press, 1997.

Kierkegaard, Søren. *Fear and Trembling*. Translated by Alastair Hannay. London: Penguin Books, 2003.

_____, "Concluding Unscientific Postscript" in *Kierkegaard's Writings*. Edited and translated by Howard V. Hong & Edna H. Hong. Princeton: Princeton University Press, 1992.

Kline, Meredith G. *Kingdom Prologue: Genesis Foundations for a Covenantal Worldview*. Eugene, OR: Wipf & Stock, 2006.

Lasch, Christopher. *The Culture of Narcissism*. New York: W. W. Norton & Company, 1991.

Lennox, John C. *God and Stephen Hawking*. Oxford: Lion Books, 2011.

_____, *God's Undertaker: Has Science Buried God?*. Oxford: Lion Books, 2009.

Lessing, Gotthold Ephriam. "On the proof of the spirit and of power (1777)" in *Lessing: Philosophical and Theological Writings*. Edited and translated by H. B. Nisbet. Cambridge: Cambridge University Press, 2005.

Letham, Robert. *The Holy Trinity*. Phillsburg, PA: P&R, 2004.

Lewis, C. S. *God in the Dock*. Grand Rapids: Eerdmans, 1970.

_____, *Mere Christianity*. New York: Touchstone, 1980.

_____, "Is Theology Poetry?" in *The Weight of Glory*. New York: HaperCollins, 2001.

London, Jack. *The Sea-Wolf*. New York: Tom Doherty Associates Books, 1993.

Luther, Martin. *The Tabletalk of Martin Luther's*. Ross-shire, UK: Christian Focus, 2003.

Lyotard, Jean-François. *The Postmodern Condition: A Report of Knowledge*. Translated by Geoff Bennington and Brian Massumi. Minneapolis: The University of Minnesota, 1983.

Magee, Bryan. *The Story of Philosophy*. London: Dorling Kindersley, 2001.

Maier, Paul L. "Josephus on Jesus," in *Josephus: The Essential Works*. Edited and translated by Paul L. Maier. Grand Rapids: Kregel, 1994.

McCall, Thomas H. "Trinity Doctrine, Plain and Simple" in *Advancing Trinitarian Theology*. Edited by Oliver D. Crisp and Fred Sanders. Grand Rapids: Zondervan, 2014.

McDonald, Lee Martin. *The Story of Jesus in History and Faith*. Grand Rapids: Baker Academic, 2013.

McGrath, Alister. *Why God Won't Go Away*. Nashville: Nelson, 2010.

Meyer, Stephen C. *Darwin's Doubt: The Explosive Origin of Animal Life and the Case for Intelligent Design*. New York: HarperOne, 2013.

_____, *Signature in the Cell: DNA and the Evidence for Intelligent Design*. New York: HarperOne, 2009.

Mill, John Stuart. *Utilitarianism*. Indianapolis: Hackett Publishing Company, 1979.

Morris, Thomas V. *Francis Schaeffer's Apologetics*. Grand Rapids: Baker Books, 1987.

Muggeridge, Malcolm. *The End of Christendom*. Grand Rapids: Eerdmans, 1980.

Murphy, John L. *Modernism and the Teaching of Schleiermacher*, Part II. Washington, DC: The Catholic University of America Press, 1961.

Murray, John. *Collected Writings of John Murray*, Vol. 4. Edinburgh: Banner of Truth Trust, 2001.

Nagel, Thomas. *Mind and Cosmos*. New York: Oxford University Press, 2012.

_____, *The Last Word*. New York: Oxford University Press, 1997.

Nash, Ronald. *Faith and Reason*. Grand Rapids: Zondervan, 1988.

_____, *The Word of God and the Mind of Man*. Phillipsburg, NJ: P&R Publishing, 1982.

_____, *Worldviews in Conflict*. Grand Rapids: Zondervan, 1992.

Newton, Isaac. *The Principia: Mathematical Principles of Natural Philosophy*. Thousand Oaks, CA: Snowball Publishing, 2010.

Nietzsche, Friedrich. *The Anti-christ.* Translated by H. L. Mencken. New York: Cosimo Classics, 2005.

_____, *Beyond Good and Evil.* Translated by Helen Zimmern. Mineola, NY: Dover Publications, 1997.

_____, *The Gay Science.* Translated by Walter Kaufmann. New York: Vintage Books, 1974.

_____, *Thus Spoke Zarathustra.* Translated by Walter Kaufmann. New York: Penguin Books, 1966.

Oliphint, Scott K. *Covenantal Apologetics.* Wheaton, IL: Crossway, 2013.

_____, *God with Us: Divine Condescension and the Attributes of God.* Wheaton, IL: Crossway, 2012.

_____, *Reasons for Faith.* Phillipsburg, NJ: P&R Publishing, 2006.

_____, "Simplicity, Trinity, and Incomprehensibility of God" in *One God in Three Persons.* Edited by Bruce Ware and John Starke. Wheaton, IL: Crossway, 2015.

Owen. John. *Biblical Theology.* Morgan, PA: Soli Deo Gloria Publications, 2002.

_____, *The Works of Owen*, 16 Vol. Edinburgh: Banner of Truth Trust, 2000.

Paley, William. *Natural Theology.* New York: Oxford, 2008.

Pascal, Blaise. *Pensées.* Translated by W. F. Trotter in "Great Books of the Western World." Gen. Ed., Robert Maynard Hutchins. New York: Encyclopedia Britannica, 1952.

Plantinga, Alvin. *God and Other Minds: A Study of the Rational Justification of Belief in God.* Ithaca: Cornell University Press, 1990.

_____, *Warranted Christian Belief.* New York: Oxford, 2000.

_____, *Where the Conflict Really Lies.* New York: Oxford, 2012.

Plato. *Plato's Republic.* Translated by G. M. A. Grube. Indianapolis: Hackett, 1974.

Poythress, Vern. *Redeeming Philosophy.* Wheaton: Crossway, 2014.

Reeves, Michael. *Delighting in the Trinity.* Downers Grove, IL: IVP, 1012.

Richards, Jay Wesley. *The Untamed God: A Philosophical Exploration of the Divine Perfection, Simplicity and Immutability.* Downers Grove, IL: InterVarsity Press, 2003.

Russell, Bertrand. *Religion and Science.* New York: Oxford, 1997.

_____, *Why I Am Not a Christian.* New York: Simon & Schuster, 1957.

Sagan, Carl. *Cosmos.* New York: Random House, 2002.

Sarfati, Jonathan. *Refuting Evolution.* Green Forest, AR: Master Books, 1999.

Sartre, Jean-Paul. *Existentialism and Human Emotions.* New York: Citadel Press, 1987.

Schaeffer, Francis. "He is There and He is Not Silent" in *Trilogy.* Wheaton, IL: Crossway, 1990.

Schweitzer, William M. *God is a Communicative Being: Divine Communicativeness and Harmony in the Theology of Jonathan Edwards.* London: T&T Clark, 2012.

Shirer, William L. *The Rise and Fall of the Third Reich.* New York: Simon and Schuster, 1960.

Singer, Peter. *Animal Liberation.* New York: HarperCollins, 2002.

Sire, James. *Naming the Elephant: Worldview as A Concept.* Downers Grove, IL: IVP, 2004.

_____, *The Universe Next Door.* Downers Grove, IL: IVP, 2009.

Spinoza, Benedict De. *Ethics.* Translated by W. H. White in Great Books of the Western World, Edited by Robert

Maynard Hutchins. Chicago: Encyclopedia Britannica, Inc. 1952.

_____, *Ethics*. Edited and translated by Edwin Curley. New York: Penguin Books, 1996.

Skinner, C. F. *Beyond Freedom and Dignity*. Indianapolis: Hackett Publishing Company, 1971.

Smith, George H. *Atheism: The Case Against God*. Amherst, NY: Prometheus Books, 1989.

Sproul, R. C. *If There's a God, Why are there Atheists?*. Wheaton, IL: Tyndale House Publishers, 1988.

_____, and Keith Mathison. *Not a Chance: God, Science, and the Revolt against Reason*. Grand Rapids, Baker Books, 2014.

Swinburne, Richard. *Is There a God?*. New York: Oxford, 1996.

Taylor, Charles. *A Secular Age*. Cambridge, MA: Harvard University Press, 2007.

Til, Cornelius Van. *An Introduction to Systematic Theology*, 2nd ed., William Edgar. Philipsburg, NJ: P&R, 2007.

_____, *Common Grace and the Gospel*. Phillipsburg, NJ: R&R Publishing, 1972.

_____, *The Defense of the Faith*. Phillipsburg, NJ: R&R Publishing, 1967.

Tillich, Paul. *Biblical Religion and the Search for Ultimate Reality*. Chicago: The University of Chicago Press, 1955.

_____, "The Depth of Existence," in *The Shaking of the Foundations*, 52-63. New York: Charles Scribner's Sons, 1948.

Turretin, Francies. *Institutes of Elenctic Theology*, Vol. 1. Translated by George Musgrave Giger. Phillipsburg: P&R, 1992.

Varghese, Roy Abraham. Preface to Anthony Flew, *There Is a God*. New York: HarperOne, 2007.

Voltaire. *The Works of Voltaire. A Contemporary Version*, 21 Vols. A Critique and Biography by John Morley. Notes by Tobias Smollett. Translated by William F. Fleming. New York: E.R. DuMont, 1901.

Vos, Geerhardus. "Theology Proper," Vol. 1 of *Reformed Dogmatics*. Edited and translated and by Richard B. Gaffin. Bellingham, WA: Lexham Press, 2012-2014.

Wald, George. "Innovation and Biology," *Scientific American*, Vol. 199, Sept. 1958.

Warfield, B. B. *"Calvin's Doctrine of the Trinity,"* Princeton Theological Review 7 (1909) 553-562. Reprinted in The Works of Benjamin B. Warfield, vol. 5, 189-284. Grand Rapids: Baker Books, 2003.

White, James. *What Every Christian Needs to Know abut the Qur'an*. Minneapolis: Bethany House, 2013.

Wilson, Edward O. *On Human Nature*. Cambridge: Harvard University Press, 2004.

Wright, N. T. *The Resurrection of the Son of God*. Minneapolis: Fortress Press, 2003.

Young, Edward. *Thy Word is Truth*. Edinburgh: Banner of Truth Trust, 1963.

Zacharias, Ravi. *A Shattered Visage: The Real Face of Atheism*. Grand Rapids: Baker Books, 1990.

Index of Names